EX LIBRIS

Matthew
Ouellett

MUSIC IN 1853

THE BIOGRAPHY OF A YEAR

MUSIC IN 1853

THE BIOGRAPHY OF A YEAR

Hugh Macdonald

THE BOYDELL PRESS

First published 2012
The Boydell Press, Woodbridge

ISBN 978 1 84383 718 3

The Boydell Press is an imprint of Boydell & Brewer Ltd
PO Box 9, Woodbridge, Suffolk, IP12 3DF, UK
and of Boydell & Brewer Inc.
668 Mount Hope Ave, Rochester, NY 14620-2731, USA
website: www.boydellandbrewer.com

A catalogue record for this book is available
from the British Library

The publisher has no responsibility for the continued existence
or accuracy of URLs for external or third-party internet websites
referred to in this book, and does not guarantee that any content
on such websites is, or will remain, accurate or appropriate

Papers used by Boydell & Brewer Ltd are natural, recyclable
products made from wood grown in sustainable forests

Designed and typeset in Bodoni Twelve ITC Std by
David Roberts, Pershore, Worcestershire

Printed in the United States of America

Contents

Illustrations

MAPS

The author and publishers are grateful to all the institutions and
individuals listed for permission to reproduce the materials in which they
hold copyright. Every effort has been made to trace the copyright holders;
apologies are offered for any omission, and the publishers will be pleased
to add any necessary acknowledgement in subsequent editions.

To all my students and friends at
Washington University in St Louis
founded in 1853

Preface

THIS book is a 'horizontal biography' of music. Biography typically follows the life of a single individual through many decades, taking in the glancing or penetrating influences of other lives. My intention here, however, is to invert the process and follow many lives through a narrow span of time, in this case a period of about ten months that more or less fits into the year 1853; I have attempted to write the 'biography' of what might, in the long term, be considered a single moment, seen through the criss-crossing lives of leading musicians of the time. Biographers are rarely able to enter into the minutiae of daily life such as those I present here, whereas my aim has been to recapture the events of the year in as vivid a manner as possible.

Why 1853? There are of course an unlimited number of such moments that could have been chosen, but I was drawn to this year since it is a period unusually rich in significant events involving the main players in the resplendent cortège of nineteenth-century music. Although by 1853 Chopin, Mendelssohn and Donizetti were dead, Berlioz, Liszt and Verdi were at the height of their powers, Wagner was on the verge of a momentous breakthrough, and a new generation, represented by Brahms, was taking its first steps in the wider world.

At some point in the 1850s the pristine Romanticism of *Winterreise*, the *Symphonie fantastique*, *Carnaval*, and the *Ballades* was laid to rest, metamorphosing into the much more dynamic, more intense world of the *Ring* and the 'Pathétique' Symphony. Musical style was undergoing profound change, passing within the dominant mode of Romanticism from early to late, and breaking up into nationalism, realism, and many other -isms of abundant variety. My chief concern here, though, is not with musical style but with the musicians who formed it. Whatever the influence of abstract forces, individuals should be fully credited with their inventive genius, especially the extraordinary pléiade of composers and writers active in the middle of the nineteenth century. The mere thought of *Les Troyens*, *Tristan und Isolde* and *War and Peace* (not to mention *Barchester Towers*, *Uncle Tom's Cabin* and Mrs Beeton's *Book of Household Management*) is enough to remind us that the 1850s were a decade when giants walked the earth. Following the example of Goethe and Napoleon, it was usual for men like Hugo, Wagner and Tolstoy to produce superhuman volumes of work, to engage in a vast correspondence, to sustain a variegated and busy social life, to nourish grandiose dreams, to be committed to political action, and never to rest. Liszt illustrates this intensely productive lifestyle, for his concern for other musicians and the cultivation of music in the public arena would alone have been enough to fill many careers even without long concert tours, conducting engagements and the uncountable compositions and arrangements that flowed from his pen.

Many cultural processes converged to make this possible, and material conditions were right. I do not claim that a close look at the daily lives of these men and women will explain their genius; in fact I am sure it will not: their achievements remain fundamentally inexplicable. But I believe that a curiosity about their works leads to a curiosity about their lives, and that it is a small step from there to a delight in details which themselves may have little to do with art. Those details in cumulation delineate the personalities in whom great thoughts took shape. From the perspective of an age when Great Men no longer exist, at least not in the creative arts, it is tempting to ask what circumstances were favourable then that we might conceivably attempt to recreate today. I leave that question for others to answer.

There was a collective energy in these men that drove their creative capabilities with extraordinary force. Some composers, such as Meyerbeer and Verdi, worked in a narrow sphere and in relative isolation, but the majority were in close touch with one another, aware of each others' travels, concerts, critical opinions and new compositions. This was no doubt part of a fraternal spirit inherited from national cultures, but it was greatly enhanced by two technical factors which I have come to regard as the pumping stations that powered this stellar group of composers: the postal service and the railways. A good mail service had been in place in most countries since the later eighteenth century, but by 1853 it reached a peak of efficiency. The post was regular, swift and reliable, with three or more deliveries a day in large cities. To a note sent out in the morning a reply could be expected in the afternoon. With writing materials always ready to hand the post was abundantly used for every kind of communication, from brief notes making appointments and organising rehearsals to tracts on aesthetic and philosophical problems. Not only did educated people write copious letters to their families and friends, an enormous proportion of this mail was saved. We can construct an almost daily record of the doings of leading nineteenth-century figures, and often, too, we can enter the more intimate thoughts of people who may have had good reason to present a different profile in public.

Trains, less obviously, contributed to the greater closeness of these individuals. The Manchester to Liverpool line was opened in 1830, a few years ahead of Continental lines. In Germany the first line opened in 1835, with the Dresden to Leipzig line completed in 1839; in France the first main line, from Paris to Orléans, came into service in 1842. By 1853 the great cities of Europe were connected by a remarkable network of railways, and although our composers commented surprisingly little on the difference it made to their lives, this was the beginning of the unlimited international travel we enjoy today. Overnight passenger services were already common. Trains were not obviously more comfortable than the stage-coaches they replaced, and as older readers will remember, steam engines bathed the traveller in smoke, soot and smuts. But they were a lot faster, so that concert engagements and tours could be undertaken more readily. The mileage that Joachim, for example, covered in 1853 alone is remarkable. There is a strong geographical dimension to the chronicle of these pages, since we can watch musicians moving from city to city, interconnecting with others, freely crossing frontiers and enjoying the international spirit which was one of the great benefits of Napoleon's overthrow.

Electricity was a technology not in daily use in 1853, and it is as well to remind ourselves that candlelight or lamplight was still the condition in which evening and nighttime events were conducted and the light by which many books were read and a lot of music composed. Many city streets were lit by gas, and the better-equipped theatres used it for stage lighting, but homes and concert halls were dependent on the chandler's craft and thus subject to the smells and smoke which everyone regarded as normal, barely ever giving it more than a passing mention.

The political map of Germany in 1853 was a quilt of semi-independent kingdoms, duchies, principalities and free cities, some quite small, like Weimar, and in most cases jealously proud of their cultural life. Musicians profited enormously from this situation and found employment in courts, churches and theatres on a scale unrivalled elsewhere. Musical activity in England and France was far more concentrated in their capitals. While I offer a chapter each in London and Paris, German, Swiss and Dutch cities are the setting for most of the events, with the constant communication between them by mail and rail one of the most striking features of the age. Although the problem of carrying and changing money across frontiers must have been a recurrent teaser (and the problem of relating monetary values a nightmare for the historian), our musicians (with the exception of Wagner) were mercifully either too discreet or too blasé to discuss money very much, so that it plays little part in the text however intensely they may have worried about it.

The international language was then French, which allowed Berlioz to conduct concerts in England, Germany or Russia without having to learn a foreign language, a skill for which he had little aptitude. Most educated Englishmen and Germans spoke some French. Liszt was bilingual, having been raised a German-speaker up to the age of twelve and thereafter living in France and adopting French as his preferred language. The Princess Sayn-Wittgenstein, Liszt's long-time partner, being a Polish-Russian aristocrat, spoke and wrote only French. Of Liszt's younger disciples Joachim, von Bülow and Cornelius were all fluent enough in French to correspond and converse in that language. Schumann and Brahms both had some French in their education but seem to have been less adept in its use.

The story begins in April 1853, when Brahms left his Hamburg home for the first time, and ends ten months later when Schumann drew a line under his creative life by jumping (or falling or stepping) into the Rhine in Düsseldorf. Midway between these two dates falls the historic meeting of Schumann and Brahms, while Berlioz, Liszt and Wagner were all at the same time engaged in complex creative enterprises that changed the landscape of music for the rest of the century.

My desire to apply the microscope to these few months of 1853 grew from my observation that Berlioz had abandoned composition in 1850, only to take up his pen again (by completing *L'Enfance du Christ*) three years later. He was persuaded to do so in December 1853 by his friends in Leipzig, raising the curious possibility that it was Brahms, a musician apparently poles apart from Berlioz in temperament and style, who was the persuader. The facts of the calendar actually eliminate this possibility, yet the conjunction of Berlioz and Brahms, for both of whom the closing months of 1853 were decisive, was part of their kaleidoscopic interaction with Liszt, Schumann, Joachim and many other musicians in Germany at that time, and it happens also to be the moment when Wagner, like Berlioz, resumed composition after a long interruption, confiding to paper the famous low E flat with which he embarked on the largest and most ambitious composition in history. Wagner was dependent on his friends for money and moral support, but never for inspiration, so it would be wrong to ascribe the beginnings of the *Ring* to the communal electricity of musical life in 1853, but for others, notably Berlioz, Brahms, and Liszt, the spirit of the times had a great deal to do with their next steps.

I was greatly impressed, too, by a similar approach to literary history found in Alethea Hayter's *A Sultry Month: Scenes of London Literary Life in 1846* (1965), an absorbing account of the close relations between Benjamin Haydon, the Carlyles and the Brownings in the summer of 1846. There too a wealth of documentation made a vivid narrative possible, and I have striven to recapture the same immediacy in recounting the events of 1853 in a different milieu. James Chandler's *England in 1819* (1998) and James Shapiro's *A Year in the Life of William Shakespeare: 1599* (2005) similarly focus on the intense literary activity of a single year, combining critical and narrative approaches. In music a useful precedent may be found in H. C. Robbins Landon's *1791: Mozart's Last Year* (1991), whose vivid sense of place contributes much to the book's evocation of the times.

None of the narrative, not even dialogue, is invented. Everything has been drawn from contemporary documents or the recollections of the participants, with the occasional 'no doubt' or 'must have' when I venture into speculation. The text is so heavily factual that it would be burdensome beyond endurance to assign footnotes to every sentence, so I have dispensed with them while assuring the reader that my sources are all to be found listed in the Bibliography. It is the writer's job to inspire trust in the reader, and I accept that obligation fully with the assurance that I have not knowingly invented facts or incidents. My sources include the massive documentation that these musicians and events have spawned, most of which has been available for over a hundred years in local newspapers or in the monographs, memoirs and collections of letters which were published in great numbers around 1900. Comprehensive modern editions of the letters of Berlioz, Schumann and Wagner have been published, but for Liszt and Brahms the sources, though abundant, are more scattered. In addition to the general bibliography there are individual bibliographies that apply to each chapter.

I have retained the standard English versions of the place-names Hanover, Cologne, Brunswick, Munich, Constance and Zurich and the old version Carlsbad, while adopting the modern forms Karlsruhe, Koblenz, Kassel, etc., since the K and C initial letters are both found in documents of the time.

I HAVE incurred many debts in assembling this account of a year's music, espe-cially to librarians and archivists in the cities which feature in the story. Among individual debts I would especially like to mention the late Charles Suttoni for help with Liszt, and Renate Hofmann, Katharina Loose and Robert Pascall for help with Brahms. Keith Graber kindly looked into the sources of William Mason's diaries for me, and Christina Bashford similarly supplied some precious information from Ella's diaries. Bertrand Jaeger checked the records in Basel, and Rainer Schmusch helped me with Baden-Baden's archives. Mark Rowe lent me his expertise on the violinist Ernst. The most obscure area of information has its expert, and in the case of Channel shipping records in 1853 that expert is Martin Price, whom I must also thank. Victoria Viebahn guided me expertly around Göttingen and its history. I have enjoyed lengthy conversations about Schumann with Gina Pellegrino and about Liszt with Kenneth Hamilton, both of whom I warmly thank for setting me on what I hope is the right track. Stephen Gage has most expertly prepared the maps. I have greatly benefited from acute observations offered by both David Cairns and Craig Monson. I especially need to express my unbounded thanks to two friends who share my passion for (in)significant detail and who have done invaluable fieldwork on my behalf: Pepijn van Doesburg has researched concert life in Germany and Holland in great depth and generously shared his findings with me; and Gunther Braam has been a source of vast reserves of information about all the musicians in the story and has been especially helpful with pictures. Without these two human storehouses the book would be much more deeply infected with error than it is.

I wish to thank the Cambridge University Press for permission to quote from *Richard Wagner: My Life*, translated by Andrew Gray and edited by Mary Whittall, Cambridge, 1983, and the University of Rochester Press for permission to quote from Hector Berlioz, *The Musical Madhouse*, translated by Alastair Bruce, Rochester, 2003.

ST LOUIS, 2011

Map 1 Germany, showing principal rail connections in 1853

CHAPTER I

Brahms Leaves Home

APRIL – MAY

O N Tuesday 19 April 1853 Johannes Brahms left his parents' house in the Lilienstrasse, in the old part of the city of Hamburg, and set off on the road. He was not yet twenty years old and his fond parents bid him farewell with anxiety. He was the second of three children, a little less than average height, with fair, straight hair and a fresh, almost babyish, complexion. Brahms, who looked so old when he was old, looked very young when he was young. His serious demeanour and taciturn manner convinced those who met him that his absorption in music and books marked him out as a young man with a future, and his talent on the piano was already evident to those who had attended his concerts, especially the performance of Beethoven's 'Waldstein' Sonata which he gave when he was fifteen. But in an age when piano virtuosi of both sexes were springing up in great numbers, youthful talent had to be nothing less than prodigious to win fame and success, and Brahms's serious-minded teacher, Eduard Marxsen, reported the Beethoven performance in terms that can only be described as cool: 'The youthful virtuoso gave most satisfactory proofs of advancement in his artistic career. His performance showed that he is already able to devote himself successfully to the study of the classics, and redounded in every respect to his honour.'

It is true that at the age of ten an American agent had offered to engage him for a tour of the United States, but adolescence led him in a more studious direction, especially towards composition, in which, according to the cautious Marxsen, he displayed 'unusual talent'. Hamburg offered reasonable opportunities for musicians. Brahms's father earned a living as double-bass player in various theatre orchestras and as horn-player in the militia band. Brahms himself was soon offered work by the local music publisher Cranz, contributing arrangements of light music for a burgeoning market. As a Free City Hamburg had no royal or ducal court, but its theatres and churches flourished (despite the catastrophic fire that swept the city in 1842), and although the city's resident musicians did not have the lustre that Telemann and C. P. E. Bach gave it in the eighteenth century, it was visited by some distinguished figures. Liszt gave concerts there in 1840 and 1841; Ernst came in 1843, Berlioz also in 1843; Joachim played the Beethoven violin concerto there in 1848, and Robert and Clara Schumann paid a visit in 1850.

Brahms did not meet any of these great musicians then, although Joachim's performance made a deep impression on him and he sent some compositions to Schumann's hotel in the hope that some encouraging judgment might be forthcoming. The parcel was returned unopened. A visiting artist, almost as celebrated as Joachim, who did respond to Brahms's talent was another Hungarian violinist

1 Brahms and Reményi in 1853 (Brahms standing)

who arrived in Hamburg in 1849. Ede Reményi was a glamorous figure who had studied at the Vienna Conservatoire under his original name Eduard Hoffmann and then transformed himself into a Hungarian nationalist in 1848 when Kossuth led the ill-fated uprising against the Austrians. Reményi joined the insurgents, but he was kept well away from the action since his commander, General Görgey, valued his violin playing too highly. At all events, when the nationalists were defeated in August 1849, Reményi had to flee for his life. A group of Hungarians headed for Hamburg since it provided easy access to America, among them Reményi, who took advantage of Hamburg's unusually liberal atmosphere to give some concerts. For one of these his accompanist fell ill, so on the recommendation of the publisher August Böhm he engaged the young Brahms for a soirée in the house of a wealthy industrialist named Helmrich. Brahms called on Reményi at his hotel. 'My name is Johannes Brahms. I have been sent by Herr Böhm to act as your accompanist and I would be delighted if I can undertake this to your satisfaction.'

Reményi, surpised by Brahms's youthful looks and high-pitched voice, found him to be a far better musician than his previous accompanist and questioned him about his career and his compositions. After they had rehearsed the programme, Brahms played some of his piano pieces and the two fell into conversation which caused them to forget their engagement for that evening and sit up late into the night. Helmrich was not pleased, and Reményi's engagements in Hamburg came to an abrupt end. In increasing fear of arrest Reményi sailed for New York, where he gave a concert on 9 January 1850. After six months in America he returned to Europe to give concerts, eluding the long arm of the Austrian police, and at the end of 1852 he appeared in Hamburg once again.

Reményi was just twenty-five, and even to the serious-minded Brahms he must have seemed a dazzlingly exotic figure. He was rather short, like Brahms, with a large head, smooth face and bright, expressive eyes. He was a man of simple tastes and strong passions, and his enthusiasm for travel was already well developed. His experience of revolution and war, his concert appearances in Paris, London and New York, and his fondness for Hungarian melodies opened up a world of which Brahms had at that time no inkling. Their temperaments were quite different, Reményi being eccentric and boastful while Brahms was intensely serious and somewhat withdrawn, but Brahms saw in Reményi a chance to reach out to the wider world of German music and to meet some of the musicians he most admired. Only thus could he hope to find a leading music publisher to take his compositions, as his parents were pressing him to do. Through Reményi he might make the acquaintance of Joachim, possibly Schumann, possibly Liszt. He had also begun to think that he was not properly appreciated in his home town. Neither his father nor his teacher Marxsen had been prepared to see in him the promise of genius that Reményi saw (or later claimed to have seen), so it was only common sense to take their talents elsewhere.

Plans for a concert tour soon formed in their minds, not to the distant capitals where Reményi had already played, but to smaller towns in north Germany. Their departure from Hamburg in mid-April may have been hastened by Reményi's renewed fear of arrest, for within half an hour of their leaving town the police called at the Brahms house in search of the errant revolutionary. Everyone except Brahms's devoted elderly mother thought it was pure folly for him to leave home with such an adventurer. The concert season was almost over and they had little money. No doubt they entertained the possibility of visiting Joachim in Hanover and Liszt in Weimar, but nothing of this kind had been arranged in advance.

Their first stop was at Winsen-an-der-Luhe, a small town just across the Elbe from Hamburg which Brahms knew well since he had spent much of his childhood there visiting the Giesemann family. Herr Giesemann, who owned a paper-mill, was a friend of Brahms's father, and his daughter Lieschen had been taught the piano by the adolescent Johannes. Reményi and Brahms stayed with the Giesemanns and gave two concerts in the town. Reményi also had friends in Winsen. His concert repertoire featured Beethoven's Violin Sonata in C minor, op. 30 no. 2, Ernst's *Elégie* and *Le Carnaval de Venise* variations, Vieuxtemps's Violin Concerto no. 1 in E major, and some of his favourite Hungarian melodies, while Brahms on his own played his arrangement of Weber's Rondo for the left hand and his own latest compositions: the Scherzo in E flat minor (later published as op. 4) and movements from his piano sonatas in C major and F sharp minor (opp. 1 and 2). They also played a violin sonata by Brahms in A minor, now lost.

It has always been assumed that Brahms and Reményi spent their first few weeks giving concerts in small towns, but the hotel records tell us otherwise. On 21 April they were checked in at the Hôtel de Russie in Hanover as 'musicians Remenissi from New York and Brahms from Hamburg'. After leaving Winsen-an-der-Luhe they took the railway which had been operating between Harburg (opposite Hamburg) and Hanover for only six years, through Lüneburg, Uelzen and Celle to Hanover. Hanover was the capital of a sizeable province of north Germany, bordered on both east and west by Prussian territory and ruled by a grandson of England's George III correctly numbered Georg V. Since by Salic law the crown of Hanover could not pass to a woman, Victoria acceded only to the British throne in 1837; the Hanoverian throne passed to her uncle Ernst August. Georg V, his son, was an old-fashioned monarch who loved music but was destined to spend his days squabbling with other German states and finally yielding his kingdom to Prussian bullying in 1866. Before the age of fourteen he lost the sight of one eye through disease and then the other, by terrible misfortune, as a result of an accident. His blindness only increased the pleasure he derived from music. He had studied the piano in London and composition in Berlin, and he composed over 200 works in the years before his succession to the throne of Hanover in 1851, including songs, choruses and piano pieces, and in 1839 he published an ambitious essay on music entitled *Ideen und Betrachtungen über die Eigenschaften der Musik,* which was also published in an English translation. He took the keenest interest in Hanover's music, especially the opera, which had been directed since 1831 by Heinrich

Angekommene Fremde, angemeldet den 21. April 1853.

Stadt Hamburg (bei Chr. Günther): Student Schweigmann aus Essen. Dr. Hohnston aus London. Lehrer Falkenhausen aus Hamburg. Polytechniker Hamel aus Altona. Dr. phil. Kraß aus Hildesheim. Pferdehändler Fränckel aus Mannheim. Kaufleute Habich aus Cassel, Salomon aus Weener, Hahloh aus Harburg, Friedeberg aus Frankfurt, Ahrens aus Münster.

Hotel de Russie (bei J. Meese): Gutsbesitzer Frhr. v. Meysenburg aus Lauenau. Dom.-Pächter Thunemann aus Königshorst. Dr. phil. Ossander aus Würtemberg. Tonkünstler Remenissi aus Newyork und Brahms aus Hamburg. Kaufleute de Kremitzini aus St. Petersburg, Anhalt aus Neusalzwerk, Pappier aus Bremen, Horch aus Leer.

2 Hotel Arrivals in Hanover, 21 April 1853

Marschner, one of the leading figures in German opera between the death of Weber and the advent of Wagner. Relations were not always easy between the King and Marschner, who had not recently produced anything to equal the remarkable *Hans Heiling* of 1833. Any music other than the performances of the court opera failed to interest him. By 1853, in a word, Marschner's vitality and influence had greatly declined, especially since in 1852 he acquired an assistant, Carl Ludwig Fischer, who was assigned the task of conducting orchestral concerts. The appointment of a brilliant star to the position of konzertmeister and principal violinist in the court orchestra shifted the focus of the city's musical life.

Joseph Joachim took up his new position in Hanover on 1 January 1853, just a few months before the arrival of Reményi and Brahms. He was only twenty-one years old but was already an international figure, known to audiences in London, Paris and many German cities (including Hamburg, as we have seen). Like Reményi he was from a family of German-speaking Jewish Hungarians, although he never identified with Hungarian causes and kept away from the insurgencies of 1848–9. He studied in Vienna with the same teacher, Joseph Böhm, and had known Reményi there as a fellow-pupil. At the age of twelve he appeared as a soloist in Leipzig with Mendelssohn conducting and it was Mendelssohn and Leipzig's leading violinist Ferdinand David who guided his artistic development until the former's premature death in 1847. In Leipzig he got to know Robert and Clara Schumann also. He played for Queen Victoria in London and under Berlioz's baton in Paris and since the autumn of 1850 he had been konzertmeister of Liszt's orchestra in Weimar. The atmosphere in Weimar was very different from that of Leipzig, stimulating in its repertoire of music by Liszt, Wagner and other progressive composers, and comradely in the fellowship of brilliant young musicians gathered around the

3 Joseph Joachim in 1853

spellbinding figure of Liszt. Joachim's position in Weimar allowed him freedom to play chamber music with other members of the court orchestra and to go on tour as a soloist. With Bernhard Cossmann, Weimar's principal cellist, in particular, Joachim developed a close friendship. Joachim was a composer as well as a violinist, and in Weimar he began to devote more time to what he may have then seen as his most promising line of work.

In Hanover, as in Weimar, Joachim enjoyed the freedom to travel as a virtuoso and to compose. His first winter concert season, in which he introduced some Wagner to the unsuspecting Hanoverians, was concluded by mid-March 1853, when he began to plan his summer engagements. With Liszt's encouragement he was also working on a substantial overture on Shakespeare's *Hamlet* (Liszt's own symphonic poem *Hamlet* was written five years later). He was already feeling isolated from his own kind, in contrast to the intense comradeship of Weimar, and out of sympathy with his two kapellmeisters, Fischer (who conducted the orchestra and liked to hobnob with courtiers) and Marschner (who conducted the opera and showed little interest in anything else). He was much better paid in Hanover than in Weimar and he had the King's support, but the musical benefits of his move were not clear.

He was still in Hanover on 21 April when his old friend Reményi arrived with a young pianist who was desperate to meet him. Leaving Brahms at the Hôtel de Russie, Reményi called on Joachim at his apartment on Prinzenstrasse. He made no secret of their shortage of funds and their desire to give a concert, making Joachim smile when he told him he had a young genius as accompanist. But when Joachim heard Brahms play he was overwhelmed by this shy, fair-haired young man playing his own compositions with unmistakable nobility. Brahms played parts of his C major Sonata, op. 1, and his E flat minor Scherzo, op. 4, and he also sang his song 'O, versenk dein Leid' (later published as op. 3, no. 1), which moved Joachim greatly. His playing, 'so tender, so imaginative, so free and so fiery', held him spellbound. This was the beginning of a great and famous friendship that was to last (with one notable interruption) until Brahms's death forty-four years later. With hindsight Joachim recalled the occasion with deep emotion, but even at the time, or at least during the ensuing weeks when the two musicians had the opportunity to know each other better, Joachim announced to his friends that an exceptional musician had joined him. 'His playing has the fire, the driving energy and the rhythmic precision that bespeak the artist, and his compositions are already more impressive than anything I have ever seen in an artist of his age.'

Reményi played some of his Hungarian melodies, for which Brahms arranged the accompaniments. A sheet of three tunes bearing a generous greeting in Hungarian to a friend (presumably Joachim) survives from this visit. But despite all that Joachim had in common with Reményi it was Brahms who aroused his interest, and he foresaw that the temperamental difference between him and Reményi would soon threaten their partnership as concert artists. It was not possible to arrange a performance for the King during this visit, and since Reményi and Brahms had a concert engagement in Celle on 2 May, they planned to return for that purpose at a later date.

Celle is an attractive town north-east of Hanover nestling beneath the King of Hanover's impressive summer residence. The travellers' hosts in Celle were Köhler, a doctor related to the rector of Winsen, and Blume, a lawyer, and the concert was remarkable for Brahms's sangfroid in the face of a piano so flat in pitch that he had to transpose all the violin accompaniments up a semitone. The Beethoven sonata had thus to be played in C sharp minor, not C minor, and although the challenge is hardly insuperable for a musician of Brahms's calibre, Reményi gave his young friend proper credit for a remarkable feat when he addressed the audience at the end of the concert. Like many a virtuoso violinist before and since, Reményi was unwilling to tune his violin down to match the recalcitrant piano.

They then continued to retrace their steps – or the railway line – most of the way back to Hamburg, to Lüneburg, where Blume, the lawyer's son, received them. They stayed in the Hotel Hoffnung. In the Blumes' house Brahms played part of his new piano sonata in C major to an audience which, at Brahms's request, included no women, not even his hostess. Here in Lüneburg, where Brahms celebrated his twentieth birthday on 7 May, he cannot have failed to visit the Michaeliskirche, the church where Bach had sung as a boy. Brahms's profound reverence for Bach was already evident, though he still had much to learn. In the house of Herr Balcke on the 9th he and Reményi played the Beethoven C minor violin sonata again and Vieuxtemps's violin concerto in E, and the same programme again on the 11th with some Hungarian melodies thrown in. Next day they packed their bags and sped back to Celle, where they made their second appearance on the following day in the Dunckers Hotel, not, one hopes, on a piano as flat as before. The rest of the month was probably taken up with concerts in smaller towns, of which no record remains, concluding on 1 June in Hildesheim, south-east of Hanover. If they were there one day earlier they would have been near misses for two meteorites that fell on the town, as the newspaper reported. Brahms later remembered playing there to a very sparse audience, after which they dined rather noisily with some friends and then took advantage of the unusually warm weather to sing and play beneath the window of the lady who was looking after their arrangements. News of the escapade – if such it was – ensured a full house for their second concert.

WHILE Reményi and Brahms continued on the road, Joachim had some out-of-town engagements of his own. On 12 May he left Hanover for Düsseldorf to take part in the thirty-first Lower Rhine Music Festival. This Festival rotated annually from city to city in the region and was assigned to Düsseldorf for 1853. It was organised this year by two of Joachim's former friends from his time in Leipzig, Schumann and Hiller, in charge of the music in, respectively, Düsseldorf and Cologne. It was Hiller's move from Düsseldorf to Cologne in 1850 that had opened the way for Schumann's move from Dresden, but the two and a half years that Schumann had spent in Düsseldorf were far from happy. His appointment carried the duty of conducting a season of concerts each year but his conducting provoked constant complaints from the Düsseldorfers; in addition his health had been intermittently alarming. In May 1853 he was enjoying a spell of better health and a flood of creative work, but relations with the city authorities were deteriorating badly and he conducted less and less of his assigned concerts, passing the baton to his assistant Tausch for almost everything except his own works.

Ferdinand Hiller was a more formidable figure in many ways. He did not have Schumann's genius as a composer, but he was heavily built, wealthy, urbane and much travelled, and he had a wide network of friends and contacts across Europe. He had spent seven years in Paris, where he was on close terms with Berlioz, Chopin and Liszt (he and Liszt were born two days apart in 1811), and a similar period in Rome. He had been close to Mendelssohn in Leipzig, he had worked with the Schumanns in Dresden. As pianist, conductor, composer and teacher he wielded great influence in Cologne and nearby cities, and his friendship with Schumann was now beginning to turn into an alliance of like-minded musicians whose principal bond was a distaste for Wagner and the threat he posed to the flourishing mainstream of German music, perceived to be a grand symphonic tradition stemming from Beethoven.

Both Schumann and Hiller had enjoyed friendly relations with Liszt, but the more Liszt took on the role of Wagner's mouthpiece the less they were able to countenance his energetic propaganda on behalf of the music of Wagner, Liszt himself, Berlioz, and a number of younger musicians of similar outlook. There was as yet no formal breach between the two schools, but the difficulty both Schumann and Hiller felt with regard to Liszt, in whom they both found much to admire, was exacerbated by Clara Schumann's unconcealed hostility to Liszt and her extreme distaste for the music and personality of Berlioz. In due course it was to be Brahms who provided the focus for their movement, but in the meantime a crucial role in the growth of resistance to the new trends would be played by Joachim. His five busy days in Düsseldorf in the company of Hiller and the Schumanns was a turning-point in his gradual desertion of Liszt and all that he stood for. He had just spent two years in Weimar working closely with Liszt and was still on excellent terms with his former boss.

Joachim arrived in Düsseldorf on the night train from Hanover on the morning of Friday 13 May. He had not seen Schumann for three years and must have noticed a certain puffiness in his complexion and the ravages of his chronic nervousness. Schumann had arranged for him to stay with a widowed banker named Scheuer in order to spare him the disturbances of a hotel. Joachim was able to attend one rehearsal later that day and two more on the Saturday, then the series of three large concerts began the next day, Whitsunday, an important holiday weekend in Germany. He played in the orchestra in the first two concerts and was the soloist in the third. Sunday's programme, conducted by Schumann, consisted of his Fourth Symphony in D minor, which dated back to 1841 but had recently been considerably

4 Robert and Clara Schumann in 1850, after a daguerrotype

revised, followed by Handel's *Messiah* as the second part of the programme. In the interval Joachim presented Schumann with a laurel crown.

For the Festival concerts enormous forces were assembled: 490 in the chorus and 160 in the orchestra. Monday's concert comprised Beethoven's Ninth Symphony after a series of vocal pieces in the first half, all under Hiller's direction, and the third concert, on the Tuesday, contained eleven items in the style of grand festival concerts of the day. Clara Novello sang 'God Save the Queen' (a well-known and popular melody in Germany), Clara Schumann played her husband's Piano Concerto in A minor, the 'Hallelujah' Chorus was repeated from Sunday's concert, Hiller improvised at the piano, and the concert ended with the first performance of Schumann's latest work, the *Festival Overture* on the Rhenish drinking song 'Bekränzt mit Laub'. This was a rousing occasional piece for orchestra with soloists and chorus joining in at the end, anticipating Brahms's *Academic Festival Overture* in many details. But the high point of the concert was unquestionably Joachim's performance of the Beethoven Violin Concerto, which Schumann had particularly requested. He had evidently not heard it before, nor had a great many of the large audience in the Geissler Garden Hall on Schadowstrasse that evening. It made a profound impression, and Clara confided to her diary that she had never before been so unforgettably impressed by any virtuoso as this.

The next morning, before taking his leave, Joachim went to the Schumanns' house on Bilkerstrasse and played through Schumann's Violin Sonata in A minor, op. 105, with Clara, again leaving a deep impression of his musicianship and artistry. Amid the flurry of rehearsals and concerts he made the acquaintance of one of Schumann's disciples, Albert Dietrich, and he told Schumann that the conviviality of musicians was much greater in Düsseldorf than in Hanover, where he had felt distinctly isolated after the intense atmosphere of Weimar. He must also have found time to tell Schumann and Hiller about the young man from Hamburg who had so deeply impressed him three weeks before. His friendship with Schumann henceforth took on a new warmth; it was Schumann rather than Liszt in whom Joachim was now more inclined to confide, and Clara recognised the depth and modesty in Joachim's character, the basis of a lifelong friendship between the two.

He would nonetheless have been far from reluctant, indeed he was full of keen anticipation, on that day Wednesday 18 May as he travelled on to Weimar, a circuitous journey by rail passing back through Hanover. He had many friends in Weimar and could look forward to some splendid music-making. The schedule was tight, for he was due to play in a concert that Friday, the 20th, in Weimar's ducal palace in honour of the marriage of Princess Amalia Maria of Sachsen-Weimar-Eisenach to Prince Henry of Nassau and Orange. Royalty from the Netherlands and Prussia and the Saxon nobility were present in strength. Joachim played Ernst's brilliant fantasy on Rossini's *Otello* for violin and orchestra, one of his regular showpieces. The orchestra played Gade's *Spring Fantasy* and a new *Fest-Ouvertüre* by Raff. The following day Liszt conducted the opening night of Flotow's opera *Indra* in the Weimar theatre; this was a work that had attracted little attention when it was first played in Paris in 1843 under the title *L'Esclave de Camoëns*, but was now appearing in an expanded German version and was spreading like wildfire from city to city. Liszt despised the work as 'shoddy goods' but had every now and then to put a good face on conducting works that the theatre management, not he, had chosen.

On the Sunday morning, as on most Sunday mornings, there was music-making at Liszt's house, the Altenburg, in which Joachim was reunited with his former quartet colleagues Stör (second violin), Walbrül (viola) and Cossmann (cello). This created a delicate situation since Joachim's successor, a brilliant young violinist from Prague named Ferdinand Laub, might have felt displaced by his more celebrated predecessor. But Joachim's authority, especially in Beethoven's quartets, was unchallenged, and his presence was warmly appreciated by all. During his two years in Weimar he had laid the foundations of his lifelong mission as a quartet leader and as an exponent of the great chamber repertoire of Haydn, Mozart and Beethoven. On the Monday Liszt arranged an orchestral rehearsal in order to try out Joachim's new overture *Hamlet* for the first time, also his violin concerto in G minor in one movement. Joachim was, privately, very disappointed with the orchestra. The strings were far below full strength and the wind were out of tune. But Liszt threw himself energetically into the task, and Joachim was gratified to discover that the overture sounded more or less as he intended, and an entry for four horns in unison designed to convey the hand of destiny came off exactly right. Nevertheless he decided to make a few revisions, the first of many, as it turned out.

He stayed in Weimar a week. A new book by Berlioz was giving much delight to all. This was *Les Soirées de l'orchestre,* a collection of essays and articles strung together under the hilarious fiction that they are stories exchanged by members of the orchestra of a provincial opera house during the performance of interminable worthless operas. More earnest reading-matter had recently arrived in Weimar from Wagner, of whom, as always, there was much talk. His privately printed libretto *Der Ring des Nibelungen* was sent to a select few, of whom Liszt was of course the first. Four consecutive evenings were devoted to reading it, and in his next letter Liszt urged Wagner, then living in Zurich, to embark on the music. Even Liszt can scarcely have imagined what a gigantic undertaking that was to be. Joachim too was still enthusiastic about Wagner. He had another opportunity on that visit to hear *Lohengrin*, which he had played many times before, and he met a devoted Wagnerian named Louis Köhler who had come all the way from Königsberg on the Baltic coast in the hope of hearing the three Wagner operas that Liszt had by now established in the Weimar repertory: *Der fliegende Holländer, Tannhäuser* and *Lohengrin*. Before leaving Weimar Joachim promised to accompany Liszt to Zurich at the end of June to pay a visit to Wagner in his Swiss exile.

JOACHIM returned briefly to Hanover for a few days to pack his bags for a longer stay in Göttingen, sixty miles south. During his brief spell at home Joachim made up a package for Schumann, to include a score of the Beethoven Violin Concerto, which Joachim sent, duly inscribed, in response to Schumann's request. Inspired by Joachim's playing in Düsseldorf, Schumann was planning to write something for violin and orchestra himself, a type of piece he had never attempted. With some diffidence Joachim included the *Hamlet* overture with the Beethoven in the hope that Schumann could spare the time to look at it. Schumann's experience and credentials as a critic were second to none, having founded the *Neue Zeitschrift für Musik* in Leipzig twenty years earlier. Joachim guessed that after his sympathetic reception in Düsseldorf he could count on constructive criticism, which he soon received in a letter written on 8 June, Schumann's forty-third birthday. Both Schumann and Clara overflowed with friendly greetings, and in the overture Schumann found much to pick out for praise. 'Don't change a thing until you've heard it several times', was his admirable advice.

By the time Joachim received Schumann's letter he was in Göttingen. Since moving to Hanover he had decided to use his free summer months to attend courses at the University of Göttingen in an attempt to enlarge what he felt had been an incomplete education in Leipzig when as a young virtuoso he had perforce spent most of his adolescent years practising the violin and giving concerts. He had invited Reményi and Brahms to visit him there, and they arrived from Hildesheim on 4 June, only a day after his own arrival. Joachim had already made up his mind about Brahms's talent in April; now the friendship began to bloom with such rapidity that within a few days Joachim could write Brahms a note of real chumminess:

My dear Johannes,
    The piano's still out, it's shy of the rain. But your sonata has nothing to fear, it'll put up a brave fight against the waters of ordinariness, like everything of yours. How about meeting at Wehner's from ten to twelve with violin, music and (last but not least) friend Reményi to breathe life into the composition, i.e. to play it? Send me a note in reply with the bearer to
    Your friend
        Joseph Joachim
    Greetings to Reményi barátom.

The sonata mentioned was the work in A minor for violin and piano, now lost, and Wehner was the hospitable head of the University's music. Reményi and Brahms both wrote entries in Wehner's autograph album, Brahms's contribution being a wistful piece for piano which resurfaced over ten years later in the second movement of the Horn Trio op. 40. According to Hermann Deiters, Brahms found himself once again in Göttingen obliged to transpose an entire Beethoven sonata up a semitone, this time the 'Kreutzer', whose transposition from A minor to B flat minor would be a far more daunting challenge than the C minor to C sharp minor he had thrown off in Celle. Joachim had some guidance to offer, since the pair were due in Hanover on the 8th to play to the King, probably the only date on which such a thing could be arranged since the King was about to leave for a visit to England and had an unusual press of business. Joachim, intent on his studies, did not return from Göttingen to accompany them, but he privately told Brahms that he thought Reményi was an unsuitable partner for him and that he would be welcome to come back later to Göttingen if he wished. Reményi attempted to stop the pendulum of a clock to mark the place and the time, as he told Joachim with characteristic vanity, when two world-famous violinists had met.

Reményi and Brahms returned to Hanover for their royal appointment. When Reményi paid his respects to the King, he was offered the services of his court pianist Heinrich Ehrlich (yet another German-speaking Jewish Hungarian) for the concert, to which the violinist replied: 'Your Majesty, I need no accompanist because I have one with me whom I regard as a great musical genius.' At the concert the King was not impressed: 'My dear Reményi,' he told him, 'I believe you are carried away by your enthusiasm; your musical genius has no genius at all.' Or, as Ehrlich epigrammatically put it, 'The violinist gave great delight; the pianist gave less.' The E flat minor Scherzo was no piece for a court concert, thought Ehrlich.

To do him justice, the King later repented of his misjudgment. Over twenty years later, having lost his throne and living in exile, he attended one of Reményi's concerts in Paris and told him: 'As for your friend Brahms, you were right and we were all wrong. I remember your prediction about that young man, and his present reputation does honour to your judgment.'

Brahms and Reményi had no certain engagements ahead, but they both had good reasons for moving on to Weimar to meet Liszt. Reményi held Liszt in awe as a fellow Hungarian and as the greatest of living pianists. They had the cachet of Joachim's introduction, and Brahms, as an aspiring composer whose music was beginning to show a new, massive style of pianism, was anxious simply to meet the great figures in German music and to experience a cultural milieu a great deal less limited than that of Hamburg. Weimar, the city where Goethe and Schiller lived and wrote, was a cultural shrine for all bookish Germans, and Liszt's presence was the most decisive factor in restoring the city to its former glory.

They were also in danger once again from the police. Wermuth, the Hanover police chief, discovering that Reményi was on the blacklist, summoned him and ordered him and his companion to move on to Bückeburg, thirty miles west of Hanover, the seat of the principality of Schaumburg-Lippe. At this point Ehrlich intervened and secured police permission for the two to go in a different direction, south-east to Weimar, where the Saxon authorities were less severe in their pursuit of Hungarian nationalists.

CHAPTER 2

Berlioz and Spohr in London

ON Saturday 14 May, while Schumann and Joachim were rehearsing in Düsseldorf and while Reményi and Brahms were travelling somewhere in north Germany, Hector Berlioz left Paris for London, sailing under overcast skies on the *Princess Helena* from Boulogne to Folkestone. It was his fourth visit to England and his third in three years. He liked London more and more, and his previous visit, in 1852, had been an enormous success. He was greatly impressed by the vastness and imperial splendour of London, and the profusion of foreign musicians working in London ensured that he would be working among friends. The social conventions that discouraged educated Englishmen from pursuing a career in the arts provided opportunities for visiting musicians from the Continent to win applause as performers and composers, and a permanent snobbery preferred musicians and artists to be foreign, or at least to bear foreign names. In addition, the disorders of 1848 all over Europe had brought many refugees to England, including such revolutionaries as Mazzini and Marx. Berlioz had been in London when the 1848 riots broke out in Paris and there were moments when he thought he might settle there himself. He was convinced that artistic enterprise was impossible in Paris and had given up trying to put on his own concerts, knowing from experience that French audiences were fickle and expenses hard to control. The tepid reception of *La Damnation de Faust* in 1846 had really brought this sad state of affairs home to him, and as his career blossomed as a guest conductor abroad – in Germany, Russia and England – his composing activities withered away. Apart from the *Te Deum* written in 1849 (and partially put together from earlier music) he had composed almost nothing since 1846 and had effectively ceased being a composer at all. In the autumn of 1850 he composed, almost by accident, a little chorus 'L'Adieu des bergers', from which he felt so detached that he presented it at its first performance as the work of an unknown seventeenth-century composer Pierre Ducré. He wrote two short flanking movements soon after, but this little triptych describing the Holy Family's flight into Egypt with the baby Jesus, entitled *La Fuite en Égypte*, had never yet been performed complete; three years later Berlioz was showing little urge to give it anywhere.

If London had offered him a permanent position as a conductor, he might have taken it; when there was talk of a position in Dresden he considered it very seriously. In the end he remained an unhappy Parisian for the rest of his life, but his best music-making was to be in London and those hospitable German cities where an enlightened court took care of the expenses of concert-giving and where audiences were sympathetic to his unusual music. In 1847–8 he conducted an opera season at Drury Lane and two concerts in Hanover Square Rooms; in 1851 he came for the Great Exhibition in Hyde Park, for which he served on the examining panel for musical instruments, but gave no concerts; in 1852 he was engaged by the New Philharmonic Society, a rival of the venerable 'Old' Philharmonic Society, to conduct their first season of six concerts in Exeter Hall, including two performances of Beethoven's Ninth Symphony which were remembered for years. His standing as a conductor was now second to none, while his appetite for composing was completely inert. He nourished some ideas for a new large work but had no intention of ever committing them to paper.

5 Hector Berlioz in 1851

A few months after his London successes of 1852 he went to Weimar for a Berlioz Festival mounted by Liszt which included a number of his concert works and a production of his opera *Benvenuto Cellini*. After its catastrophic failure at the Paris Opéra in 1838 Berlioz had abandoned hope of ever hearing it again. But Liszt, with his wholehearted devotion to the cause of advanced music and his flair for promoting the works of others, took *Benvenuto Cellini* into the Weimar repertoire to join three of Wagner's works and to serve as a model for the eager young German musicians who were discovering Berlioz's music for the first time. The news of Liszt's successful Weimar revival prompted the management of the Royal Italian Opera in London to approach Berlioz with an invitation to conduct the work himself at Covent Garden in the summer of 1853. It was to prepare these performances that he now crossed the Channel for his fourth visit.

He was accompanied by Marie Recio, with whom he had been living for almost ten years, following a painful separation from his wife Harriet Smithson. Harriet was immobile from a series of strokes and had to be nursed day and night, while their son Louis, now eighteen, was training for service in the navy and awaiting his next ship in Cherbourg. Berlioz and Marie, who travelled as Monsieur et Madame Berlioz, arrived in London on 14 May and took lodgings at no. 17 Old Cavendish Street, a few doors down from his previous year's lodgings and close to the houses in Harley Street and Queen Anne Street where he had stayed on his first two visits. That area north of Oxford Street was now a familiar haunt. Their landlady was a dressmaker, Mrs Elizabeth Turnour, but the building has since been demolished and replaced.

London boasted less opera than Paris but a much more active concert life. Scarcely a day passed without one of the major musical organisations offering a concert, so that at the height of the season, which ran roughly from March to July, the leading musicians of the capital were in tremendous demand. This concert *richesse* has always been a feature of London life since the later eighteenth century, and the comfortable wealth of Queen Victoria's leading citizens supported spectacular opera with the world's best singers and long concerts with many soloists. There was a new burgeoning taste for chamber music, while a typically English devotion to large-scale choral music, an inheritance from Handel, filled the larger halls with oratorios and cantatas sung by many hundreds of voices.

German critics, flaunting the great tradition from Bach to Beethoven, harped endlessly on the notion that England was a land without music, but they were wrong. English composers since the seventeenth century may have been of little significance, but the generous English appetite for music and its active cultivation by amateurs were vigorously healthy elements of cultural and economic life. As Ernest Newman put it, 'There was the usual crowd of professional and amateur-professional practitioners, several of whom were such manifest mediocrities that to us of today it is a mystery how they escaped a knighthood.' At the same time dilettantism was rife, and criticism, though conducted by persons of unimpeachable literary distinction, was simply out of touch with the latest Continental currents of style and taste. Ernest Newman continues: 'There was the *Times*, already bearing with conscious dignity the heavy burden of the responsibility that had been laid upon it by Providence of giving the cosmos its A.' While all Germany debated the issue of Wagner and the new music, London was still wedded to the comfortable idioms of Spohr and Mendelssohn. Schumann was coupled with Wagner as a dangerous modernist, and the suspicion attached to their works shows how far London critics and audiences were from a true understanding of the real critical issues. Berlioz, too, was regarded as a purveyor of shock, but being starkly individual in style and manifestly independent of any school he was not thought to pose a serious threat, as some German composers were, to the health of the musical organism.

Four principal organisations were giving regular concerts in the 1853 summer season: the 'Old' Philharmonic Society, the New Philharmonic Society, the Sacred Harmonic Society, and the Musical Union. The Philharmonic Society, founded in 1813, performed on alternate Mondays in Hanover Square Rooms, giving long concerts with substantial orchestral works mingled with vocal and choral music in the manner of the day. Their conductor was Michael Costa, by far the most influential conductor in London, as Habeneck had been in Paris twenty years earlier. Of Italian birth, Costa had a reputation for firm discipline and for attracting the best players. Berlioz recognised his qualities as a conductor but deplored his habit of reorchestrating the works of the masters, a practice that was common well into the twentieth century. As a composer himself, Costa no doubt felt as qualified to take on that task as Mahler did in his turn. But Berlioz took a different view:

> That composers are great masters, armed with great authority, that they are called Mozart, Beethoven, Weber or Rossini, matters little. Mr Costa has for a long time thought fit to give them lessons in instrumentation.

Costa's tastes were soundly conservative. Although the Philharmonic had put on the *Benvenuto Cellini* overture in 1841 and had unsuccessfully attempted to engage Berlioz as conductor in 1843, they had since showed little inclination to attempt his kind of music.

The New Philharmonic Society was founded in 1852 principally to correct this lack of a modern orchestral repertoire in London's music. It fielded an orchestra of 110 players, including some of the best London musicians, and it was managed by Dr Henry Wylde, a professor at the Royal Academy of Music with aspirations as a composer and conductor; his abilities were limited but his taste in music was mildly adventurous. His partner was Frederick Beale, a music publisher on the look out for new successes. The New Philharmonic played much less regularly than the Old, usually on Wednesdays three or four weeks apart, and their concerts were held in the large Exeter Hall (on the site now occupied by the Strand Palace Hotel). As their conductor for the first season Berlioz had launched the orchestra with considerable élan, but Wylde and Beale fell out over whether to re-engage him for the next season, and when Wylde, who wielded the money, refused to do so,

Beale resigned. Berlioz was disappointed, but he knew that Wylde's pretensions as a conductor would not tolerate the competition. 'He just wants a one-eyed or blind conductor, and I don't even wear glasses,' he wrote.

So for the 1853 season Wylde, allowing one or two appearances on the rostrum for himself, invited two elderly German conductors of sterling reputation who had been presiding over their respective cities' music for over thirty years: Lindpaintner from Stuttgart and Spohr from Kassel. Lindpaintner was a modest composer whose conducting was much admired by Mendelssohn and also by Berlioz when he visited Stuttgart in 1843. Spohr was triply honoured, for in addition to his celebrity as a conductor he was also recognised as a great violinist (though never to be compared with Paganini) and as a leading composer within the central German tradition; in fact in England his standing as a composer was so high that when Mendelssohn died in 1847 Spohr was widely thought to have inherited the mantle of the greatest living composer. In Germany there were few who would go so far, yet he was none-theless highly respected as a composer both for his fluency in all forms and for his deft harmonic language that derived from Mozart and had probably influenced Schubert. Wagner in turn was to learn far more from Spohr than he would ever care to admit.

Lindpaintner had not been to England before, but it was Spohr's sixth visit to a country where he was always warmly welcomed. His tall, impressive bearing and his impeccable moral integrity won the approval of the Queen and her court, but although English choral societies had taken Spohr's choral works to their hearts, his operas had made little impression there. His *Faust* (one of the earliest operatic treatments of a favourite subject) had been a triumph at Covent Garden in 1852, so in 1853 the management decided to mount *Jessonda*, by common consent his finest opera and already well known all over Germany, and they invited Spohr to conduct, an invitation identical to that extended to Berlioz to conduct his *Benvenuto Cellini*. Spohr, now sixty-nine, and Berlioz, now forty-nine, were entirely unlike in upbringing, temperament and style. They had never met, and although they must have been introduced during their overlapping sojourns in London, there is no record of any exchange or amity between them. Berlioz was now beyond the stage where he would be aching to tease memories out of elderly musicians who had known Goethe, Beethoven and Weber. In their idiosyncratic ways they represented one version of the polarity between the old and the new.

Of the other leading musical organisations the Sacred Harmonic Society was a choral society of over twenty years standing, made up of amateur singers of all classes and devoted to the uplifting choral works that reposed so centrally in the Victorian musical consciousness. They performed on alternate Fridays under their conductor Costa, and their repertoire in 1853 was *Israel in Egypt*, *The Creation*, and *Elijah*, each performed twice.

The Musical Union was the brainchild of the violinist John Ella who founded a series of chamber concerts in 1845. He was much applauded for the novel idea of providing programme notes for each concert, but he deserves greater credit for his unflinching commitment to high standards and for engaging world-class musicians, the stars of the day, most of whom were inevitably foreign. His regular players were the French violinist Sainton, the Italian cellist Piatti and the German pianist Karl Halle (now franco-anglicised as Charles Hallé), and in 1853 he also presented the Belgian violinist Vieuxtemps, the Italian virtuoso double-bassist Bottesini, and an eight-year old Portuguese prodigy curiously named Arthur Napoleon. The Musical Union's concerts took place on alternate Tuesdays at Willis's Rooms in King Street, St James's (now Christie's London auction rooms). Ella had travelled widely on the Continent and had met Schumann, Wagner, Berlioz and many others. His sympathetic understanding of these feared composers was a salutary counterblast to the weight of critical opinion in the press marshalled against modern music and its much-touted 'ugliness'.

Numerous other concert organisations jockeyed for London venues and audiences, as they still do – some orchestral, some choral, some mixed. Scarcely any concert fielded fewer than four or five soloists, and while solo numbers in mixed concerts were frequent, solo recitals by pianists or singers were virtually unknown. A number of distinguished European musicians came to London for engagements by one or more of these managements. This year the five leading visitors were all well known to Berlioz and the object of considerable admiration: the singers Staudigl, Pischek and Pauline Viardot, and the pianists Wilhelmine Clauss and his old friend Ferdinand Hiller from Cologne, fresh from his successful appearance in the Lower Rhine Festival in Düsseldorf.

At the summit of musical prestige stood the Royal Italian Opera in its Covent Garden home. Until a year earlier there had been two rival Royal Italian Opera seasons, one at Covent Garden managed by Frederick Gye, the other at Her Majesty's Theatre in the Haymarket managed by Benjamin Lumley. After six years of cut-throat rivalry Lumley was forced to concede and many of his company, including his conductor Costa, deserted to Covent Garden. These events, falling at exactly the moment that Gye was deciding to mount *Benvenuto Cellini,* have some bearing on the fate of Berlioz's opera at Covent Garden. For the 1853 season Gye felt comfortably assured of success, and he engaged a formidable roster of European stars. He had the two greatest tenors of the day, Mario and Tamberlik, a fine baritone Ronconi, the French bass Tagliafico and the German bass Formes; his sopranos were Mme Bosio, Mme Jullienne, Mme Castellan, and Mme Didiée. Only four of these – Mario, Tamberlik, Ronconi and Mme Bosio – were Italian, and none of them was English. It was the practice of the company to sing all operas in Italian regardless of their original language, so both Berlioz's and Spohr's operas had to be translated into Italian. The repertoire was predominantly Italian, and within a space of four months no less than seventeen operas were performed by this company: Mozart's *Don Giovanni,* Rossini's *Barbiere di Siviglia, Otello* and *Guglielmo Tell,* Bellini's *Norma* and *I puritani,* Donizetti's *L'elisir d'amore, Maria di Rohan* and *Lucrezia Borgia,* Verdi's *Ernani* and *Rigoletto.* From the French repertoire (besides Rossini's *Tell)* Auber's *Il Masaniello* and Meyerbeer's

6 Frederick Gye

three classics, under their Italian titles *Roberto il diavolo, Gli Ugonotti* and *Il profeta*, were all played during the season. The three main novelties were *Rigoletto*, without its composer, and *Benvenuto Cellini* and *Jessonda,* both conducted by their composers. Costa conducted everything else, and his principal singers sang in nearly all the operas. It is hard to comprehend how such an enormous repertoire can have been presented in so short a period by so few singers, or how the technical and scenic complexities were handled in an age when décor was elaborate and vividly representational.

ACTING without any expectation of commercial gain, Beale played a part in persuading Gye to put on *Benvenuto Cellini*, the negotiations for which proceeded in a businesslike way. Berlioz had checked the material and revised the Italian translation to enable rehearsals to begin before the beginning of May. He arrived in London in time to devote six weeks to rehearsals, a generous but necessary period in view of the complexity of the score. Of all Berlioz's works it displays the most vivacious and complex rhythmic idiom, not easily learnt by singers and players familiar with the quite different style of Italian opera. Meyerbeer's French operas, with their four-square periods and stolid rhythms, were no preparation for Berlioz's teasing cross-rhythms and breakneck speeds. Nonetheless Berlioz was delighted with the cast and the production. He felt Tamberlik was exactly the tenor he had in mind when he composed the role of Cellini, and Augustus Harris (father of the famous impresario of the same name) did an excellent job of putting the work on the stage. These were rewarding weeks of serious music-making in which the task of putting on a difficult opera proceeded unhindered.

Berlioz's correspondence from his stay in London is almost exclusively concerned with his preoccupations with the opera; he scarcely mentions contact with other musicians or the musical goings-on of the capital, and we have almost no notion of what he did in his spare time, if he had any. He did not need to confine himself to the company of his French friends, since educated people everywhere spoke French. He spoke no German, and his English remained surprisingly sketchy even after three previous visits and despite having married an Irish actress.

If we may suppose that Berlioz and Marie were glad of the opportunity to hear their friends performing without the disagreeable duty of having to write a notice of the concert afterwards (which was normally the case in Paris), they could have attended the following events during their first week in London, which was sunny and unusually warm. On Monday they might have stepped the few yards across Oxford Street to hear the Old Philharmonic Society's concert in Hanover Square Rooms, in which Costa conducted Beethoven's Eighth Symphony and Mendelssohn's 'Italian'. Vieuxtemps, whom Berlioz liked and admired, played one of his own concertos. Old Sir Henry Bishop, a relic of a past age, was wheeled out to conduct his cantata *The Departure from Paradise*. Famous as the first British musical knight, Sir Henry had enjoyed unprecedented success thirty years earlier concocting operas out of bits by Mozart, Rossini, Weber and himself.

On Tuesday they would certainly have gone to the Musical Union's concert in Willis's Rooms since Berlioz was a friend of the organiser, John Ella, who had always vigorously upheld the composer's music. Berlioz and Ella went with their Parisian friend Emile Prudent to take tea as the guest of Vieuxtemps before the concert at which Piatti and Bottesini played a Tartini sonata for cello and double bass, and Vieuxtemps and Wilhelmine Clauss played a Beethoven violin sonata. Berlioz would have greatly enjoyed this since the same two players, with Weimar's cellist Cossmann, had played Schubert trios in Berlioz's apartment in Paris only a few months before. A Mendelssohn string quintet was also played.

On Wednesday they might have gone to Exeter Hall to hear an oratorio, *Jerusalem*, by one of the most original English composers of the day, Hugh Pearson, known as Henry Hugo Pierson since his removal to Germany, a country which he found to be more sympathetic to his musical aims. Pierson had no patience with the conventionality of most English music and preferred a more unpredictable idiom wedded to poetry in vocal and programme music. He was naturally linked to the modern German school, and the English critics were not kind to him. Davison, critic of the *Times*, associated him with the 'aesthetic' school of Schumann and, loosely, with Wagner, the two names that were certain to send warning signals to conservative audiences, while Chorley, the outspoken critic of the *Athenaeum*, spoke of the 'crude and fierce noises' in the oratorio. Although Pierson undoubtedly had much in common with Berlioz in outlook, Berlioz was rarely inclined to seek out originality in younger composers, and we must doubt whether he would have troubled to hear him on this occasion, even though the performance was conducted by Julius Benedict, whom Berlioz had first met in Naples in 1831 and then again in London in 1848. Benedict occupied a house nearby in Manchester Square where Berlioz sometimes went for late-night conversation and cigars.

If he did not go to hear the oratorio he might have gone back to Willis's Rooms to hear a concert given by the German violinist Molique, whom he had known in Stuttgart in 1842 and again in London in 1848.

On Thursday it would be agreeable to imagine that the Berliozes went to the third performance of *Rigoletto* at Covent Garden. First performed two years before in Venice, Verdi's great drama had not yet been performed in Paris. Berlioz had never met Verdi and had only ever seen three of his operas: *Jérusalem* (the French version of *I Lombardi)* in 1849, *Attila* in London in 1848, and *Luisa Miller*, which was staged in French at the Paris Opéra without much success the previous December. On this basis he could hardly have anticipated the intense dramatic force of *Rigoletto,* and the British press had received it only coolly. (It had been poorly received in Hanover only a month earlier.) Mario sang the Duke, and Ronconi Rigoletto. Berlioz would at the very least have been curious to see Harris's staging, which was greatly admired, as a foretaste of what he might do with *Benvenuto Cellini*. But alas there is no evidence that he ever heard *Rigoletto*, now or later.

On Friday Haydn's *Creation* was performed at Exeter Hall by the Sacred Harmonic Society under Costa's direction. While Saturday was often a big night at Covent Garden, most concert organisations left their patrons free to leave town for the weekend. Berlioz spent the Sunday at Tolbecque's house in Rutland Street (now Mackworth Street), off the Hampstead Road, rehearsing with Mme Didiée, who was singing the role of Cellini's apprentice Ascanio, with the nineteen-year-old William Ganz playing the piano. From there he doubtless walked across to the Finchley Road where every Sunday evening Frederick Beale kept open house. Foreign musicians were his chief guests on those occasions. Vieuxtemps was there, as well as a young man from Darmstadt, Adolph Schloesser, who remembered Berlioz's visit to that city ten years earlier and the composer's insatiable appetite for cups of tea.

In his second week in London Berlioz continued working at Covent Garden. Rehearsals were going well and the chorus were particularly taken with the opera. At the same time they were preparing a revival of Verdi's *Ernani* for the Saturday night, probably another Verdi opera Berlioz failed to hear, since at this point he turned his attention to the Old Philharmonic Society, who had to everyone's surprise invited him to conduct half a concert during his stay. At first he proposed the *Symphonie fantastique*, which had never been heard before in London, but since they could not offer him more than a single rehearsal he refused to risk it and substituted *Harold en Italie*, which was familiar since it had been played more than once by many of the same players during Berlioz's first London visit in 1848. The viola soloist on that occasion, Henry Hill, brother of the violin-maker William E. Hill, was unwell, so the viola solo was played by the French violinist Sainton, leader of the Philharmonic's orchestra. Two short works were also programmed: the *Carnaval romain* overture, which had also been played in 1848 and which served as an appetiser for *Benvenuto Cellini,* and *Le Repos de la Sainte Famille*, the third movement of *La Fuite en Égypte,* which had never been heard anywhere before.

This short and very gentle work, billed as a 'Descriptive Air', required a small choir of angels and a tenor soloist. Gardoni, one of the Italians put out on the street by the demise of Lumley's company at Her Majesty's Theatre, was engaged. He sang, as Berlioz reported, 'deliciously', and at the concert, on Monday 30 May, his piece had to be encored. The critics were surprised by its gentle, archaic style, especially beside the fiery orchestral wizardry of the *Carnaval romain* overture and the noisy finale of *Harold en Italie.* One rehearsal was manifestly not enough for this difficult music, but the press acknowledged Berlioz's mastery, and J. W. Davison, one of Berlioz's most esteemed friends, used the occasion to arouse eager anticipation for the much greater test of presenting an opera at Covent Garden. Berlioz was paid ten guineas for his services.

The second half of the concert, which Costa did not invite Berlioz to conduct, comprised Beethoven's Fifth Symphony, a Weber overture, Bottesini playing one of his own double bass concertos, Gardoni singing a Donizetti aria, and one of Berlioz's favourite singers, the great Bohemian bass Pischek, singing a Spohr aria. Berlioz noted wryly that a third of the audience, who had evidently come to hear just him, left at the interval.

The day before the concert, being a Sunday, the Berliozes, the Vieuxtempses, the Ellas and the Baugniets had taken a train to Kingston-upon-Thames. Did they go just to breathe the country air, or to visit anyone in particular? We don't know. Charles Baugniet was a Belgian portraitist who had been working in London since 1841. As a souvenir of his Musical Union season, Ella commissioned from Baugniet a group portrait of all the leading musicians who were in London that season, including (from left to right) Bazzini, Blagrove, Goffrie, Blumenthal, Vieuxtemps, Lazarus, Pratten, Jarrett, Hiller, Baumann, Lindpaintner, Spohr, Molique, Berlioz and Ella himself (pen in hand, as the author of the programme notes). Baugniet has cleverly given due prominence to the five distinguished foreign visitors: Vieuxtemps, Hiller, Lindpaintner, Spohr and Berlioz.

The morning after the concert, if the opera rehearsals allowed, Berlioz might have gone back to Hanover Square Rooms to hear Pischek and Gardoni singing in an unusual matinée organised by Harriet Beecher Stowe, who presented a black American singer, Elizabeth Greenfield, with an astonishing vocal range. Mrs Stowe, whose *Uncle Tom's Cabin* was published just the year before, had managed

7 Musicians in London in 1853: standing with violin, Vieuxtemps; seated centre, Hiller; standing hands clasped, Lindpaintner; seated with score, Spohr; seated in profile, Berlioz; standing with pen, Ella.

8 Cheque for ten guineas paid to Berlioz, 22 June 1853

to secure the patronage of four duchesses, two marchionesses, three countesses and a viscountess. On the day following there was yet another opportunity to hear Pischek, when he appeared in the New Philharmonic's concert in Exeter Hall in some pieces by the conductor, Lindpaintner. One song in particular, 'The Standard Bearer', provoked a 'hurricane of applause'. Berlioz's Parisian friend, Emile Prudent, played a fantasia of his own for piano and orchestra. This concluded Lindpaintner's engagement with the orchestra, and he returned to Stuttgart with applause ringing in his ears.

With Pischek still in town, another singer of world class arrived in London. Pauline Viardot was the daughter of the singing teacher Manuel Garcia and the sister of the great diva Maria Malibran. She had developed a lustrous mezzo voice of great range, and the apogee of her fame came with her impersonation of Fidès in Meyerbeer's *Le Prophète* in 1849. She was well known to Berlioz and to London audiences, for she had sung the orchestral version of *La Captive* in Berlioz's London concert in 1848, a song which she very much made her own. From thinking earlier that she was too wedded to the Italian style and too fond of early music such as Bach, Berlioz gradually recognised that she sang Gluck to perfection and a close friendship developed from that bond. Her celebrity was such that the day after her arrival in London she sang to the Queen at Buckingham Palace, and for the full month of June she appeared in one concert after another in all the best London venues except, of course, Covent Garden. The *Illustrated London News* described her as the 'grandest singer of her age', noting that the Sacred Harmonic Society were lucky indeed to have her singing *Elijah*. For the Philharmonic Society on 13 June she sang Handel's 'Lascia ch'io pianga' and, with Formes, a duet from *Les Huguenots*, and appeared two days later to sing some French romances (Berlioz's *Captive* perhaps?) to Mlle Clauss's accompaniment. For Ella's Musical Union on the 14th Hiller put together a Beethoven Trio and played a sonata of his own. On the 22nd Julius Benedict gave his annual concert in Hanover Square Rooms in which the dazzling constellation of Arabella Goddard, Hiller, Vieuxtemps, Piatti, Bottesini, Reichart (flute), Sainton, Pischek, Sims Reeves, Gardoni, Mmes

Viardot, Marchesi, Lablache, Clara Novello, and many others all took part. Pauline Viardot's performance of Balfe's *Scherzo* was 'rapturously encored'.

It is likely that Berlioz heard at least some of these concerts, and at least joined his friends for lunch, dinner or even tea, but the only certain thing is that rehearsals at Covent Garden were unremitting. On 11 June, when it was announced that *Benvenuto Cellini* would open in a few days time, Berlioz was less sanguine, giving it a week or two still to go. He wrote to Auguste Barbier in Paris strongly urging him to come to hear the opera whose libretto he had written. Splendid staging, marvellous tenor, superb orchestra, *adequate* conductor! Tamberlik, his Cellini, invited Berlioz and all the cast to dinner up in Hampstead. On 125,000 francs a year, Berlioz felt, he could easily run to this, and liked him for being a straightforward, normal person. 'He can't help having a golden voice.'

That week two of Berlioz's most sincere admirers arrived in London in the shape of blind King Georg of Hanover and his Queen Maria. As Crown Prince of Hanover Georg had first met Berlioz ten years earlier and been much taken by his music. He had come to London to stand godfather to his cousin Victoria's latest child, Prince Leopold. They arrived at Woolwich on the 16th and between military parades and the usual ceremonials the pair attended a concert in Buckingham Palace on the 20th and paid a visit to Covent Garden on 21 June to hear *Rigoletto*, which the King had already heard and liked in Hanover. Knowing that they would also be keen to attend the opening of *Benvenuto Cellini*, Berlioz had every reason to be optimistic. If he had suspicion of plots against its success, nothing reached his ears until a couple of days before. When the opera finally opened, on Saturday 25 June, a remarkably distinguished audience filled the auditorium, led by Queen Victoria, Prince Albert and their royal guests, the King and Queen of Hanover, all four – even the Queen – decently accomplished musicians. Liszt's patron, Duke Carl Alexander of Weimar, was there too, unknown to Berlioz. Spohr had just arrived from Kassel for his stint with the New Philharmonic; Hiller was there, also Pauline Viardot, George Eliot, the principal London critics, such as Davison, Holmes and Chorley, and, we may assume, many members of London's prodigiously varied musical community (though Ella for some reason stayed at home).

Just before curtain up, Marie Recio left Berlioz's dressing-room to join their Belgian friend Eduard Silas in his box. There was a conspiracy, she told him, to fill the air with hisses and boos; this was led by Italians and their supporters from Her Majesty's Theatre, nursing a bitter grudge against Covent Garden for forcing them out of existence, and resenting the intrusion of so many non-Italians at the Royal *Italian* Opera. Berlioz was cheered as he appeared on the podium, but the hisses and boos did not wait long. They began before the singers even opened their mouths. The entire performance was stifled by prolonged noise from groups within the house whose disruption appeared to all competent judges to have been, as we now say, orchestrated. Even the *Carnaval romain* overture, so well received two weeks before at the Philharmonic, was shouted down when played as an entracte

9 The King and Queen of Hanover

before Act II. Pauline Viardot, having sung in *Elijah* the night before and now sharing a box with her husband and the critic Edward Holmes, turned to the latter and asked him if it wasn't wrong to hiss an opera like that. The presence of royalty was no deterrent. The clamour continued right to the end.

It was a second catastrophe for this unhappy opera, so roughly handled in Paris in 1838. Berlioz's faith in it was not one whit diminished, and he was thrilled by the performance itself; Fieramosca's Air in Act II and Ascanio's Air in Act III were actually encored, and he felt he had conducted well. But he knew he could neither appear on stage at the end to take a bow nor allow any further performances to take place. Francis Hueffer later reported that Berlioz had invited the leading artists to a supper after the performance. But it had bombed so badly that none of his guests dared appear, with the sole exception of Davison of the *Times*. Berlioz was moved to tears by the tact and politeness shown by his solitary guest.

Next day, a wet and windy Sunday morning, Hiller paid him a call to offer condolences and found him downcast, still in bed. Berlioz then wrote Gye a letter which was published in a number of newspapers soon after:

> I cannot again expose myself to such acts of hostility as those which we had to undergo last night. [...] I regret infinitely to have exposed you and the distinguished and kind artists who took part in the performance to so much trouble and annoyance by accepting your offer to produce my work.

Was it truly a pro-Italian conspiracy? Berlioz always thought so. Some even ascribed it to Costa, nettled by Berlioz's published comments on his integrity as a conductor, although Berlioz himself doubted this part of the theory since Costa had offered every kind of assistance in rehearsing the opera and would hardly be in favour of a disaster in the house of which he was the musical director.

But other theories have been put forward. Berlioz also thought some of his enemies had come from Paris specially to boo. No one claimed Berlioz's music was easy listening for an audience brought up on Italian opera and the comfortable German classics. He rarely received wholehearted approbation either from his audiences or from the press; in Paris he had his regular detractors in both categories. Spohr probably spoke for many well-intentioned listeners when he said: 'In Berlioz's opera there are some fine things, but no sooner has one become interested in it than something so bizarre and harsh happens that all the pleasure is destroyed.' In her diary Queen Victoria put the same observation in less civil terms: the opera struck her as

one of the most unattractive & absurd Operas I suppose anyone could ever have composed. There was not a particle of melody, merely disjointed and most confused sounds, producing a fearful noise. It could only be compared with the noise of dogs & cats! The 2 1st acts kept us in fits of laughter, owing to their extreme foolishness.

Only by the last act was Her Majesty not amused. King Georg must have been appalled by the boorishness of his English cousin.

The press were similarly reluctant to praise the work while praising the performers. Some picked on infelicities in the libretto, the principal target of abuse in Paris in 1838, some complained of the oddity of Berlioz's style and the impossibility of grasping it at one hearing. Many found it too noisy, with too much percussion. Gruneisen in the *Illustrated London News*, Davison in the *Times*, and Holmes in the *Atlas*, who all held Berlioz in profound respect, argued for a more serious appreciation. Holmes even hinted that it was supporters of the New Philharmonic (who 'listened with so much complacency to the platitudes of Dr. Wylde and Lindpaintner') who shouted the opera down. 'For ourselves we feel both grief and shame – grief that a man of genius should be so insulted, and shame that Englishmen should have been the dastardly insulters.'

There was surely no dissatisfaction within the Covent Garden company itself. On the Monday over 200 London musicians signed up for a testimonial concert to be given on Berlioz's behalf to compensate him for the collapse of his opera. A committee, comprising Beale, Ella, Osborne, Benedict, Smart, Sainton, Mori, Davison, Gruneisen and Chorley, planned a concert in Exeter Hall, to be given a week or so later. But the hall was not available on the chosen date and the musicians were mostly booked to leave for the Norwich Festival, so the plan fell through. In compensation the committee agreed to give Berlioz £100 for the English rights to *La Damnation de Faust*. This was exceedingly generous since only four months earlier Berlioz had sold the copyright for all countries except England to the Parisian publisher Richault for 700 francs (less than £30). The £200 raised by subscription was to go toward the publication of a vocal score of *La Damnation de Faust* with English translation. Berlioz wished it might have been a score of *Benvenuto Cellini* instead, but in any case neither score appeared at that time; perhaps the money helped pay for the vocal score of Berlioz's *L'Enfance du Christ*, published by Beale in 1856 with an English translation by Chorley.

Berlioz and Marie left London for Paris on 9 July, having spent their last evening with the Ellas. The display of goodwill by London's musicians and Gye's suggestion that he write a new opera for his theatre went some way to soften the pain of his visit, even though he had no intention of submitting himself to a Covent Garden audience ever again. With supreme civility he wrote to Costa, Beale, Sainton, Smythson (chorus-master at Covent Garden), and probably many others, thanking them for their support and friendship, and in the *Musical World* he published a letter expressing his profound gratitude to the musicians who had offered to give the testimonial concert.

COVENT Garden then switched gear to work on the less alarming strains of Spohr's *Jessonda*. From the new to the old ... There was no likelihood that old Spohr would be subject to the same humiliation as Berlioz. The Philharmonic audience that took their seats in Hanover Square Rooms on the Monday evening following the *Cellini* fiasco (which many of them may have attended) were no doubt relieved to be hearing German music which offered nothing so 'bizarre and harsh'. The great Spohr himself was there to hear Costa conduct his Sixth Symphony, known as the 'Historical', a teasing conception that evokes Bach, Handel, Mozart and Beethoven in its first three movements, and then paints 'the most modern period, 1840' with a noisy finale satirising the kind of music Spohr most detested, as his remarks about Berlioz make clear. When first heard in London in 1840 the audience failed to get the joke and hissed it. Now, perhaps, the target of Spohr's humour was nearer at hand, still ringing in their ears. Mme Viardot sang Agathe's aria from *Der Freischütz*, then, joined by Mme Castellan, sang duets from *Jessonda* and *Così fan tutte*. Hiller was the soloist in his own piano concerto, and the orchestra also played Beethoven's Fourth Symphony and an overture by Lindpaintner.

Only two days later Spohr conducted Beethoven's Choral Symphony in Exeter Hall with the New Philharmonic Society. Since the Society had last performed it under Berlioz's baton the year before, direct comparisons were inescapable. Spohr's tempos were much too slow, even the Adagio, evoking the words 'monotonous' and 'wearisome' in the press, the very opposite of the effect Berlioz had produced. There must have been many yawns in the audience since, besides the symphony, they were offered one overture by Beethoven and two by Spohr himself, a Mendelssohn piano concerto, a flute solo, and two vocal arias including Mozart's Queen of the Night.

Spohr doubtless attended an extra concert given by the 'Old' Philharmonic on 4 July, put on by command of the Queen, since she had had to miss their concert three weeks before. The programme, selected by the Queen and Prince Albert, surprisingly contained no music by Spohr, but featured Beethoven's Seventh Symphony and *Egmont* overture, Weber's *Euryanthe* overture, and Mendelssohn's *Midsummer Night's Dream* music. Viardot and Gardoni singing Handel and Mozart were once again the vocal attractions.

Spohr's contract with the New Philharmonic required him to conduct one more concert, and that took place on 8 July. The programme was again immense, with the usual lining of overtures and vocal pieces. The main item was another Spohr symphony, this time the Seventh, an ambitious work from 1841 with the subtitle 'The Earthly and the Godly in Human Life', an essay in metaphysics depicting the conflict between spirituality and passion. A small orchestra represents the spiritual, while the full orchestra is to be identified with the baser human urges. Certainly this was a bold idea for musical representation, anticipating some of Liszt's symphonic poems, and the formal design of the work is original, but despite Schumann's admiration it never outlived its composer in the concert repertoire. On this occasion the press observed that, as so often happens, the representation of the immoral was more appealing than that of the moral. 'The effect of the symphony was dull and dreary,' alas. Beethoven's Second Symphony, played immediately after, only reinforced the impression. All in all, concluded Gruneisen in the *Illustrated London News*, the New Philharmonic's invitation to Lindpaintner and Spohr was a mistake. Molique and Benedict, both resident in London, could have done better, he thought.

Spohr and his wife were staying with a Dr Farre, who laid on two musical evenings for the entertainment of his guests, one a soirée in which a group of singers gave extracts from Spohr's operas, the other a domestic performance of Spohr's oratorio *The Last Judgment* sung with piano accompaniment by twenty-eight of the doctor's medical colleagues. This pleased the composer especially for its faultless precision and for not displaying the habitual English taste for massive instrumentation. A private performance of his Nonet earlier arranged by Wylde also pleased him for the same reason.

Rehearsals of *Jessonda* at Covent Garden were delayed since other operas had to be put into the dates originally planned for performances of *Benvenuto Cellini*, and they all needed some rehearsal. In addition, Mario, in the main tenor role of Nadori, withdrew from the cast, so that Tamberlik (who had sung it before in Germany) replaced him. The result was that *Jessonda* did not open until 6 August, over three weeks after Spohr himself had had to return to Kassel to resume his duties there. Costa conducted it instead. Being very late in the season, summer holidays were taking Londoners away, and although Spohr said it was a 'brilliant success', he was either misinformed or deluded. The singing, playing and staging were all, by common consent, up to the finest standards, but *Jessonda*, with its unmistakable pre-echoes of Wagner, received only two performances, never to be revived.

For all Spohr's ambitious intentions in this and other works, there was no mistaking the fact that his music was that of a passing generation and that his style was rooted in the early years of the century. Most people believed that the future, however unattractive, lay with composers like Berlioz and Schumann. In fact it lay with Wagner and Brahms, both as yet unknown in London, but both on the verge of great things.

———◄—

CHAPTER 3

Brahms and Liszt in Weimar

JUNE

RemÉnyi and Brahms left Hanover on Friday 10 June and arrived in Weimar at a moment when the city was preparing to celebrate the Silver Jubilee of the Grand Duke's reign. Carl Friedrich, Grand Duke of Sachsen-Weimar-Eisenach, had succeeded his father, the remarkable Carl August, patron of Goethe and Schiller, in 1828. He was now seventy years old, but he had personally contributed little to Weimar's cultural life in comparison with the achievements of his father and with the lively support for music and theatre displayed by his consort Maria Pavlovna, sister of Tsar Nicolas I of Russia, and by his son and heir Carl Alexander. It was Carl Alexander who had lured Liszt to Weimar, and who followed the theatre's *Spielplan* with close interest; his wife Sophie, a princess of the house of Orange, was Liszt's pupil.

So small a city as Weimar could not but be dominated by the ducal presence, with the imposing (but not beautiful) palace in the centre of the town and the daily formalities of court preoccupying the population, most of whom were in one way or another in the ducal employ. It was no secret that the treasury had been seriously depleted by the turbulent events of 1848–9, and it was becoming clear that the small political units of which Germany was largely made up, though larger in size and fewer in number since Napoleon's depredations, were scarcely viable in the railway age. Nevertheless the round of state visits and dynastic marriages continued, as, for example, when Joachim's services were required at the royal marriage three weeks before; on that occasion Carl Alexander's sister married his wife's brother, doubling the link between the Dutch and Saxon lines.

On Tuesday 14 June, the day before the Jubilee, King Friedrich Wilhelm IV of Prussia arrived with his family, including his sister-in-law Princess Augusta, the Grand Duke's daughter. The list of royal guests was otherwise rather undistinguished; many had chosen to come to the wedding on 19 May rather than to old Carl Friedrich's Jubilee. Weimar was decked out in flags and flowers. At five o'clock on the morning of the 15th church bells rang out all over the city, followed by festal music in the palace courtyard at six. At eight the royal party processed to church amid crowds of waving children in traditional costume. The Grand Duke rode in an open carriage beside the King of Prussia. The weather was perfect. After the church service the rest of the day was spent in audiences and deputations, and of course a banquet. In the theatre that evening an 'Allegorical Festival Play' was mounted, with music by Carl Stör, Joachim's second violin and a modest composer. This was followed by Auber's *La Part du diable*, a comic opera about the castrato Farinelli and his elevation at the Spanish court. Liszt conducted. All

33

10 Franz Liszt in 1854

the houses were lit up as the royal party wound their way back from the theatre to the palace. The following two days were filled with similar ceremonies; trees were planted, foundation stones were laid, statues were unveiled, speeches were delivered, and hymns were sung. On the evening of the 17th a grand ball was held at the palace, and a huge banquet on Sunday 19th concluded five days of festivities.

Reményi and Brahms arrived in Weimar just before the celebrations began and could hardly have expected to give any public concerts in such extraordinary circumstances. Their purpose, in any case, was to meet Liszt. Although the wider musical world viewed Liszt as the central pillar of Weimar's cultural life, his position was not that of the benign musical autocrat that many imagined. From the day he arrived in Weimar in 1848 he had to contend with small-town rivalries arising from the theatre's divided functions as play-house and opera-house, and from the lesser musicians of the court who felt overshadowed by his powerful presence. In addition his domestic circumstances were not entirely acceptable to the more fastidious members of Weimar society, since he had brought with him to Weimar a remarkable Polish-Russian aristocrat, the Princess Carolyne von Sayn-Wittgenstein, whom he intended to marry. Being married already to an uncooperative Russian nobleman who resisted her requests for a divorce, she was compelled to establish a *ménage* of which Liszt officially was not a part, although in practice they were to live in Weimar as man and wife for ten years. While Liszt lived officially at the Erbprinz Hotel, she and her daughter, the sixteen-year-old Princess Marie, took the lease of a large rectangular four-storey house on a hill just across the river Ilm from the centre of Weimar. This house, the Altenburg, now one of nine buildings occupied by Weimar's Liszt School of Music, was to be the real centre of Weimar's musical life. Here Liszt was to compose the great orchestral works of the 1850s; here, earlier this year, he had just completed the great Sonata in B minor; here he was to plan his campaigns for the new German music; here a whole generation of brilliant young musicians were to gather to make music and to sit at the feet of the most palpable musical genius of their time; here Liszt was immune from the gossip and jealousy of the town; and here, for all the trials and tribulations that he and Carolyne had to face – her permanently troublesome health, her unattainable divorce, his ambivalent position in Weimar, and the regular attacks of his enemies in the musical press – here they achieved a distinct brand of happiness. It was not the idyllic home of the muses that Weimar had been in Goethe's and Schiller's time, but it was an inspiring fountainhead of music to which musicians flocked from all over the world.

Reményi and Brahms lodged at the Russischer Hof, then as now one of Weimar's principal hotels and the site of famous meetings involving Liszt, Wagner and the Schumanns. There is no sign of their presence at the regular Sunday music-making at the Altenburg that Sunday, the 12th, when Laub and his three colleagues played Schubert's recently published G major string quartet and also a Beethoven quartet. They probably had to wait for an opportune moment to meet Liszt. As Reményi recalled these events twenty-five years later, he first went alone to the Altenburg to call on Liszt. He was ushered into the main drawing room, and when Liszt appeared, he was profoundly struck by the sight of his fine Dante-esque face. He produced Joachim's letter of introduction. Liszt put him at his ease, being naturally well disposed towards a fellow Hungarian. He agreed to give Reményi some instruction, and then asked him if he had any money. (Since Liszt never accepted fees for teaching, this question is not as pointed as it seems.)

'Little or none.'

'Where are you living?'

'At the Russischer Hof.'

'Get your things together and come and live with me.'

Reményi was overwhelmed. 'But, *mon cher maître*, I am not alone.' Reményi told Liszt about his encounter with Brahms in Hamburg and their two months on the road.

'Oh well,' replied Liszt, 'that's fine. Both of you come and live here.'

THE next morning Brahms and Reményi packed their bags, walked through Weimar's festooned streets past the ducal palace, across the picturesque Kegelbrücke and up the steep steps to the Altenburg. Liszt had sent word to his pupils that there were to be visitors that morning, so Brahms was to meet some of the young musicians who had aligned themselves with Liszt and who worked

11 The Altenburg, Weimar

with and for him in various capacities. Joachim Raff, at thirty-one, was the oldest of the group. He had worked in Zurich, Cologne, Stuttgart, and even for a while in Hamburg for the music publisher Schuberth, so it is possible that he had met Brahms before; he and Brahms would at least have had acquaintances in common. Since 1850 he had been in Weimar working as Liszt's principal amanuensis while continuing to turn out a stream of compositions of his own in all genres. Liszt had conducted his opera *König Alfred* in Weimar in 1851. In admiration of Wagner he had just embarked on a five-act opera to his own libretto on the story of Samson, destined never to be published or performed. But he was not happy in Weimar and was hoping to find a position as kapellmeister somewhere that would allow him to work on *Samson* and feel more independent. Liszt was not resentful of these feelings; indeed he wrote Raff a splendid testimonial. But the latter had accumulated a mountain of debt, and it was some time before he was able to leave Weimar.

Karl Klindworth, a brilliant virtuoso with a heroic physique, was twenty-two, at the beginning of a long and illustrious career that took him for long periods to London, Moscow and Berlin. At Weimar he imbibed from Liszt a profound commitment to the music of Berlioz, Wagner and Liszt himself. He was busy studying Liszt's Sonata in B minor which had been completed only four months before. Dionys Pruckner, only nineteen, was another piano student, whose youthful promise did not in his case flower into a successful career. But his fellow-students greatly appreciated the supply of beer from his father's Munich brewery.

Two of Liszt's most interesting pupils were not in Weimar at this time: Hans von Bülow, at twenty-three, was probably the finest pianist to pass through Liszt's hands, and after two years' study in Weimar was on his first concert tour as a soloist. After two months in Vienna he was now enrapturing the public of Pest. Liszt, with his particular interest in all things Hungarian, followed his successes there closely. Peter Cornelius, aged twenty-eight, whom we shall meet later, was already a confirmed member of Liszt's circle; he was not a pianist, but a poet and composer and a man of great civility and culture. Since Liszt preferred to speak and write in French rather than German (though he was fluent in both languages), Cornelius was often engaged to translate Liszt's articles from French for publication in German. He was away at this particular time on a visit to his mother in Mainz.

Usually present at all musical events in the Altenburg were, of course, Carolyne Sayn-Wittgenstein, the mistress of the house, a woman of formidable intellect, and her daughter Marie. Liszt's mother, who normally lived in Paris, was also staying with them at this time in the vague expectation that she would be there to witness her son's marriage. The marriage looked less and less likely; meanwhile a fractured foot kept her in Weimar.

A recent arrival in Weimar was a young pianist from Boston, William Mason, who most prudently kept a diary during his sixteen months in the city. Mason was thus able to confirm the vivid account that Reményi gave of Brahms's meeting with Liszt, a historic encounter in the annals of music, even if no one present could have guessed it at the time. Brahms must have formed some expectation of

12 William Mason in 1847

the atmosphere in the Altenburg from Joachim, but nonetheless this gathering of self-aware musical talent around the charismatic figure of Liszt, with much of the conversation conducted in French, overwhelmed the shy young musician whose Hamburg teachers had never given him much confidence in his own abilities as a pianist. So when Liszt said to him, 'We are interested in hearing some of your compositions whenever you are ready and feel inclined to play them', Brahms retreated in shyness and declined. But he had brought his manuscripts, which Mason had sneakily observed lying on a table, noticing that the Scherzo in E flat minor, which lay at the top of the pile, was almost illegible. To the alarm of both Mason and Raff, Liszt then took the manuscript of the Scherzo and proceeded to play it fluently, commenting on the piece as he played. Brahms was overwhelmed, Reményi greatly moved. When Raff observed a likeness between the opening phrases of Brahms's Scherzo and Chopin's Scherzo in B flat minor, Brahms simply replied that he had never seen or heard any of Chopin's compositions, which should not surprise us, given the narrow background of Brahms's upbringing. Liszt also read through part of Brahms's Sonata in C major, a work unfit for any but the mightiest techniques.

A little later, as was usual on such occasions, Liszt played some of his own music. To everyone's delight he proceeded to lay down the solemn octave G's that open his Sonata in B minor. Who would not pay a king's ransom to hear the greatest of pianists playing the greatest of his own works? When he came to the *cantando espressivo* section, he glanced around and saw Brahms in his armchair with his eyes closed. Was he truly asleep? It is hardly likely. Reményi, who recounted the tale when his admiration for Brahms had long faded, said he 'calmly slept, or at least seemed to do so'. Mason admits he could not see what happened, although when he met Reményi many years later in Boston he corroborated the story. Liszt completed the performance and left the room.

It would be absurd to attribute the rift between Liszt and Brahms, which was undoubtedly a factor in their later alignments, to this imagined slight. Liszt never once alluded to it, indeed he extended his hospitality to Brahms for a further two weeks and wrote to the publishers Breitkopf & Härtel in Leipzig urging them to take some of Brahms's compositions, which they did. Much more obvious to everyone at the Altenburg was the rift between Brahms and Reményi, who were finding their temperamental differences too serious to allow their collaboration to continue. They stayed in Weimar about three weeks, but the atmosphere was tense and it is hard to know exactly what they did there. Liszt seized on Reményi's knowledge of Hungarian folk song since he was working on his book on the gypsies and their music and had already published thirteen of his *Hungarian Rhapsodies*. While Liszt and Reményi chatted endlessly in French about Hungarian melodies and how best to arrange them, Brahms, who had only recently learned to share Reményi's enthusiasm for Hungarian music, was left without any obvious function. On 22 June, a week after the Grand Duke's Jubilee, Reményi inscribed a manuscript containing nineteen Hungarian melodies with a fulsome dedication to Liszt, a manuscript that is now attached to a similar manuscript collection in Liszt's hand containing various Hungarian melodies by different composers. With Liszt's habitual and astonishing capacity to work on many projects at once, he was able to pursue his collection of Hungarian melodies and his study of Hungarian gypsy music at the same time as he prepared both recent and older piano works for publication – the B minor Sonata, the second Ballade, the brilliant *Scherzo und Marsch*, and a revised version of the *Années de pèlerinage* – not to mention his commitment to a stream of advanced orchestral works.

Brahms was undoubtedly looking over the shoulders of his two Hungarian friends. Within a year he was playing Hungarian dances to Clara Schumann. One of the melodies in Liszt's part of the manuscript was to turn up sixteen years later as the ninth of Brahms's published (and very popular) *Hungarian Dances* for piano duet, while Reményi's group of pieces supplied both composers; his second piece was used by Liszt (with due acknowledgement) in his oratorio *Die Legende von der heiligen Elisabeth*, first performed in 1865. The third piece became the theme of Brahms's *Variations on a Hungarian Song*, probably composed in 1856 and published in 1861.

The fifth and eighth pieces reappeared in almost identical form in Brahms's *Hungarian Dances* nos. 3 and 7. Part of the latter was already familiar from Liszt's eighth *Hungarian Rhapsody*. Hungarians always acknowledged that many of their national melodies were passed from one arranger to another, but it was later to be a source of pain to Reményi that Brahms, with no Hungarian blood and no apparent sympathy for Hungarian causes, had such enormous success with his *Hungarian Dances* without acknowledging any sources. Brahms even claimed, in a private letter to his publisher Schott, that he and Reményi had supplied Liszt with some of his material.

Here, surely, is the root of Brahms's rupture with Reményi in Weimar in June 1853. Brahms had by no means turned away from the Hungarian idiom at this time, but their very different tastes prevented them from continuing their work together. He had glimpsed a world of more serious and sympathetic music-making in the company of Joachim while failing to harmonise artistically or personally with the inhabitants of the Altenburg. He no doubt wished that Liszt would pay more attention to him, but whereas Joachim had found Brahms to be the more stimulating musician of the two, Liszt was more drawn to Reményi. When Liszt's book *Des Bohémiens et de leur musique en Hongrie* appeared in 1859, its last page was a fulsome encomium of Reményi:

> Alone among contemporary violinists Reményi possesses the authentic tradition, the true form and the esoteric sense of this art. [...] One happy day, at a lucky hour, this young Hungarian may place his foot on one of the summits symbolised by the antarctic volcano Erebus, which throws its nocturnal fires into the ancient ice-floes all around ...

Liszt had to leave soon after, compelling his guests to make plans of their own. He presented Brahms with a leather cigarette case as a souvenir of his visit. On 28 June he travelled to Karlsruhe to prepare plans for a large-scale music festival to be held in August under his direction. He had programmes to draw up, musicians to meet, and details to fix with the administration. From Karlsruhe he planned to head south for Zurich to spend some days in the company of Wagner. He was still expecting Joachim to join him there and he left Weimar unaware that Joachim had changed his mind. Was Joachim too absorbed in his university studies to leave Göttingen for a few days? Did he already sense that his mission was opposed to that of Wagner and Liszt and lay in a new direction? Or did he simply prefer to spend the time in the company of Brahms? For Brahms, in a candid report on the unhappy state of affairs in Weimar, wrote to Joachim the day after Liszt left Weimar begging to join him in Göttingen. He was depressed. Reményi's behaviour was exasperating. He was desperate to find a publisher for his music and could not return to Hamburg without having found one, and he acknowledged Liszt's help in this regard. Joachim responded enthusiastically and cancelled his plan to go to Zurich, so on 3 July back to Göttingen in joyous anticipation went Brahms. Late the previous evening he called on Raff with a discreet request for money.

Raff was inconsolable a day or two earlier after his fiancée Doris had left for Wiesbaden, where she was a member of the Court Theatre troupe. She was the daughter of Eduard Genast, director of the Weimar theatre. The gang attempted to cheer him up. They started with some drinks, then harnessed a wagon and took him the seven or eight miles to Bad Berka, a nearby spa. Reményi reminisced about his heroic participation in the Budapest uprising of 1848, Mason sang some negro spirituals, while Klindworth challenged Reményi to a race, only to fall and hurt his knee. Perhaps Brahms was part of the party, though Raff did not mention him in his letter to Doris the next day.

Reményi, Brahms thought, was planning to travel on in a different direction. In fact he stayed on in Weimar for many months, transfixed by Liszt's personality. Liszt was equally charmed by Reményi and his endless stories, not all of them true. Early in July Reményi found himself almost alone: Liszt was in Zurich, Brahms in Göttingen, the Princess and her daughter in Dresden, Laub in Prague, Cossmann in Baden-Baden, and Klindworth back in Hanover where he had been brought up. Reményi kept company with Pruckner, Mason and Liszt's mother, nursing her broken foot.

In later life Reményi no doubt wished to think that it was he who had discovered Brahms, and his part in launching Brahms's meteoric celebrity was certainly important. But in truth the two men were ill-matched partners (as Joachim had already observed), finding artistic collaboration daily more difficult. Reményi remained a wanderer all his life. After seven more years on the road, including a spell in London, he was allowed back to Hungary in 1860. He worked intermittently there and in Rome with Liszt, who is said to have sketched a violin concerto for him. Eventually he toured the United States and was one of the first European musicians to tour Australia, south-east Asia and South Africa. He died in 1898 in San Francisco while playing a concert. His recollections of those distant months with Brahms were always to be a source of both pride and regret: pride that he had introduced so great a composer to the world, regret that he and Brahms had failed to form a lasting or fruitful artistic partnership.

CHAPTER 4

Wagner and Liszt in Zurich

O N Sunday 22 May 1853 in Zurich, Richard Wagner celebrated his fortieth birthday. Birthdays always meant a lot to him, and he marked this important day by giving a series of concerts devoted to his own music, the first time he had ever done such a thing. Apart from his chronic shortage of money, life was treating him well, considering that he was banned from living and working in Germany as a result of his ill-advised involvement in the failed revolutionary rising in Dresden in 1849. He had been lucky to escape. Some of his fellow revolutionaries were caught and condemned to death, though their sentences were later commuted. Wagner himself fled Dresden on 9 May 1849, passing through Weimar to visit Liszt and reaching Switzerland on 28 May of that year.

After four years living as an exile in a city that had adopted him with considerable warmth, he was becoming restless. He shared his life with his wife Minna and her illegitimate daughter Natalie, who was now seventeen and was thought by the world (and even by Natalie herself) to be Minna's younger sister. They had no children of their own. Minna's dream of a secure bourgeois life was at odds with Wagner's turbulent attachment to radical causes and with his impossibly grandiose plans for long, unperformable operas, yet they clung perilously to a relationship that survived over twenty rocky years before beginning a final disintegration at the end of Wagner's time in Zurich. She cannot possibly have grasped the import of his visionary energy, and she was often left out of his plans. He needed, and sought, friends with whom he could share his torrential thoughts, friends who believed in him, and friends who could lend him money. Almost as important to Wagner as his wife were his parrot Papo, who could whistle the opening of Beethoven's Eighth Symphony, and his dog Peps, who accompanied his master everywhere.

They lived in a series of apartments, starting west of the river Limmat which, flowing north from Lake Zurich to join the Rhine, divides the old city in two. Then for over a year they lived on a street close to the lake in the suburb of Enge, a little way from the city and not far from where Wagner would later live as the guest of his benefactors the Wesendoncks. By 1853 they were back closer to the city centre on Zeltweg, five minutes walk from the cathedral and the river bridges. In April of that year they moved from a ground-floor flat at no. 11 to a larger, lighter apartment on the second floor next door at no. 13, now commemorated by an impressive memorial tablet. This was to be Wagner's home for the next four years, where *Das Rheingold* and *Die Walküre* were to be composed.

The suite of rooms was elegantly furnished. Wagner admitted that *Üppigkeitsteufel*, demon luxury, seized him when they moved in. The curtains and

13 Richard Wagner in 1853

upholstery were velvet. His study contained a grand piano and his library, with a
high desk next to the piano. There was also a sofa on which he would recline and
read. Furnishing the apartment to meet his fastidious tastes cost a great deal of
money, nearly ten times what he paid in annual rent to Clementine Stockar-Escher,
the proprietor; she was the sister of millionaire businessman Alfred Escher and
an amateur portrait painter who regarded it as an honour to house the composer.
The Wagners kept a good table and liked to entertain, although Minna could
hardly conceal the fact that she disliked Zurich and many of her husband's friends.
He went regularly to the Café Littéraire on Weinplatz to mix with the large group

43

of German exiles who would congregate there, but he preferred to spend long evenings at home with his many new acquaintances discussing art and philosophy and expounding his copious thoughts on all subjects while Minna retired to her own room. Jakob Sulzer, for example, cantonal secretary of Zurich, was a frequent visitor, with the advantage that he was a wealthy bachelor who liked fishing and hunting and from time to time brought game and wine to the table. There was Wilhelm Baumgartner, a young composer who had been briefly in Dresden and who arrived one day with a hare he had shot; Franz Hagenbuch, another local official, and Ludwig Ettmüller, a professor of literature who knew the Nordic sagas well; and Ignaz Heim, a local composer and neighbour whose wife was an excellent singer. Karl Ritter was a young musician who had attached himself to Wagner in Dresden and now spent a lot of time in Zurich, even lodging with the Wagners in their earlier quarters; his widowed mother was wealthy enough and devoted enough to supply Wagner with a generous pension that was withheld at times when the relationship hit a bumpy passage. Also Bernhard Spyri, a lawyer who edited one of the local newspapers, the conservative *Eidgenössische Zeitung*; he admired Wagner too much to care about his revolutionary record (the other local paper, the more radical *Neue Zürcher Zeitung*, consequently ignored him).

Membership of Wagner's circle required an essential faith in his greatness, but his personality was so potent and his mind so active that a variety of people, both men and women, were happy to risk their pockets in befriending him. Despite his small stature his was a commanding presence in any company, and while most of his friends did more listening than talking, some individuals could match him in political ardour and philosophical discourse. Chief among these was Georg Herwegh, poet and revolutionary from Stuttgart, who played a part in the uprising in Baden-Baden in 1849 and arrived with a gaggle of refugees in Zurich in 1851. Having spent some time in Paris, he had been a close friend, perhaps lover, of Marie d'Agoult, the mother of Liszt's three children. Friend and follower of Marx and Bakunin, he was a classic Cadillac Communist, living comfortably at the Hotel Baur au Lac. His association with the great Russian thinker Alexander Herzen had led him into a messy open affair with Herzen's wife, which eventually led Herzen to challenge him to a duel and caused Herwegh's long-suffering wife Emma to leave him in favour of the Italian revolutionary Orsini (who later attempted to assassinate Napoleon III). Like Wagner, Herwegh depended on others for an income – in his case, Herzen and his own wife Emma, so that alienating both was not a wise move. In May 1853, at the time of Wagner's birthday concerts, Emma abandoned Orsini and came back with her children to live with Herwegh, restoring his comforts. She made no secret of her dislike of Wagner, whom she described as a 'heartless egoist who behaves like a hysterical woman'. Herwegh and Wagner shared a passion for radical politics and luxurious living. They also enjoyed long mountain hikes together, for which their Swiss surroundings provided magnificent opportunities and which illustrated yet another aspect of Wagner's relentless energy. While Wagner's socialist convictions were undergoing a profound transformation in these years, Herwegh's remained

14 Otto and Mathilde Wesendonck

constant, ending his career as honorary correspondent of the First Socialist International. It was Herwegh who introduced Wagner to Franz Wille, who, like both Wagner and Herwegh a political exile with an eventful past, had come from Hamburg in 1851 with his English wife Eliza to live a few miles along the lake at Meilen, where Herwegh and the Wagners sometimes spent two or three days as their guests. Heinrich Heine compared Wille's deeply furrowed face to that of an 'academic youth who has inscribed himself with sword-cuts'. It was Herwegh who was later to introduce Wagner to the philosophy of Schopenhauer, with immense consequences for his thinking and his art.

No couple could have offered Wagner more precious life-giving friendship than Otto and Mathilde Wesendonck, whom he first met in 1852 shortly after their arrival in Zurich. They were both from Elberfeld, now part of Wuppertal. Otto had amassed a fortune in the silk business in New York, and they now lived in style in the Hotel Baur au Lac, like the Herweghs. Otto was two years younger than Wagner, his wife fifteen years younger, and they had a baby, Myrrha. Mathilde was young, beautiful, passionate, fond of poetry, and transfixed by Wagner's music, while Otto was wealthy and generous, a combination perfectly calculated to draw Wagner into their orbit, and they were to provide, respectively, the spiritual and material succour which was always his greatest need.

There were distant friends too, with whom Wagner kept up a voluminous correspondence. Every day at eleven he impatiently awaited the first postal delivery. His nieces Johanna in Berlin and Franziska in Schwerin stayed in touch; August Röckel, behind bars, was out of reach, but Theodor Uhlig, a young violinist in the Dresden

45

orchestra who had developed an admiration not just for Wagner's music but also for his ideas about the theatre and the future of music, was a willing correspondent who had visited Zurich in 1851 and taken long mountain walks with his disgraced kapellmeister. Uhlig significantly named his son Siegfried. Long letters passed regularly between Zurich and Dresden in which every step of Wagner's artistic pilgrimage was reported and dissected. Certainly Uhlig's passion for discussion and argument is reflected in Wagner's writings. Of the greatest importance was, as ever, the figure of Liszt, busy with his own affairs and his own creative concerns in Weimar but ever willing to assist Wagner and share his thoughts and dreams. Their correspondence records an extraordinary artistic closeness even though they had not met since Wagner's hurried visit in May 1849. Liszt had given the world première of *Lohengrin* in Weimar in August 1850 and also sustained *Der fliegende Holländer* and *Tannhäuser* in the Weimar repertoire, the first city to showcase all these works together. He was also, from time to time, a source of much-needed funds, which would alone have encouraged Wagner to keep their relationship in good order.

From the day he set foot in Zurich in 1849 Wagner had been producing a steady stream of work. Almost none of it was music. His last composition was the score of *Lohengrin*, finished in April 1848, a year before the débâcle that ended his Dresden career. But it was not exile that shut off the flow of music, it was the profound conviction that his artistic future lay in a radical transformation of the art of opera. His intuition was leading him to a new type of music-drama, a new conception of melody, harmony and orchestration, and a new relationship between ideas, words and sounds, all of which required long hours of profound thought. Wagner's chosen medium of thought was, besides conversation and correspondence, the prose essay. From his desk came a remarkable sequence of tracts and books, leading to the drafting of the libretto of *Der Ring des Nibelungen*, the most ambitious and far-reaching opera ever conceived.

The first essay was *Die Kunst und die Revolution* ('Art and Revolution'), which he wrote in fourteen days in July 1849 and published soon after in Leipzig. It is a thirty-four-page attack on Christianity and its suppression of the virtues embodied in Greek drama. Still breathing fire, Wagner sees world revolution as the only means by which art can fulfil its true purpose, in the form of the ideal theatre of the future. If he later said that writing this had the effect of 'removing the poison from his system', at the time he was powerfully committed to such ideas. They were undergoing change, however, and we can trace the evolution of more coherent, more constructive views on art and its role in society as the stream of writing continued. *Das Kunstwerk der Zukunft* ('The Artwork of the Future') followed a few months later and was also published in Leipzig. This book is four times as long as the previous one, couched, like all his writings of this period, in almost impenetrable German prose. Wagner is still insistent that current opera is elitist and commercial, and that in the future theatres will be built solely for the ideal presentation of music and drama, not for ostentation or social adornment. The Greeks' union of dance, music and poetry was to be once again the ideal harmony of the arts in a new perfectly combined form. The book was dedicated to the philosopher Feuerbach, whose ideas on religion had profoundly influenced Wagner to the point where the gods who play such a large part in the *Ring* are truly reflections of human behaviour, just as Feuerbach had argued.

More prose followed. *Kunst und Klima* ('Art and Climate') was a brief rebuttal of charges that he had neglected the importance of climate in culture. It was not climate that brought about the degradation of art, he argued, but modern civilisation with its devotion to industrial development and bad art. The next essay, *Das Judenthum in der Musik*, was an ill-considered rattle of anti-semitism that did Wagner no good then, and has been even more damaging to his standing in the twentieth century. The latter part of 1850 was largely given up to writing the longest of these important prose works, *Oper und Drama* ('Opera and Drama'), over 300 pages of dense argument from which emerges a vision of a future music-drama quite different from anything the world had seen before. We have to remember that Wagner was not trying to formulate a method or a system by which he could construct his next work; his appeal to the Greeks and his hostility to modern manifestations of commercially driven art were a necessary step in clarifying the ideas that would eventually re-form as the music-drama. He was trying to articulate in prose a basis for the musical and dramatic framework that was simultaneously taking actual shape in his mind as drama.

Before *Oper und Drama* appeared in print in Leipzig in 1852 Wagner read it aloud to his friends, including Herwegh, in twelve sessions. But the well was not exhausted, and there followed another hundred pages entitled *Eine Mitteilung an meine Freunde* ('A Communication to my Friends'), finished in July 1851. This rounded out the series with the exhortation to his friends to believe that to love the art one must love the artist, and included many direct references to the great work of art that was now to take over his creative energy. Ever since finishing *Lohengrin* in 1848 he had known that his next opera was to be about the mythic hero Siegfried, and the draft libretto of *Siegfrieds Tod*, the basis of what later became *Götterdämmerung*, was ready that year. But everything in Wagner's spirit told him that this was only the kernel of an immense conception that would require years of profound thought and even more years of hard labour. Never one to flinch from material difficulties, he forged his ideas in these voluminous writings, coming to the conclusion, expressed clearly in *Eine Mitteilung an meine Freunde*, that this work would fill three evenings and a preliminary evening and would require a new kind of theatre and a new kind of audience.

While still at work on that book he had already drafted the libretto of *Der junge Siegfried*, which was to preface *Siegfrieds Tod*, and then, realising that the story needed the fuller exposition of two more preliminary evenings, went on to outline *Das Rheingold* and *Die Walküre*. Before the end of 1851 he already had a broad idea of the whole conception both as theoretical exegesis and as draft scenario. He had even attempted some musical sketches for *Siegfrieds Tod* and noted down the tune of the Valkyries' Ride that would eventually be one of his best-known melodies. But another profound instinct told him that composition was premature. The poems were finished in verse form on 15 December 1852 and recited aloud by their author to Herwegh and the Willes a few days later.

S o Wagner's first action in 1853 was to send his completed poem to the printers. Fifty copies were run off on high-quality paper by Erwin Kiesling, who published the local theatre journal and who had recently published the libretto of *Der fliegende Holländer* and a book by Wagner's philologist friend Ettmüller. Ten copies were sent to Weimar for Liszt to distribute. Uhlig, alas, was destined never to see the finished poem about which he had heard so much, for he died of tuberculosis in Dresden on 2 January, aged only thirty. Wagner was deeply affected by his death. In February a group of friends gathered at the Hotel Baur au Lac, where the Herweghs and the Wesendoncks lived, to hear Wagner read the entire poem on four consecutives nights. After the first reading Wagner became hoarse, the treatment of which recommended by the doctor was to drink two or three cups of weak tea and not to talk all next day, a prescription which he would normally find exceedingly difficult to follow. But he did, and the remaining readings went well. They were indeed very well received. Yet how, they must have wondered, could such a colossal drama ever be set to music, especially if the composer was in no special hurry to begin the score? Why was it not in traditional rhymed verse, as every libretto had been since the beginning of opera? How exactly did such a grand scheme fit with the oceans of prose that had preceded it? How were these gods, giants, dwarfs, dragons, Gibichungs and Valkyries ever to be represented on the stage?

The mixture of admiration and bewilderment that greeted the poem caused Wagner some distress. An opera cannot live unless it has music, and without music the *Ring* was merely an unconventional libretto of unprecedented length. Even his admirers might be forgiven for having serious doubts as to whether it was achievable, let alone the key to the future of music. Wagner's tendency to elaborate all discussion of the work in cascades of historical and philosophical discourse cannot have made it any easier for them. Even Liszt, who acknowledged it to be an extraordinary work and had complete faith in Wagner as a composer, refrained from offering the detailed critique that he craved, possibly because in the midst of putting on all three operas *Der fliegende Holländer*, *Tannhäuser* and *Lohengrin* in Weimar, and amid all his other occupations, he scarcely had time to write it. Some of those to whom Wagner sent copies made no response at all.

His mood in the spring and summer of 1853 was consequently a see-saw from visionary optimism to profound despair. He set in motion any manoeuvres he thought might end his banishment, working on various contacts who had access to the Dresden authorities. Zurich had come to seem an inadequate, provincial location for the great task on which he was now embarked, especially since interest in the existing operas was growing daily in German cities. None of these approaches bore fruit, and he would not set foot in Germany for nearly ten years. If he had been ready to begin composition of his huge score, he might have felt less restless; but he was not. We cannot tell how freely his inner ear filled with music in these months, for nothing was yet written down.

He distracted himself with the three concerts timed to mark his birthday. In addition to the voluminous thinking, talking and writing that consumed his time in the early Zurich years he had not neglected his role as a conductor, which had, after all, been his professional métier in Würzburg, Leipzig, Magdeburg, Riga and Dresden. Within a few months of his arrival in Switzerland, on 15 January 1850 in the tiny Casino hall, which seated no more than 400 (today the cantonal courthouse on Hirschgraben), he enthralled the local Music Society audience with his performance of Beethoven's Seventh Symphony. That same year he arranged for his protégé Karl Ritter to be appointed conductor of the Zurich opera, which played in the Aktien Theatre, opened just next door to the Casino in 1834. Ritter, however, was not up to the job, so Wagner had to take over much of the season himself, including *Der Freischütz* on opening night. Hans von Bülow, just twenty

15 The Aktien Theatre, Zurich

years old, whose talent was superior to Ritter's and whose devotion to Liszt and Wagner was fired by hearing *Lohengrin* in Weimar, arrived in Zurich in time to help out and gain some conducting experience under Wagner's tutelage. Wagner himself conducted at least six operas in the 1850–51 season, some of them more than once. The modest payments were not unwelcome, of course. At season's end he published a long essay *Ein Theater in Zürich*, which proposed developing a core of local talent and a repertoire to match so that the theatre could become the spiritual heart of the community, a theme he developed elsewhere from time to time. This was published by the local bookseller Friedrich Schulthess, a friend of Bernhard Spyri. A year later he conducted four performances of *Der fliegende Holländer* which satisfied him perhaps more than the original production in Dresden.

Between 1851 and 1855 he conducted twenty-two concerts by the Music Society, sharing the podium with Franz Abt, whose followers, if not Abt himself, resented Wagner's manifestly greater authority in Beethoven and the larger symphonic repertoire. He resisted the tendency to fill concert programmes with innumerable solo novelty items and always put the main symphony last, in what has become the universal modern practice. On 16 March 1852 he conducted the *Tannhäuser* overture and Beethoven's 'Pastoral' Symphony in a concert which was probably the concert that first brought Wagner's personality and music to Mathilde Wesendonck's notice. A year later, in March 1853, it was the turn of the 'Eroica' and the Seventh Symphonies. The Zurich public clearly had an appetite to hear his music, so when he proposed a series of three concerts to the committee of the Music Society, they made strenuous efforts to raise the money that he needed in order to augment the orchestra by bringing in out-of-town musicians, some from as far away as Frankfurt and Wiesbaden, and to modify the platform to his special designs. At Otto Wesendonck's urging sufficient guarantors came forward. Wagner had his hands full throughout April recruiting musicians and preparing the orchestral material. In preparation for the concerts, which were all to have the same programme, he gave preliminary readings of the librettos of the three operas from which the main part of the programme was drawn: *Der fliegende Holländer* on 10 May, *Tannhäuser* on 12 May, and *Lohengrin* on Saturday 14 May (the day on which Joachim was rehearsing with Schumann in Düsseldorf and Berlioz was crossing the Channel to London). This in itself was a remarkable experience, if only because conductors or composers did not normally write their own librettos, and none ever gave public readings. But Wagner needed to familiarise his audience with the background and poetic tone of these works; Zurichers knew the *Holländer* from the previous year's performances, but the other two works were new to them. Wagner, having himself never heard any of *Lohengrin*, was particularly anxious to hear the Prelude. Surely he knew that it was one of the most perfectly crafted compositions he had yet written, but he still needed to hear it. As word spread, audiences were more numerous at each session, overwhelmed by his vivid and dramatic style of reading.

— 777 —

Musikaufführung

in Zürich

am 18. Mai, wiederholt am 20. und 22. Mai.

Zur Eröffnung:

Friedensmarsch aus „Rienzi".

Erster Theil:

„Der fliegende Holländer".

1. Ballade der Senta.
2. Lied norwegischer Matrosen.
3. „Des Holländers Seefahrt" (Ouverture).

Zweiter Theil:

„Tannhäuser".

1. Festlicher Einzug der Gäste auf Wartburg.
2. „Tannhäuser's Bussfahrt" und Gesang der heimkehrenden Pilger.
3. „Der Venusberg" (Ouverture).

Dritter Theil:

„Lohengrin".

1. „Der heilige Gral" (Orchestervorspiel).
2. Männerscene und Brautzug.
3. Hochzeitmusik und Brautlied.

Der Billetverkauf findet am 14. und 17. Mai, sowie an den Tagen der Aufführung selbst, Vormittags von 10—12 Uhr, an der Theaterkasse statt. Bestellungen zu Billets werden bis dahin von Herrn Theaterkassier Keller im St. Johannes an der Oetenbachergasse angenommen. Ausgenommen in den Logen sind noch in allen Plätzen Billets zu haben.   Die Konzertkommission
der allgemeinen Musikgesellschaft.

Vorlesungen.

In Verbindung mit den oben angezeigten Musikaufführungen, und zur Ermöglichung eines leichteren Verständnisses der in ihnen vorzutragenden Tonstücke, beabsichtigt der Unterzeichnete an drei verschiedenen Abenden dieser Woche die Dichtungen der drei Opern, aus denen jene Musiksätze gewählt sind, öffentlich vorzulesen, und zwar:

1. Dienstag den 10. Mai: „Der fliegende Holländer".
2. Donnerstag den 12. Mai: „Tannhäuser".
3. Samstag den 14 Mai: „Lohengrin".

im grossen Saale des Kasino, Abends um 7 Uhr.

Jeder, der eine der Musikaufführungen zu besuchen gedenkt, ist zu diesen Vorlesungen freundlichst eingeladen.

Richard Wagner.

16 Wagner's concert, 18 May 1853

On Sunday 15 May, Whitsunday, at seven in the evening Wagner asked the musicians to come to the theatre for a pep-talk, itself an unheard of requirement, presumably to win them over to an understanding of what they were about to spend the week playing. Choral rehearsals had begun a week earlier, while orchestral rehearsals, from which the public was excluded, began at ten o'clock on the Monday morning. He had a string strength of twenty violins, eight violas, eight cellos and five double basses. The harpist, Ottilie Nägeli, daughter of one of Switzerland's most distinguished musicians, insisted on knitting during rehearsals and had to be replaced.

The first concert took place at seven o'clock on the Wednesday evening. It is significant that Wagner chose to give these concerts not in the Casino, where the Music Society normally gave its orchestral concerts, but in the larger Aktien Theatre, home of opera. The programme was constructed in three parts (each with three items) with a preliminary piece, a programme which Wagner could not have devised without intending its similarity to the plan of his *Ring*

51

poem, with its three evenings, each divided into three acts, and a preliminary evening:

Opening: Friedensmarsch (*Rienzi*)

Part I *Der fliegende Holländer*
   1 Senta's Ballad
   2 Norwegian Sailors' Song
   3 Overture

Part II *Tannhäuser*
   1 Entry of the Guests into the Wartburg
   2 Tannhäuser's journey and Pilgrims' Song
   3 Prelude

Part III *Lohengrin*
   1 Prelude
   2 Men's Scene and Bridal March
   3 Prelude to Act III, Wedding Music and Bridal Song

Ignaz Heim's wife Emilie was the singer in Senta's Ballad. There was an orchestra of seventy and a chorus of a 110. Assuming two intervals, the concert would have lasted two and a half hours. On the evening after the first concert he invited the orchestra and chorus to the Café Münsterhof for a post-mortem and further words of exhortation, and the next two performances, on Friday and Sunday, were an even greater success. On the intervening Saturday Wagner's plan was to take the musicians on a steamer trip down the lake to Horgen, but it proved impossible to arrange and they settled instead for a dinner at the Casino at which old Ott-Imhof, president of the Music Society, toasted Wagner's health. Wagner was presented with a silver goblet and a laurel wreath. He replied that the goal of his endeavours was not fame or riches or a brilliant position in the musical world, but to express his feelings warmly and truly and to convey, in words and music, his vision of what was noble, pure and godlike, so that his audience could feel with him and be blessed in love. Dinner guests would surely have understood what he meant if the sublime phrases of the *Lohengrin* prelude were still echoing in their ears, as they were in his. Wagner's offer to pay for the orchestral players' dinner was declined by the committee.

So great was the demand for tickets to the concerts that there were pleas to give another performance the following week and to take the programme to other cities. But backed up by his friend Hagenbuch Wagner refused these requests, conscious that he had created a Wagner Festival which could not be duplicated elsewhere. As a precedent for the Bayreuth Festival it was not without relevance. In any case the third concert fell on an important milestone in his life, 22 May 1853, his fortieth birthday. That evening he was showered with wreaths and bouquets, and one of the singers recited a poem in his honour written by 'a lady' – no doubt Mathilde. The concert series as a whole still made a loss of 7,000 francs, which was covered by Wesendonck and seven other sponsors. To Liszt, who would certainly have come to hear the concerts had he not been obliged to remain in Weimar for the ducal wedding that weekend, Wagner wrote: 'I laid the whole festival at the feet of *one* lovely woman'. He was already ensnared by a complicated passion for Mathilde Wesendonck that would have profound consequences in the next few years.

The *Eidgenössische Zeitung* declared 'We have a King in our midst who delights us with his grace and favour. But his kingdom is art.' The once fanatical republican was beginning to enjoy being described in such regal terms. Zurich was beginning to seem a more congenial city than he thought, especially since, unlike Dresden, it was not ruled by a hereditary monarch who kept a tight grip on the cultural reins. Here in his own domain he could be a prince himself.

WHETHER or not it was the stimulus of hearing his own music again, in the week following the concerts he composed a piece of music for the first time in over five years. It was, to be sure, on a scale diametrically opposed to what we think of as Wagnerian: a mere twenty-three bars of light music for the piano in the style of a polka. He presented it to Mathilde on the 29th with the cryptic inscription 'Yesterday's frost here melted.' Was it a peace offering of some kind? The glaring insignificance of the music is dwarfed by the momentous fact of Wagner once again scratching out notes on a page of music paper, even though no one, least of all himself, had ever doubted that there were great works yet to come, greater even than the three fine operas of which Zurich had just heard some 'bleeding chunks'.

On 1 June Wagner invited the Wesendoncks in for the evening, promising Mathilde not to invite anyone else so as not to spoil their 'sacred' evening. They were about to leave for a visit to Bad Ems, the fashionable spa near Koblenz frequented by crowned heads and Europe's high society. Wagner was not at all happy at the prospect of spending the month of June 'alone'. He had been pressing Liszt to join him, but having just served the Weimar court for the ducal wedding, Liszt had to stay on for the Grand Duke's Jubilee and for Carl Alexander's birthday at the end of the month. He did not yet know he would also be receiving Reményi and Brahms as guests. Expecting to escort his mother back to Paris at the end of the month, he could see no prospect of getting to Zurich before the middle of July.

A set-back arrived in mid-June when Wagner learned that his appeal for amnesty had once again been turned down by the Dresden authorities. At a concert in Weimar on 6 June in honour of the King of Saxony, Grand Duke Carl Friedrich had at Liszt's urging attempted to convince his guest to pardon Wagner. The King himself might have been sympathetic to the plea, but his ministers and the reactionary forces in power were swayed by reports of Wagner's extravagant living in Zurich and of the subversive company he kept. A Dresden police bulletin of 11 June described him as one of the most prominent members of the revolutionary faction: 'If he is caught he must be arrested and handed over to the Royal Court of Justice in Dresden.' It was a severe blow, not only because the feeling that he belonged

17 The Hotel Baur au Lac, Zurich

heart and soul to Germany was stronger than ever, but also because his inability to hear *Lohengrin* (other than a few extracts) left a void in his musical consciousness, whether or not it inhibited his plan to embark on the *Ring*.

With the three concerts still ringing in his ears Wagner composed some more music. It was still not the immense tetralogy for which he needed the right surroundings, the right mood and the right moment, but another piece for Mathilde, a little more substantial this time. Many years later he said it was a thankyou for a beautiful sofa-cushion she had given him. It was a piano sonata in one movement in A flat major, whose opening notes strangely prefigure the beginning of the Liebestod from *Tristan und Isolde*, still a few years in the future. Its second section hints at *Die Meistersinger*. It is tempting to suppose that the sonata is in a single movement in emulation of Liszt's great single-movement piano sonata completed a few months earlier, but Wagner did not yet know the Liszt work, and he may not even have known of its existence. The correspondence between the two composers is much concerned with Wagner's works and barely mentions Liszt's. In any case Wagner scarcely attempts the heroic pianism or the complex formal design for which Liszt's sonata is justly famous; it is merely a richly melodic slow movement in some semblance of sonata form rising to a dramatic climax in the middle section.

At the head of the manuscript Wagner wrote the words 'Wißt ihr wie das wird?' – 'Know ye what is to come?' – quoting the three Norns from *Götterdämmerung* (later echoed by Brünnhilde in her immolation scene). This might be interpreted in a variety of ways, referring either to Wagner's coming flood of inspiration in writing the *Ring*, or to the incipient passion for Mathilde that was rising in his veins, or, more vaguely, to a philosophical uncertainty about fate in general. It was completed by 20 June when he sent it to Otto in gratitude for many debts incurred, asking him to give it to his wife. She spent a few days at the piano with her piece, puzzling over the epigram at the top, then wrote a long letter to Minna to thank her husband for the presentation. The sonata was not published until 1878 when

Wagner reluctantly allowed Schott to print it in settlement of some debts and in return for *not* printing the *Siegfried-Idyll*. Its published title was at first to be *Sonata Sketch* but ended up as *A Sonata for the Album of Frau M.W. composed in 1853*.

Having despatched the sonata Wagner and Minna spent a week in Interlaken with Emilie Ritter, daughter of his benefactress Julie Ritter, and sister of the two musicians Karl and Alexander. There, sheltering from incessant rain, he drew up a plan for the restructuring of Zurich's musical life, thinking, no doubt, that he was now likely to have to remain there several years more.

Finally the long-awaited visit of Liszt took place. Wagner had been begging him to come since he settled in Zurich, but Liszt's obligations in Weimar and his occasional engagements elsewhere had up till now stood in the way. He planned to come with Joachim and Robert Franz, a composer of fine songs whom both Liszt and Schumann admired. But at the last minute both defected. Joachim, as we have seen, now preferred the company of his new friend Brahms, and Franz, who spent his whole life in the city of Halle, did not manage to make the visit until four years later. The Princess Sayn-Wittgenstein was intending to take the waters in Carlsbad. So at 1.00 p.m. on Friday 1 July Liszt, accompanied by his manservant Hermann, having stopped in Karlsruhe for a couple of days to settle arrangements for the forthcoming festival still planned for late August, took the train from there to Basel. Swiss trains, now one of the most celebrated of railway systems, were then many years behind the rest of Europe. By 1853 hardly any lines had been built. So Liszt had to take the night diligence from Basel that reached Zurich on the Saturday at seven in the morning.

Wagner was there at the coaching stop to meet him. Having not seen each other for four years the two friends fell upon one another in a hearty embrace. For a quarter of an hour they wept and laughed, then went back to Wagner's apartment to spend the rest of the day in ardent conversation. Liszt was struck by Wagner's luxurious surroundings, and when he observed that his style was scarcely democratic, Wagner assured him that he had completely severed his connections with revolutionaries and refugees. Twenty times that day Wagner threw his arms around him and rolled on the ground with his dog Peps. His conversation reminded Liszt of a Vesuvius throwing out streaks of flame alternating with bouquets of roses. Minna, he noticed, had put on weight, while Wagner himself had lost a good deal. Eventually, after a dinner to which a dozen friends were invited, Liszt returned to his hotel, the Baur au Lac. He had always loved lakes, and this one did not disappoint. From his bedroom window he could see the lake washing up almost to the ground floor of the hotel. The hotel served an excellent honey for breakfast, which pleased him too.

The two great musicians had much to talk about. In the course of the eight-day visit Wagner felt that he got to know Liszt properly for the first time, and Liszt too felt that they achieved a mutual understanding 'above and beyond verbal exchange'.

Wagner's immense correspondence kept him well informed on musical affairs in Germany, but he still had much to learn about Liszt's network of disciples and friends and about prospects for presenting the kind of opera he dreamed of. They might have wondered why Joachim failed to be there, but did Liszt mention the shy young man from Hamburg who had recently accompanied Joachim to Weimar? Liszt was full of plans for the forthcoming Karlsruhe Festival. They would have talked about Berlioz's visits to Weimar and the production of *Benvenuto Cellini* there, but they would not yet have learned that the opera had hit a storm of abuse in London only a week before. Wagner undoubtedly felt that he and Liszt were moving into a new world of music, leaving Schumann and his supporters far behind. What, Liszt must have wondered, would the music for the *Ring* sound like? There is no record that Wagner sat at the piano to reveal the new musical language forming in his brain, but we know that Liszt did play repeatedly for Wagner, probably including the Sonata in B minor, and probably including some of the symphonic poems he had been working on since their last meeting: *Orpheus*, *Prometheus*, *Mazeppa*, full of sounds that clearly left their mark on Wagner's later style. Was it this music that prompted Wagner finally to embark on the huge task he had been contemplating for so long? Optimistic as always, Wagner convinced Liszt that a Nibelungen Festival could be presented in a new theatre, yet to be built, in Zurich in 1856.

On Liszt's second day, amid protestations that he had renounced politics for ever, Wagner took Liszt to see Herwegh, whom he had met several times in Berlin in 1843 and as a member of Marie d'Agoult's circle in Paris (and perhaps at breakfast in the hotel). On the Monday and Tuesday evenings Wagner gave readings of the *Rheingold* and *Walküre* poems, and on Wednesday afternoon they set off with Herwegh for an excursion to Brunnen. They took the steamer along Lake Zurich and then a carriage by road for four hours across to Brunnen, on Lake Lucerne, arriving late at the inn Oberst auf der Maur. Early next morning they crossed the lake by boat to visit the Grütli, where it was supposed that the Swiss Confederacy had been declared in 1305. To symbolise the union of the three cantons the three men drew water from three sources and swore eternal brotherhood, in imitation, as they all no doubt knew, of the scene for Gunther and Siegfried in *Siegfrieds Tod*. Liszt and Herwegh then discussed the idea of an oratorio entitled *Christus*, although whose idea it was first is hard to guess. This work did not come into being for over a decade, and then with no participation from Herwegh.

The three men then took a boat back across the lake to one of William Tell's chapels (the subject of an engraving by Turner made in 1827). Liszt must have known that this was not the chapel he had evoked in his mighty piano piece *La Chapelle de Guillaume Tell*, composed after his elopement to Geneva with Marie d'Agoult in 1835. Tell, after all, is no more than a mythical figure of Swiss legend whose exploits are marked by at least three chapels, one of them on Lake Geneva, another on Lake Lucerne. The three friends returned to Zurich the same evening by a different route, taking a boat along Lake Zug.

18 The Chapel of William Tell, Lake Lucerne

The Friday and Saturday were absorbed in yet more conversation and more music, and on Sunday evening (10 July) Liszt left, heading back again through Basel. Wagner and Herwegh saw him off from the coach station. He promised to come for at least a month next year. Wagner gave him a pale pink hat which he had admired. The euphoria Wagner experienced after his three concerts had now evaporated, and with Liszt's departure he sank into a state of inertia which, with hindsight, we can now see to be the necessary recoil *pour mieux sauter*.

———————

CHAPTER 5

Berlioz in Baden-Baden and Frankfurt

O N Saturday 9 July, the day before Liszt's departure from Zurich, Berlioz and Marie returned from London to their Paris apartment on the Rue de Boursault with wounds to lick. The humiliation of *Benvenuto Cellini*'s reception in Paris in 1838 was now matched by another, that of Covent Garden. Berlioz thought wistfully of Liszt and his successful resurrection of the opera in Weimar the year before and wrote him a long letter with a full account of the London débâcle. Liszt was intending to revive it, and there was talk of productions in Marseille and St Petersburg. Berlioz certainly never expected to hear *Cellini* in Paris ever again. He never expected anything at all in Paris any more and had no plans to compose or conduct any more music in his home city. Journalism was almost his sole resource, since more people were keen to read his articles, it seemed, than listen to his music. His book *Les Soirées de l'orchestre*, published the previous December, was doing well and was ready for a new printing. Readers of the *Journal des débats* were ready for another feuilleton having not had one from his pen for over two months.

He put together a mordant essay comparing musical life in London with that of Paris. Many musicians of the day were in a position to write such a piece, but none could have done it with such insight and wit. The poverty of Paris's music, especially the stale repertoire of the Conservatoire concerts, fares badly, naturally, against the superabundance of London's, even if Londoners were fatally uncritical about what they hear. 'In London,' he writes, 'they don't just consume music, they relish it, and they particularly love grand, large-scale works, unlike certain Parisian consumers who turn up their noses at pineapple and prefer sour apples or brambleberries.'

Liszt replied to Berlioz's letter with an account of his visit to Wagner in Zurich. Although we don't have the letter, he must have mentioned something Wagner had said or written that Liszt felt needed to be explained, probably the bruising reference to Berlioz in *Oper und Drama*. Berlioz was not troubled:

> Like you I am convinced that Wagner and I can easily mesh together if he'd just put a little oil on the wheels. I've never read the lines you mention, but I don't resent them in the least. I've taken enough pot-shots at passers-by in my time not to be surprised at a few stray bullets coming in my direction.

He had some cleaning up of the *Cellini* material to do, which justified having a complete new full score copied. The original autograph score had been revised and messed around so many times that it was no longer serviceable. He also had piles of proofs to read. *La Fuite en Égypte* had already been published in Paris, but his music would only be performed in Germany if it was translated into German, and this was a constant source of trouble. The original German versions of both *Roméo et Juliette* and *La Damnation de Faust* had been expensive disasters. With the full score and vocal score of *La Damnation de Faust* now in the press with a revised translation he was anxious about that, as well as the problem of finding someone to take on the much smaller *Fuite en Égypte*. Liszt's friend Auguste Gathy, who lived in Paris and wrote for several German newspapers, was his first choice, but an elusive one, and the problem was not solved until the end of the year when Peter Cornelius, whom Berlioz had not yet met, stepped forward and became not only a faithful and skillful translator, but also a true disciple.

Five minutes' walk away in the Rue Blanche Berlioz's wife Harriet clung to pathetic shreds of life. She was paralysed from a series of strokes, could hardly speak, and had to be nursed day and night. When he reflected on what she had once meant to him, the agony was unbearable. At least their son Louis, now nearly nineteen, was taken care of. He had been assigned to a ship, the *Corse*, which took him from Cherbourg westward around the British Isles to the Shetlands and was heading for Edinburgh. He proudly reported on municipal and military receptions on land, and had been hunting. He was paid forty francs a month and was well liked by his superior officers.

Louis's career in the navy held more promise perhaps than his own. 'There's a great battle in my mind,' he told Liszt,

> between art and disgust, between impatience with the known and the desire of the unknown, between obstinacy and the cry of reason: 'it can't be done'. Our art, as we understand it, is a millionaire's art. But not one monarch, not one Rothschild, understands that. Could we possibly be just plain idiots with our absurd pretensions ...?

With no plans to write music and no intention of giving any concerts in Paris, there remained only two options: one was to carry on as critic of the *Journal des débats*, a métier at which he excelled but which he heartily detested; the other, much more alluring, was to give concerts abroad. By good fortune there had just arrived an invitation to give a concert in Baden-Baden, the most fashionable of all the spas in Germany, and there were feelers out for concerts in Frankfurt and Munich also. Berlioz had developed some useful experience in negotiating with German cities, and although the financial outcome was never certain, the musical rewards were infinitely higher than any to be had at home. The two long tours of 1842–3 and 1845–6 introduced his music to receptive German audiences, and the visits to Russia and England in the last six years cemented his reputation as a conductor of outstanding gifts.

A T the end of his four-week break at home, he received a visit from Meyerbeer who was in Paris working on his opera *L'Étoile du nord* in preparation for its première at the Opéra-Comique. Then he and Marie left for Baden-Baden, with an immense trunk to carry all the orchestral and choral parts he needed, mostly hand-written. They arrived on Wednesday 3 August, which allowed him just a week in which to prepare his concert. The railway connection to Strasbourg was recently completed, but the journey required an overnight stop and a ferry crossing of the Rhine. Many Parisians were making the journey because this was the height of the spa season and Baden-Baden was at the very top of the list of fashionable summer resorts for the well-to-do. Baden-Baden was exceptional in that the manager of the casino, Edouard Bénazet, drew on his gambling profits to promote serious classical concerts and opera. It was Bénazet's idea to invite Berlioz to give a concert this year, which he eagerly accepted, having heard that Bénazet had a particular talent for attracting the right people and keeping the riffraff away:

> It's not enough [he wrote in the feuilleton published on 26 July] to set about charming elegant society by putting its members in company with the wittiest men, the most ravishing women and the greatest artists, and laying on magnificent entertainment for them; beyond that, these jewels of the fashionable world must be protected from the very approach of individuals who are disagreeable to see or hear, and whose presence alone is enough to put a damper on a ball, or strike a jarring note at a concert. Ugly women, vulgar men, fools, scatterbrains and imbeciles, in a word all bugbears, must be kept out of the way.
>
> This is something no impresario before Monsieur Bénazet had ever tried to do. But now it seems certain that neither Mme ***, so stupid and ugly, nor Mlle ***, whose appearance is so grotesquely outlandish, nor the deathly dull Monsieur ***, nor Monsieur ***, his worthy rival, nor many others just as dangerous, will appear again in Baden for a long time.

Since Berlioz never found it easy to conceal his contempt for the great unwashed, the rumour of Baden-Baden's exclusiveness was more than welcome. Even more welcome was his discovery that Bénazet, who had briefly studied at the Paris Conservatoire, liked him both as a composer and a conductor and was willing to accede to what many others would have regarded as unreasonable demands in terms of rehearsal time and musical authority. The whole atmosphere of the little town was new to him, and he liked it.

Perhaps it was the inefficacy of nineteenth-century medicine that led so many to put their faith in 'the waters', but you did not have to be unwell or hypochondriac to submit to the various water regimes that were offered in all of Europe's great spas. Sun-bathing and sea-bathing were derided as messy and undignified, whereas the inland resorts usually offered mountain scenery and healthy air, away from the smog of cities and away from the tiresome presence of the plebs. Doctors analysed the chemical constitution of different mineral waters and prescribed various cures for various ailments. Hotels offered packages which included daily attendance at treatment centres; visitors and patients were usually required to consume torrents

19 Edouard Bénazet

of the elixir waters. For Europe's upper classes this was the standard summer holiday throughout the nineteenth century.

Then as now, there were many who were seriously concerned about their health and were willing to put themselves in the hands of spa doctors, rigorously following a prescribed regime. Wagner was constantly undergoing hydrotherapy of different kinds, drinking water all day and determined to find a cure for his chronic ailments, including erysipelas. From Zurich he was regularly visiting Switzerland's many *Kurorte*. Others went for purely social reasons, since the leading spas attracted crowned heads and the best international society. Many a diplomatic deal was done in the summer months at spas. Both Napoleon III and Queen Victoria visited Baden-Baden, which was also a particular lure for the Russian aristocracy and the Prussian royal family, while the Austrian imperial family preferred Bad Gastein and Bad Ischl. The future Edward VII took his pleasures in Marienbad. The wealthy Wesendoncks, as we have seen, had been to Bad Ems and were now at Bad Schwalbach.

Others went for the music. All spas had resident orchestras that played for nightly dances throughout the season, in fact the particular tint that light music developed in the 1850s was largely a product of the frivolous tastes of holidaying celebrities. Offenbach, who was for many years in charge of the music at Bad Ems, perfectly embodies the frothiness of popular music, 1850s-style. Brahms was to be a regular visitor to Baden-Baden in the 1860s, where he enjoyed the company of Clara Schumann, and in later life, always an admirer of Johann Strauss, he made regular visits to the Austrian spas not to play but to listen.

Others went for the gambling. While Britain and France prohibited or discouraged gambling, the German spas drew thousands to their casinos and enormous sums of money changed hands. While Turgenev was leading the literary life in Baden-Baden (his novel *Smoke* is set there), Dostoyevsky was pursuing his demon in the casinos of Wiesbaden, Bad Ems, Bad Homburg and Baden-Baden. His story *The Gambler*, the basis of Prokofiev's opera, set in the imaginary German spa Roulettenburg, is a vivid evocation of this less admirable side of spa culture. The sexual license that was also discreetly understood to be part of the scene was encouraged by the mixed bathing that some spas permitted and by the honest belief that certain water treatments would overcome infertility.

Hemmed in by steep wooded slopes on either side, the town of Baden-Baden clings to the river Oos which flows westward into the Rhine. The town bulges northward up to the new castle, above which, at the top of a steep hill, stand the ruins of the old castle. From hard rock in the centre of the town the *Ursprung*, one of more than a dozen such springs, delivers a constant stream of hot water, to be bathed in or drunk by the spa's patients, and whose vapour was held to be a particularly effective treatment for ailments of the ears and eyes. Close to the *Trinkhalle* on the south side of the Oos stood the focus of the town, the Salle de la Conversation,

20 The Salle de la Conversation, Baden-Baden

fronted by massive Corinthian columns with a broad open promenade in front. It contained a series of lavishly decorated halls assigned to dancing, gambling, music, and of course conversation. In this centre of Baden's social life most of the conversation was, naturally, in French. The town's theatre had burned down a few years before, but Bénazet, having taken over the reins at his father's death in 1848, was busily expanding the attractions of the town with new promenades, a new church, and was already planning to build a new theatre.

Berlioz and Marie lodged in the house of a Herr von Lora in the Steingasse where it meets the Gernsbacherstrasse, not far from the new castle. The house no longer exists, having given its space to an open area in front of the convent of St Sepulchre. The local newspaper listed the town's visitors, including such exotic persons as Mrs Shakespeare and family from London, Contessa Gualtieri and suite from Sicily, Prince Galitzin from St Petersburg, and many less exalted names from England and America. Princess Augusta of Prussia was there too. She spoke warmly to Berlioz about Liszt, whom she had just seen in Weimar, but she was unable to attend Berlioz's concert, being then in mourning for her father, the Grand Duke.

Among the musicians in Baden-Baden were Berlioz's old friend Heinrich Ernst, the great violin virtuoso, who had been engaged to give a series of trio concerts in the Salle de la Conversation with another of Berlioz's friends, the cellist Hippolyte Seligman from Paris, and the pianist Heinrich Ehrlich from Hanover, who had been in Paris earlier in the year. Ehrlich blamed Baden-Baden's gamblers for not supporting the chamber music series, which was abruptly curtailed. If he and Berlioz spoke of their mutual friend Joachim, perhaps Reményi and the young Brahms came up in the conversation too. Berlioz was very fond of Ernst, who was born in Moravia in 1812 but now lived mostly in Paris when he was not touring. Both were accompanied by ladies who were not yet their wives and whose presence is discreetly not mentioned by the *Badeblatt*. Ernst's Amélie was a young actress whose glamour and early success must have reminded Berlioz of his ailing wife back in Paris, especially if he was able to hear her giving one of her recitations, which were part of the city's programme of entertainments. Another friend was the cellist Bernhard Cossmann from Weimar. Berlioz's old friend Johann Peter Pixis, pianist and composer, whom he had known in Paris in the 1820s, was now living permanently in Baden-Baden. Baron Donop, an amateur pianist from Detmold, was about to hear Berlioz's music for the first time and about to become one of his most ardent admirers.

Ehrlich found Berlioz unusually reserved. One evening, at Berlioz's request, he and Ernst played some Bach, probably a violin sonata, at his lodgings on Schloss Strasse. Assuming that Amélie and Marie were there, a third lady present was the Countess Kalergis, niece of the Russian Chancellor, Count Nesselrode. She was thirty-one years old, half Russian and half Polish, and had made a rash marriage to a wealthy Greek named Kalergis at the age of sixteen. She had studied the piano with Chopin in Paris and continued to play well. Her charms had cast their spell on Liszt, Heine and Gautier, and she had gone especially to Dresden in 1845 to hear *Tannhäuser* and to meet Wagner. Berlioz greatly admired her playing too. She was staying at the rather grand Hôtel d'Angleterre, about as close to the Salle de la Conversation as it was possible to get. The conversation turned to the nature of truth. Berlioz took exception to Boileau's dictum that only truth was beautiful, and only truth could be loved. 'Is there anything more absurd than that?' he asked. 'Truth doesn't always have to be beautiful,' Ehrlich replied, 'but the beautiful is always true, though not perhaps in the usual sense. The absurd can often seem clever, but it's always insecure, while truth doesn't have to be clever.'

Ehrlich then played from memory some passages from Berlioz's music drawing attention to things which seemed true and beautiful and to things which seemed merely cleverly done. Astonished that Ehrlich was so familiar with his music, Berlioz apologised for his divergence of opinion and was extremely civil to him on every occasion thereafter. Almost a year later Berlioz remembered this conversation and remarked, as a postscript to a letter to Ehrlich: 'The absurd is clearly true, because if the absurd were not true, God would be cruel to have put such a passion for the absurd into the hearts of men.'

The entertainments on offer during that week were a performance of Bellini's *I Puritani* in the city theatre on the Thursday; on the Sunday both a German comedy and a concert of light music featuring the great cornettist Arban, whom Bénazet had engaged to play in Berlioz's orchestra; the Tuesday offered a 'Soirée fantastique', but the local paper gave no details of what to expect. Berlioz had no taste for Bellini, and, despite his admiration of Arban, no inclination to attend concerts. In any case he was too busy. Baden-Baden had no orchestra and no chorus capable of performing Berlioz's music, so Bénazet had engaged the resident orchestra and chorus from Karlsruhe, thirty miles to the north. Every morning Berlioz travelled with the soloists on the 7.45 a.m. train to Karlsruhe where he rehearsed with the ducal orchestra until 12.30. They were then given lunch in a garden restaurant, paid for by Bénazet, after which they took the train back to Baden-Baden, whose station was then, unlike the modern station, conveniently within the city, on Lange Strasse. Only for the final rehearsal, on the day of the concert, Thursday 11th, did the Karlsruhe musicians come in to Baden-Baden to rehearse in the hall. Such intense preparation was unheard of in the world of concert-giving, where a maximum of two rehearsals was normal. Berlioz was right to recognise Bénazet as an impresario of exceptional quality.

They had a long and difficult programme to put together. Unlike the modern fashion, concerts then preferred to put the most demanding work at the beginning, and close with something bright, in this case the *Roman Carnival* overture. The first two parts of *La Damnation de Faust* opened the concert. Since the work's first performance in Paris in 1846, Berlioz had only ever programmed the first two parts, probably because the remaining two parts make greater demands on the soloists and because the first two contain such rousing pieces as the *Hungarian March* and the *Chorus of Soldiers and Students*, as well as the *Song of the Rat* and the

Grande salle de la Conversation.

JEUDI 11 Août, à 8 heures précises du soir:

GRAND CONCERT
VOCAL ET INSTRUMENTAL
DIRIGÉ PAR
Mr HECTOR BERLIOZ.

Programme.

PREMIÈRE PARTIE.

1° Les deux premiers actes de la **Damnation de Faust.** Légende en quatre actes de Mr. **H. Berlioz.**

1re Acte. (Plaines de Hongrie.)
Faust seul au lever du soleil.
Ronde de Paysans — chœur.
Récitatif.
Marche Hongroise.

2me Acte. (Faust seul dans son cabinet de travail.)
Récitatif sur une fugue instrumentale.
Hymne de la fête de Pâques — chœur.
Entrée de Mephistophélès. Récitatif (Cave de Leipzig.)
Chœur de Buveurs.
Chanson de Brander ivre.
Fugue vocale sur le thème de la chanson de Brander.
Chanson de Mephistophélès.
(Bosquets et prairies des bords de l'Elbe.)
Chœur de Sylphes et de Gnômes.
Sommeil de Faust.
Ballet des Sylphes.
Récitatif. Chœur de soldats.
Chanson latine d'Etudiants.
La chanson et le chœur ensemble. Final.

Faust; M. EBERIUS. Mephistophélès: M. OBERHOFFER. Brander: M. BREGENZER.

2° Duo de „Semiramide" de *Rossini,* chanté par Mlle **Sophie** et **Marie Cruvelli.**

3° Fleurs Rossiniennes, fantaisie pour la clarinette avec orchestre, composée et exécutée par Mr. **Cavallini.**

4° Air de „Semiramide", chanté par Mlle **Marie Cruvelli.**

DEUXIÈME PARTIE.

1° Fragment instrumental de la Symphonie avec chœurs de **Romeo et Juliette** de Mr. **H. Berlioz.**
(Mélancolie — Bruits lontains de Bal et de Concert — Grande fête chez Capulet.)

2° Andante suivi du carnaval de Venise (demandé) composés et exécutés par Mr. **Ernst.**

3° Air „d'Ernani" de *Verdi,* chanté par Mlle **Sophie Cruvelli.**

4° Chant grec varié pour la clarinette, et exécuté par M. **Cavallini.**

5° Ouverture du Carnaval Romain de Mr. **H. Berlioz.**

Places réservées 10 Fr. — Billets d'entrée 5 Fr.

On peut se procurer des billets à l'avance à la Librairie de Mr. MARX.

21 Berlioz's Concert on 11 August 1853

Song of the Flea. It was sung in German with three German singers to sing Faust, Mephistopheles and Brander.

Modern audiences would call for an interval at this point, but appetites were keener then, and they were no doubt anxious to hear a twenty-seven-year-old diva who had already sung a string of Italian opera roles in Milan, London and Paris. Despite her Italian-sounding name, Sophie Cruvelli came from Bielefeld, in Germany, and she performed on this occasion with her sister, Marie, a contralto, in selections by Rossini and Verdi. The first half of the concert also included a show-piece for clarinet played by the Italian virtuoso Ernesto Cavallini.

These soloists all appeared again in the second half of the concert alongside the celebrated Ernst, who had often been compared to Paganini in his meteoric career. For his one appearance he chose to play his *Carnival of Venice*, a dazzling display of violin virtuosity which he had played all over Europe. Audiences never tired of hearing it, it seems. The second half was framed by two of Berlioz's most stirring orchestral works, both requiring a top-class orchestra, or at least an orchestra that has been thoroughly well rehearsed: first, *Roméo seul – Grand Fête chez Capulet*, which progresses from an expressive Andante malinconico to an exuberant depic-tion of the Capulets' ball, and second, the *Roman Carnival* overture, still today a favourite showpiece for the world's great orchestras. The hall was full to over-flowing and the applause deafening. Some 500 more people were listening from outside under the colonnade.

Berlioz had been assisted in Karlsruhe by the city's kapellmeister, Joseph Strauss, a man of sixty years who had known Beethoven in Vienna. He went up to Berlioz after the concert and told him:

> Allow me to shake your hand, Monsieur Berlioz. I listened to all your rehearsals of *Faust* with great interest. The music is so new that my reactions were rather confused until this evening when the light dawned and I now see and understand it all. I give you my word of honour: this is a masterpiece.

There was much talk of Liszt, since he was already planning the Karlsruhe festival, now scheduled for late September, with kapellmeister Strauss. Berlioz was sorry not to see him in Baden-Baden. Strauss already knew Ernst from many earlier visits to Karlsruhe during Strauss's long kapellmeistership. He must have known that they both came from the city of Brünn (now Brno), in Moravia, where Strauss's father taught the violin.

Berlioz and Marie stayed on an extra day or two in Baden-Baden. He had never felt better. The air, the mountains, the river, the sunshine, all revived him. He showed no interest in taking the waters or in any cure, and he was disgusted by the gambling. What pleased him above all (apart from the closure of the casino on the night of his concert) was finding an organisation that allowed him to select his own programme and his own soloists and to have as much rehearsal as he needed. Eight years later he remembered Bénazet's invitation as if it had been a blank cheque. 'O Richard, O my king,' he claimed to have replied.

Is there any sovereign capable of so much? You'll actually let me do what I want? You actually choose a musician to direct a music festival? You go against the trend of the whole of Europe by not selecting a naval officer or a cavalry commander or a lawyer or a jeweller to run things? You will be horribly compromised. Monarchs will withdraw their ambassadors.

'Don't worry,' replied Bénazet, 'Even if the balance of power in Europe is overthrown, my mind is made up. I count on you.'

The success of this Baden visit had a far-reaching effect on Berlioz's later career. He did not return until 1856, but from then until 1863 he went every year, presenting a major concert and enjoying the same careful music-making that Bénazet guaranteed. Socially too, Baden-Baden was congenial to him, and as a new opera house became more urgent in Bénazet's mind, Berlioz was the obvious choice for a commissioned work with which to open it. So *Béatrice et Bénédict*, Berlioz's last work, was performed in the new theatre in August 1862, its happy mood a reflection of the relief he felt every year as he made that ever speedier journey from Paris. After 1859, when his health seriously deteriorated, he found, like many others before and since, that spas like Baden-Baden did both mind and body nothing but good.

B ERLIOZ and Marie left probably on Sunday 14th for Frankfurt, where he was due to give two concerts. They took the railway connection via Heidelberg, a swifter journey than the boat they had taken in 1843 down the Rhine and up the Main. In any case the level of the Main was so low that steamers were restricted, and a large rock known as the Good Wine Rock had become visible this year as it did in very hot summers when the grapes were ripening well.

Frankfurt was no spa. It was a busy commercial city with no particular appeal to tourists, apart perhaps from the house where Goethe was born. Berlioz knew it from some frustrating visits ten years before, when every attempt to put on a concert came to nothing. He heard *Fidelio* there and wrote extensively about the city's music in his travel journal, but the place did not know his music. The kapellmeister then was an unhelpful individual named Guhr, but he had now

Frankfurt a. M.

Hektor Berlioz, der berühmte französische Componist und Kritiker, ist hier eingetroffen und wird einige seiner großen Tongemälde im Schauspielhause zur Aufführung bringen. Als solche sind bezeichnet: Die große Symphonie „Harold in Italien", die zwei ersten Acte von „la damnation de Faust" und „die Rast der heiligen Familie", ein Fragment im älteren Style. Bei dem außerordentlichen Ruf, welchen die Compositionen von Berlioz in seinem Vaterlande erlangt haben, dürfte die Aufführung der genannten Tonstücke den hiesigen Kunstfreunden von hohem Interesse seyn, um so mehr, als uns bis jetzt noch nicht Gelegenheit geworden, dieselben hier zu hören und kennen zu lernen.

22 Report of Berlioz's arrival in Frankfurt

been replaced as director of the theatre's music by Liszt's friend Gustav Schmidt. Schmidt was very sympathetic to Berlioz's music and had proposed two concerts to be held in the theatre. His situation was similar to that of Liszt in Weimar, in that he was dependent upon the theatre's overall director whenever he needed to give a concert there. The director, Johann Hoffmann, was not as obstructive as some, and offered Berlioz terms which allowed him half of the receipts after deducting 170 francs for expenses. From Berlioz's point of view this was not at all like the Baden-Baden situation where everything was paid for and he took away a proper fee. It all depended on ticket sales, and in Frankfurt there was nothing like the overflowing audience he had seen in the Salle de la Conversation. For neither concert was the theatre anywhere near full. But the compensation was that Frankfurters were a good deal more discerning than the aristocrats and health freaks who came to hear his music in Baden-Baden.

Although they had heard him in London, Berlioz and Marie were free on days when he was not rehearsing to hear Pischek again. He was in Frankfurt playing in *Don Giovanni* on the 19th, Spohr's *Faust* on the 21st, with a benefit performance on the 26th and *Don Giovanni* again on the 28th. They would probably go to Auber's popular hit *Le Maçon*, sung in German, on the 17th since the three soloists lined up to sing in *La Damnation de Faust* also had principal roles in that.

Berlioz's concerts were given in the handsome thousand-seat Comoedienhaus which stood from 1782 to 1878 in what is now Rathenauplatz. The first was originally planned for 7 p.m. on the 22nd, but was not given until Wednesday 24 August. The heat was oppressive, but the audience were tremendously enthusiastic in response to a programme made up entirely of Berlioz's own music. Unusually for the age, there were no vocal solos, no clarinet variations, no cheap thrills. The first part of the concert consisted of *Harold en Italie*, with the viola solo played by Posch, a member of the Frankfurt orchestra. No doubt Berlioz wished that Ernst had followed him to Frankfurt since he had played the solo part previously in Vienna in 1846 and in St Petersburg in 1847, but he may have been suffering already from the illness that laid him low in October. In the absence of star viola players in Berlioz's time, the soloist in this work was often a violinist; Joachim had played it under Liszt the year before, Sainton was the soloist in London a few months earlier, and David would take it on in December, all primarily violinists. Of all Berlioz's works it is the one that he most consistently programmed throughout his career, at least the second movement, the 'Marche des pèlerins', if not the whole symphony. Berlioz had originally planned to start the concert with excerpts from *Roméo et Juliette*, but later opted for *Harold* instead.

This was followed by *Le Repos de la Sainte Famille*, of which Gardoni had given the first performance in London only recently. The tenor solo was sung in German, the translation rapidly put together by Schmidt at Berlioz's request. The soloist was Friedrich Caspari, a member of the theatre troupe, whom he had heard in *Fidelio* in Frankfurt in 1843 and who later sang the title role in *Benvenuto Cellini* in

Weimar. 'He has a tenor voice,' wrote Berlioz later, 'for which they would pay huge sums in Paris if he knew any French and if he knew... how to sing.'

The final section of the concert consisted of the first two parts of *La Damnation de Faust,* as performed in Baden-Baden, though with an entirely different orchestra, chorus and soloists, who had little more than a week to learn their music. Caspari sang Faust, Dettmer sang Mephistopheles, and Leser was Brander. For the second concert five days later on Monday 29th, Caspari was evidently unavailable, so *Le Repos de la Sainte Famille* was replaced by Weber's *L'Invitation à la valse* in Berlioz's orchestration, and the part of Faust was sung by Carl Baumann, who had just moved to Frankfurt from Riga.

Schmidt worked tirelessly to help in rehearsals, and so did another Hoffmann, Carl-Adolph, who was in charge of the chorus. Berlioz had help from the theatre's assistant conductor, Goltermann, known to all cellists as the composer of concertos and studies for their instrument. One of the violinists, Eduard Eliassohn, remembered Berlioz from his days in Paris as a student of Baillot. He now became a true admirer and took up the cause of promoting Berlioz's music. Two years later he wrote to Berlioz to say how fondly the Frankfurt musicians remembered his visit. 'On vous aime,' he told him.

Proof of their enthusiasm was the dinner given in his honour after the concert at the Holländischer Hof, whose chef, Herr Bayha, excelled himself for the occasion. There were speeches, toasts, and laurel wreaths. Carl Gollmick, a member of the orchestra, read a poem. The local military band played an arrangement of his overture *Les Francs-juges* at the window of his hotel. These tributes and the obviously congenial company of musicians made up for the rather dismal takings from the concerts. Above all, Berlioz was now completely convinced, if he had not been before, that for serious music-making he had to go to Germany. Proof that Germans took music seriously was provided by the partisanship that was emerging between the supporters of the new music (of which Berlioz was definitely seen as a representative) and the conservatives who believed that the great tradition of Mozart and Beethoven was being undermined.

One member of the audience in Frankfurt was definitely in the latter camp. Anton Schindler's fame already rested on his familiarity with Beethoven, whose biography he had published in 1840. He had worked as Beethoven's amanuensis and factotum for most of the last seven years of the master's life, and it was not yet known that he had allowed his imagination to gloss some of the facts he recounts and that he had destroyed a great number of the curious conversation books which the deaf Beethoven used for communicating with visitors. On a visit to Paris in 1839 he had heard one of the first performances of *Roméo et Juliette* and soon after presented Berlioz with a copy of his book. Berlioz thanked him by sending a score of the *Requiem.* A later stay in Paris made Schindler more familiar with modern French music, most of which he disliked intensely. Time did not mellow him. Hearing Berlioz's concert now in Frankfurt filled his ink-well with vitriol. By selectively drawing on Berlioz's writings from the 1830s, he demonstrated that Berlioz regarded himself as a genius and a madman, and because he had taken exception to the Tuba mirum of Mozart's *Requiem*, Schindler claimed he condemned all Mozart's music in its entirety. He was enraged by his very presence.

'Six rehearsals! What impertinence! For whose benefit? An empty hall! The net takings were forty gulden. That proves that the music's no good.' Schindler thought the *Hungarian March* and the *Ballet de sylphes* were original, but nevertheless concluded that Berlioz was a worthless fraud, a pretender and impostor, certainly not the successor to Beethoven 'as he claims to be'. And who better than Schindler to judge?

This report appeared on 3 September in the *Niederrheinische Musikzeitung*, a music journal recently founded in Cologne by Ludwig Bischoff. With Ferdinand Hiller's support (which meant a lot in Cologne), Bischoff's principal mission was to mount a crusade against Wagner and all his works. With Liszt and Berlioz as secondary targets, Schindler had no hesitation in contributing his polemical review to an early issue of the journal. By the time it appeared, though, Berlioz was back in Paris, and it is more than possible that he never saw the article. In any case he could not read German. He was moving on. Schmidt had a plan for some kind of *Hamlet* concert in Frankfurt and was keen to include Berlioz's *Hamlet* pieces from the collection *Tristia*. Berlioz's mind was now full of plans for his next visits to Germany, perhaps Frankfurt and Munich, certainly Brunswick, certainly Hanover.

CHAPTER 6

Joachim and Brahms in Göttingen and Bonn

WHERE was Brahms meanwhile? We left him on Sunday 3 July making his departure from Weimar in order to join Joachim in Göttingen, happy to leave Liszt's rather clinging coterie at the Altenburg. Liszt had already left for his trip via Karlsruhe to visit Wagner in Zurich. Joachim had been in Göttingen for a month and had already settled into his lodgings in the Krüger Garden House at 21 Nikolausberger Weg, now a busy road leading into the town from the northeast. His landlord was a bookseller named Vogel, but the house no longer exists. Göttingen was a quiet town of 10,000 inhabitants dominated by the university founded by George II over a hundred years before and boasting one of the finest libraries in Germany. Heinrich Heine some thirty years earlier said that Göttingen's inhabitants were of four types: 'students, professors, Philistines, and cattle, all distinct. The cattle are the most important.' It was not uncommon to see sheep and cows wandering about the town. Everyone kept pigs, and the local wurst was famous. When lectures finished at noon, the streets were filled with students, to be met by 'crowds of girls with basketfuls of bilberries or stewed plums', as an alumnus recalled. At four o'clock it was the custom to run twice round the town on the city walls.

Scholars gathered from all over Germany to work in Göttingen's library. This summer an important visitor was the poet and political reformer Hoffmann von Fallersleben, who was writing a history of church music and also editing the writings of Theophilus of Antioch. He claimed to work up to twelve hours a day on these tasks. His faith in a united Germany aroused opposition from those who clung to the complex web of princedoms and duchies into which Germany was divided, and his poetry reinforced a romantic vision of Germany's past. He was also an accomplished musician.

Joachim matriculated on 14 June and sat at the feet of the eminent professors Heinrich Ritter, who had just completed a twelve-volume history of philosophy, Theodor Waitz, a brilliant young philosopher from Marburg who was laying out the foundations of psychology, and the art historian Carl Oesterley, court painter to King Georg of Hanover.

When not attending class Joachim played his part in the beer and merriment for which German students were famous. He may have been King Georg's konzertmeister, but he was only twenty-one, after all. He joined the Saxonia Corps which met every Tuesday and Saturday evening (and probably many evenings in between) at the bar on Weenderstrasse next to the Jakobikirche. One of his fellow-members Ludolf von Bismarck-Briest recalled that Göttingen's beer, with the exception of

23 The Krüger Garden House, Göttingen

Alte Fink, was dreadful. They sat in this cramped room drinking beer, smoking cigars and pipes, and singing songs like 'Mein Lebenslauf ist Lieb und Lust'. Brahms joined in with gusto and from time to time he and Joachim performed the 'fox-ride', galumphing noisily around the table astride a chair. His impressions of these jovial evenings came to the surface twenty-six years later when he wrote his *Academic Festival Overture* on receiving an honorary doctorate from the University of Breslau.

Joachim's stay in Göttingen was never intended to be a retreat from music; a retreat from the violin perhaps, but outside his class studies his main concern was composition; he was working on his G minor violin concerto in order to send it to Schumann. Whether he was aware of it or not, his May visits to Schumann in Düsseldorf and to Liszt in Weimar in quick succession triggered a turn in his allegiances and ambitions, and the catalyst was almost certainly Brahms's appearance out of nowhere. Cancelling the trip to Zurich with Liszt to visit Wagner can clearly be interpreted in this light, and the intense comradeship of Joachim and Brahms in the next two months sealed both their personal friendship and their stand as representatives of the nameless group soon to be aligned against Liszt and Wagner.

The leading musician in the town was Arnold Wehner, director of the university's music, and a pupil of Spohr and Mendelssohn. He was actually Spohr's nephew. He lived at 82 Weenderstrasse, the main north-south street of the town, and it was at his house that Reményi had played Brahms's A minor violin sonata a few weeks before. On 18 July Wehner held another soirée. Joachim played some unaccompanied Bach and one of his own compositions with Wehner on the piano. Hoffmann von Fallersleben was there, though he did not mention Brahms in his reminiscence. He was convinced that Joachim was one of the leading violinists in Europe.

Four days later, in the Krone hotel on Weenderstrasse (now a bank), Brahms made an appearance as pianist, playing one of Bach's concertos for two pianos, probably the concerto in C major, with Wehner at the other piano. This work, which had surfaced only recently in an 1846 publication by Peters of Leipzig, was probably unfamiliar to everyone present. This was followed by Beethoven's Piano Trio in G, op. 1 no. 2, and then the Bach unaccompanied *Chaconne* played by Joachim.

On the morning of Sunday 24 July Joachim found himself being serenaded by Wehner, Hoffmann von Fallersleben, Brahms, and a law-student named Otto Brinkmann. They performed a 'Hymn for the Glorification of the Great Joachim Offered by Some of His Innumerable Admirers, Gioseppo, Ottone & Arnoldino, Artists from Arcadia.' This is a brief waltz for two violins and double bass with two false starts and some crude tuning of the strings composed into it. Who played what? It's hard to say. Hoffmann von Fallersleben said it was a 'sort-of' birthday party for Joachim, although his actual twenty-second birthday was a month earlier. After lunch they all (with Wehner's wife) went on an expedition to the castle ruins at Hardenberg a few miles north of Göttingen, enjoyed the view and ended with a 'rustic' dinner at the inn there.

Ex. 1 Brahms, *Hymn for the Glorification of the Great Joachim*, bars 1–7

The next day Joachim wrote a letter to Brahms's father. With Brahms's lengthy stay in Weimar, the break-up with Reményi, and now a longer stay in Göttingen, his parents were understandably concerned that the original purpose of his journey had been deflected. They were mystified that he seemed not to need more money, anxious perhaps that he was too dependent on Joachim's generosity. Joachim felt some reassurance was needed: 'Allow me,' he began, 'to write to say how infinitely fortunate I feel in the company of your Johannes. [...] Your Johannes has given me new encouragement in my career as an artist; to strive with him towards a common goal is a fresh encouragement on the difficult path which we musicians have to pursue through life. His purity, his youthful independence and the unusual rich- ness of heart and mind find expression in his music, just as his whole being will bring joy to all who come in spiritual contact with him.' Jakob Brahms was moved and delighted by these words; with some help from a more educated hand he wrote a gracious and polite letter of thanks.

Joachim's letter goes on to hope that some great work will come forth to reveal his true artistic powers. While Joachim was in class Brahms was working diligently at home, regarding lectures as a boring way to acquire knowledge; he preferred books, he declared. His main task was to build up an impressive portfolio of his own

24 Joachim in 1853

compositions, but he was also watching Joachim's scores come to life. The *Hamlet* overture was done, the new violin concerto almost ready, and another Shakespeare overture, *Henry IV*, taking shape. Without telling his friend, Brahms made a transcription of the *Hamlet* overture for piano duet. With Hoffmann von Fallersleben at hand Brahms set three of his poems to music, 'Wie sich Rebenranken schwingen', and 'Ich muss hinaus, ich muss zu dir', later published as 'Liebe und Frühling I and II', op. 3 nos. 2 and 3, and 'Weit über das Feld durch die Lüfte', op. 6 no. 5. According to Brahms's biographer Max Kalbeck, the first of these makes delicate allusion to Zerlina's aria 'Batti, batti' in *Don Giovanni* because the composer had been charmed by a girl he had heard singing that role, presumably in Hamburg, though possibly on his recent travels.

He also set a poem by Friedrich Bodenstedt, who translated extensively from Russian and Arabic. This Lied, with a Russian theme, was grouped with the others as op. 3 no. 4. Bodenstedt's Persian-flavoured verses were enjoying huge popularity at the time, which suggests that Brahms's nickname for Joachim, 'Jussuf', might have been taken from this source.

In Göttingen too Brahms composed one of his most unusual piano pieces, the Andante espressivo from the F minor sonata, op. 5. Uncharacteristically (or at least never repeated in his later piano music) he attached three lines of a poem by Sternau to set the mood and evoke a typically romantic scene:

> Der Abend dämmert, das Mondlicht scheint,
> Da sind zwei Herzen in Liebe vereint
> Und halten sich selig umfangen.
>
> The twilight falls, the moonlight glows,
> Two hearts are united in love,
> Held in a blessed embrace.

Its delicately romantic start develops into something more adventurous, and he attached to it a shorter piece headed 'Retrospect' which moves from a reminiscence of its simple theme to a much darker tone. Only in the context of the full five-movement sonata, of which these were to be the second and fourth movements, do these pieces make any sense; following the two big piano sonatas he had already written, Brahms was now planning a third. He could hardly have known that he would write no more sonatas for the piano thereafter.

The artist William Unger, who made an etching of Brahms in old age, was then just sixteen years old. He visited the Krüger Garden House several times that summer.

> We often had the good fortune to hear the divinely gifted Joachim playing in that house, and our joy was even greater when a slim young musician with long shoulder-length hair came to visit him. We had many opportunities for hearing them both playing. It was the young Brahms, whom I saw again much later in Vienna when he was a world-famous composer.

Brahms, Unger remembered, liked to take walks in the cornfields next to the house reading a book or writing in a notebook. One afternoon his walk took him all the way back to the ruins at Hardenberg. Exhausted in the heat, he took a nap somewhere within the site only to find as evening fell that the gates had been closed. Happily it was a warm night, but his absence alarmed Joachim as well as Unger and his young friends who had been sent out to look for him.

T HE month of August continued as before, a profoundly happy time for both young men. University classes came to an end and the emptiness of vacation overtook the town. Joachim was not needed in Hanover until the beginning of September. Sometime in August they gave a concert together and drew an immense paying audience. The proceeds allowed Brahms to pursue his plan to explore the river Rhine, something he had always wanted to do. The Rhine was central to all Germans' myth-making about themselves as it was central to Wagner's colossal new opera. Not to see the Rhine would have been unthinkable for Brahms if the opportunity were to present itself, as it now did.

Schumann's name was constantly on their lips. It was evident to both of them that Brahms should meet him soon, but shared concerns about Schumann's health and Brahms's vivid memory of the silent rejection he had suffered three years before required some delicacy in the approach. Even if Joachim had mentioned Brahms during his visit to Düsseldorf in May, he felt he should not only provide Brahms with a letter of introduction but also pave the way in person by going to Düsseldorf himself. They would then reunite in Hanover in October.

Toward the end of August, therefore, Joachim went north, calling briefly in Hanover before taking the westerly train to Düsseldorf. After a couple of days of intense music-making with the Schumanns he was back in Hanover by 1 September and ready for duty. Brahms meanwhile headed south, via Kassel and Frankfurt to Mainz. Little did he know that he was leaving behind in Göttingen an eighteen-year-old girl named Agathe von Siebold that he would meet on his next visit to the town five years later and fall in love with. Little did he know that he passed through Frankfurt between the two days on which Berlioz gave concerts in the Comoedienhaus there. They were soon to meet, but not quite yet.

In Mainz he stayed at the Drei Reichskronen hotel on Brandplatz and then set off down the Rhine with walking-stick and knapsack, full of delight at the amazing river scenery, his head teeming with tales true and imaginary and also, no doubt, with music. In their haste to bring him to Schumann's door, Brahms's biographers hurry him along through the next few weeks as if it were a mere holiday without incident. But he was himself in no such hurry, and we should therefore enjoy with him the unforgettable experience of such an adventure; it surely remained vivid throughout his life. He took with him a travel guide in which he marked without comment only the towns he visited and the places he spent the night. What sights he sought and what pleasures he derived from them is left for us to guess.

The course of the Rhine from Mainz to Bonn is one of the most spectacular

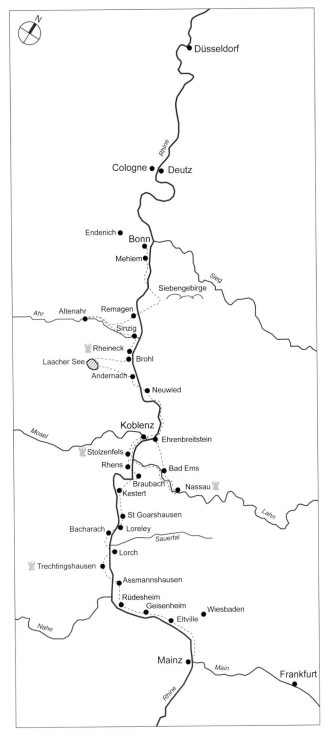

Map 2 Brahms's hike down the Rhine

riverscapes in Europe, much celebrated by painters and memoirists, especially in the Romantic period. Flanked by steep vine-clad hills on either bank, many of them topped by castles and fortifications of unknown antiquity, the river flows majestically north, too wide to be bridged (at that time). Travellers and tourists today crowd the roads and rails on either bank, but in 1853 there was almost no road traffic since the river was a swifter, surer artery for people and goods, and there was no railway line. On the water there was a constant swarm of boats moving up and down stream: rowing boats, sailing craft, barges and lighters, and an increasing number of steamboats, while ferrymen rowed passengers across at regular intervals. Apart from a few determined hikers like himself Brahms would have met only local people walking or riding from one village to the next. It was an unusually hot summer; river levels were low and the harvest was poor, so the price of grain, and hence beer, went up. The locals spoke of *Hundstage*, dog days.

His first day took him along the right bank of the river through Biebrich, Schierstein (both now suburbs of Wiesbaden), Eltville (where Gutenberg once lived), Erbach, Oestrich, Mittelheim, Winkel and Johannisberg to Geisenheim, where he spent the night of 27 August. He covered over a dozen miles, no doubt studying points of local interest in each village as he passed through. The next day he went via Eibingen to Rüdesheim, where he did some sightseeing of a town he was to get deeply attached to after 1874 when his friends Alwin and Laura von Beckerath invited him to stay there several times. The Third Symphony was composed there in 1883, and it was also the scene of his romantic attachment to the singer Hermine Spies. Being at the heart of the Rheingau wine business, Rüdesheim is still a magnetic spot for visitors following in Brahms's steps. His path now led along the Rheingauer–Riesling route around the river's sharp right-hand bend to the north. At Assmannshausen he took the ferry to the opposite bank to see the splendid mediaeval castle at Trechtingshausen. Originally the seat of the archbishops of Mainz, it had recently been restored and named 'Rheinstein' by its owner, Prince Friedrich of Prussia, who liked to entertain such guests as Queen Victoria there. Brahms spent the night in more humble lodgings.

Monday 29th took him through Niederrheimbach (two castles) then back across the river to Lorch with detours to Wispertal and Sauertal, then across the river once more to Rheindiebach and Bacharach, with its famous ruined Wernerkapelle above the town. On, downstream, to view the extraordinary fortress, Burg Pfalzgrafenstein, on a rock in the river near Kaub, then to Oberwesel with its profusion of old buildings and churches which Brahms doubtless sped past in his eagerness to see the famous Loreley rock on the other side of the river at the narrowest point in its course. The legend of the beautiful maiden who lives on the rock and lures men to their death in the foaming waters below had been familiar to all Germans since Clemens Brentano's ballad of 1801, and especially since Heine had composed his Loreley poem in 1824. At the time of his death Mendelssohn was planning an opera on the subject later taken up by Max Bruch and completed in 1863. Steeped in German Romantic poetry as Brahms was, he felt a deep sense of

25 Rheinstein castle

identification with such a place and such a legend. He spent the night at the Adler hotel in St Goarshausen, just down the river from the rock, on its east bank.

Brahms's steady progress of twelve to fifteen miles a day (with many detours) continued for the week. On Tuesday he passed through Ehrental, Kestert, Kamp, Osterspai, Braubach (with its splendid Marksburg castle high above the town), then across the river to Rhens, where the famous fourteenth-century Königsstuhl had recently been rebuilt after being destroyed by the French army in 1803. Since it was here that the Rhine Electors were said to have voted for their king, its rebuilding signified a renewed faith in German unity. He reached Stolzenfels, just short of Koblenz, for the night. Its castle was one of the most spectacular of the many along his route, for like Rheinstein it had recently been thoroughly restored in the Gothic style by King Friedrich Wilhelm IV of Prussia and adopted as a summer residence. It was currently occupied by the King's brother Wilhelm and his wife Augusta, Liszt's friend and admirer.

Koblenz was the largest town between Mainz and Bonn, an important trading centre because of its location at the confluence of the rivers Lahn from the east and Mosel from the west. The Romans had bridged the Rhine here, but in 1853 there was still no bridge, the first being built in 1864 to carry the railway across from Koblenz to Pfaffendorf on the eastern shore.

Abandoning his pack at Koblenz's Rheinberg hotel early next morning, with its precious content of manuscripts and books, Brahms devoted Wednesday to an expedition away from the Rhine. He crossed the river to Ehrenbreitstein whose high fortress no doubt invited the vigorous young man to climb to the top. From there he went cross-country to Bad Ems on the river Lahn. Brahms had perhaps never confronted the aristocracy *en masse* before, not even in Hanover, but here they were assembled in great numbers to take the waters, although the season was rapidly coming to an end. Wagner's friends the Wesendoncks had been there a month or two before. Offenbach's engagements in the town were some years in the future, but the spa was already enjoying enormous favour with Germany's rich and famous, who no doubt looked in horror at the weather-beaten Brahms stepping into their domain in his hiking gear. His fondness for spas in later life when he was himself rich and famous might have been implanted here at Bad Ems.

He did not linger but moved on along the river Lahn to Nassau, an ancient town with yet another spectacular castle on the other side of the river. To return to Koblenz he followed all the way down the Lahn until it reached the Rhine, then back across the river to his hotel. Thursday was 1 September. Through Vallendar, Bendorf, Mühlhofen and Engers, with its fine late baroque palace, he followed the river's right bank. The gradual shift from wine-growing areas into a region of more industrial activities such as mining would have struck him as he passed. Engers is today a suburb of Neuwied, whence he took the ferry across to the town of Andernach, with its mediaeval walls mostly intact and a famous sixteenth-century treadmill, still working, that lifted cargo from barges using the labour of six men. His goal in Andernach was his newly acquired friend Hoffmann von Fallersleben, whose nomadic career brought him and his wife at intervals to take refuge here. It was already getting dark when Brahms arrived. Hoffmann's wife was astonished to open the door to this slender young man who introduced himself in his boyish voice as Johannes Brahms.

He spent the night with his hosts, and the following day von Fallersleben led the three of them on an expedition away from the river. Five miles away was the Laacher See, a large lake, five miles in circumference, formed by a volcanic eruption around 11,000 BC. Surrounded by hills, it has no natural outlet, and the water is cold and bitter to the taste. The visitors went round the lake to the abbey of Maria Laach on the opposite shore, one of the finest romanesque buildings in Germany with its six towers dating from the twelfth century.

They returned on a different course through Wassenach and Tönnistein (a minor spa) to Brohl, the next town down the Rhine from Andernach. At Rheineck, where they viewed the tall twelfth-century tower on the top of a hill with a brand new castle attached, Brahms and his friends parted company. Hoffmann von Fallersleben had enormously enjoyed their conversation. Brahms told him all about his musical studies and ambitions and explained 'why he was so underdeveloped, physically'. After so much vigorous walking, we might more readily suppose that Brahms was in excellent shape. While his hosts returned south, Brahms carried on north through Breissig to Sinzig, where he spent the night.

The next day, Saturday, he continued the pattern of exploring towns and valleys away from the Rhine itself. He headed west up the valley of the Ahr, noted for its red wines, and, passing through Ahrweiler, another town with more or less intact mediaeval walls, reached the village of Altenahr. He retraced his steps down the river and ended the day in Remagen, not far from Sinzig where he had set off.

From this point on Brahms omitted to mark in his travel guide the places he visited and stayed at. He was a day's journey from Bonn, where the newly appointed conductor of the Concordia choral society was Wilhelm von Wasielewski, a violinist who had studied with David and Mendelssohn in Leipzig and had there been part of the group of brilliant students that included the boy Joachim, ten years his junior. An introduction from Joachim and the aura of the city as Beethoven's home town drew Brahms to Bonn, although perhaps he first headed across the river to visit the area known as the Siebengebirge ('Seven Mountains'), now a national park of exceptional beauty with many more than seven hills to climb and explore. The fantastic dream castle of Drachenburg, comparable to Ludwig II's more celebrated Neuschwanstein in Bavaria, was not yet built. From there it was a short crossing of the river to Bonn.

Wasielewski was surprised to find a good-looking fair-haired young man at his door with one of Joachim's visiting cards and was impressed by his natural manner. They got on well, and quite soon Brahms was seated at the piano playing one of his two completed sonatas, which greatly impressed his host, with whom he also played his version of the Rakóczy March, a relic of his concerts with Reményi. He was invited to stay a few days, during which a visit to Beethoven's childhood home in the Rheingasse and a sight of the Beethoven statue in the main square near by, erected through Liszt's efforts in 1845, would have been essential. Wasielewski had just spent two years in Düsseldorf as Schumann's principal violinist and was, despite his awareness of Schumann's shortcomings as a conductor, a devoted friend of both him and Clara, and was later to be Schumann's first biographer. He had attended the Lower Rhine Music Festival in May and he spoke warmly of the Schumanns to Brahms.

From Mainz to Bonn without any deviations is a distance of nearly a hundred miles. Brahms had walked it in about ten days in unusually hot weather with at least three excursions away from his route. At the Wasielewskis' house he was no doubt glad to rest his sore feet and get back to the piano. The weather had now turned sour, which was another reason to be settled. It was here perhaps that he received the letter from his anxious mother worried about him falling amid the rocks or going out in a thunderstorm, since she knew people who had died on adventures such as his. She would have been relieved to learn that he was at last back in civilised surroundings.

Wasielewski introduced Brahms to the Deichmanns, a well-to-do couple who lived in Mehlem, just south of Bonn. Wilhelm Deichmann was from a Cologne banking family and his wife Lilla was a prominent hostess, especially well disposed towards musicians. They were friendly with all the leading musicians around, including Hiller and Reinecke in Cologne, and they were great admirers of

Schumann's music in particular. They had met the Schumanns in Bonn in February when Clara played in a chamber concert with Wasielewski. They liked Brahms immediately and within three days took him into their home. Wasielewski would not have been offended that Brahms accepted their hospitality and moved from his more modest lodgings in Bonn to the Deichmanns' large riverside villa in Mehlem. This was to be his home for nearly three weeks. Their three sons, probably teenagers, liked him too.

At the Deichmanns he was immediately introduced to two visiting musicians: Christian Reimers he might have known in Hamburg since he came from Altona nearby; he was now living in Düsseldorf and playing the cello regularly with the Schumanns. The other was Franz Wüllner, a twenty-two-year old pianist with whom he was to establish a lifelong friendship. (Wüllner was destined to be the first conductor of *Das Rheingold* and *Die Walküre* when those operas were staged in Munich against Wagner's wishes before the creation of Bayreuth.) These two arrived by steamer on the 8th, Reimers from Düsseldorf, Wüllner from Frankfurt, and if the weather had not prevented it the three would have taken a trip somewhere together. After a few days at the Deichmanns Brahms wrote to Joachim, postponing a narrative of his Rhine journey since he found letter-writing arduous, but exclaiming at the warmth of his reception in Bonn. Despite his shyness he had made many new friends. He was working through the Deichmanns' copies of Schumann's music, much of which he had never seen before. Hearing Brahms's enthusiastic account of his travels, Frau Deichmann paid for Brahms to take the boys on a steamboat trip back up the river and to retrace his excursions into the surrounding countryside. Thus he revisited as a tour guide the beautiful Ahr valley, the Laacher See and the abbey of Maria Laach, and then the river Lahn perhaps as far as Bad Ems. The boat took them back from Koblenz to Bonn. They must have been three or four days away.

It was not yet clear to Brahms what his next move should be. He told Wasielewsi he was heading back to Hamburg. As the September days slipped by he thought about going to the Karlsruhe Festival to hear Joachim play and to hear Beethoven's Ninth, which he'd never heard before, under Liszt's baton. He knew he ought to go to Leipzig since that was the capital of the music publishing business, and his first priority as a composer was to get his first works printed and in circulation. He was definitely anxious to meet the Schumanns and was encouraged to do so by all his friends, but he was also anxious that such a meeting might misfire owing to his own diffidence or Robert's uncertain mental and physical condition, of which there was much talk. 'Don't take that incident personally,' Wasielewski told him, referring to Brahms's Hamburg experience with Schumann. 'From my own experience I know how friendly and kind Schumann is towards aspiring artists.' Brahms gave him no reply but in the end resolved to go neither to Karlsruhe nor to Leipzig but to head further down the Rhine to Cologne. Here, on the recommendation of Göttingen's Arnold Wehner, Wasielewski and the Deichmanns, he paid a visit on Carl Reinecke, a composer and teacher at the Cologne Conservatoire who was later to lead the Leipzig Conservatoire at the peak of its fame at the end of the century. Reinecke later remembered, as everyone else did, this good-looking young man with long fair hair and rather girlish looks. After some introductory talk Brahms offered to play him his Scherzo, which astounded Reinecke both for its compositional skill and for the fluency of Brahms's piano playing. Reinecke introduced him to Cologne's leading musician, Ferdinand Hiller; both of these new friends had close links with Schumann. As if to make sure of his next step, Reinecke took Brahms across the river to Deutz, the town on the other bank, whence the train ran directly to Düsseldorf. As a parting gift, Brahms gave Reinecke a photograph of himself, which Reinecke treasured all his life. Having met so many distinguished, even famous, people on his recent travels, Brahms might have wondered, as the train puffed its twenty miles north, if meeting Schumann might not be simply another name to cross off on his pilgrimage. On the contrary, it turned out to be a turning-point in his destiny and a swift countdown to fame.

CHAPTER 7

Liszt in Frankfurt, Weimar and Carlsbad

JULY – SEPTEMBER

BEFORE parting company with Wagner on 10 July Liszt received a telegram from Weimar reporting the death of his monarch, the Grand Duke Carl Friedrich. While his respect for the new Grand Duke, his son Carl Alexander, was profound, it says much for the father's lack of cultural endowment that Liszt showed no desire to hasten back for the funeral. His services at such an event were neither required nor appreciated. After returning to Basel in the bumpy diligence with his servant Hermann, and exhausted from all the late nights with Wagner, he went to Badenweiler, one of the smallest of German spas, a few miles north of Basel, to meet Eduard Devrient, whose wife and daughter were taking the cure. Devrient had a spectacular career as singer, librettist, actor and theatre manager, and had worked with Mendelssohn in Berlin and with Wagner in Dresden. He was now in charge of the theatre in Karlsruhe and a key figure in the forthcoming Karlsruhe Festival which was much on Liszt's mind. They discussed their plans and then paid a visit to Meyerbeer's wife and daughters who were also staying there, Meyerbeer himself being busy in Paris with preparations for *L'Étoile du Nord*. In the evening he heard a brilliant young cellist from Meiningen named Hippolyte Müller.

From there he pressed on north. Making a quick stop in Karlsruhe to attend to festival plans, he got into trouble with the police since the pink hat Wagner had given him was suspiciously close to being a *bonnet rouge*. He carried on to Frankfurt the same day. The musician in charge of the Frankfurt theatre, Gustav Schmidt, whom we met in Chapter 5, was a progressively minded musician, well known to Liszt and an admirer of Wagner. Schmidt had already staged *Tannhäuser* and was preparing to mount *Lohengrin*. Liszt planned to hear Schmidt's perfor-mance of *Tannhäuser* but it was cancelled, apparently because Johanna Wagner (adopted daughter of Wagner's brother) would not sing. She had sung the role of Elisabeth in the first performance of *Tannhäuser* in 1845, and was now sufficiently celebrated to permit her to act like a diva. She had sung in Meyerbeer's *Le Prophète* the night before, and on the day of Liszt's arrival sang three Schubert *Lieder* in a benefit concert, but for some reason the *Tannhäuser* was cancelled. Liszt was nonetheless happy to book her to sing both Elisabeth and Ortrud (a mezzo role) in *Lohengrin* in Weimar in the coming season. The traffic of celebrated musicians through Frankfurt was not unlike that of London. Marschner was there, from Hanover, and Vieuxtemps too was making an appearance. Berlioz was booked for the following month.

Another reason for Liszt to go to Frankfurt was a desire to renew contact with one of the leading diplomats of the day, Baron von Prokesch-Osten, Austrian

26 Liszt in 1854

delegate to the Federal Diet in Frankfurt and formerly ambassador in Berlin. Three years earlier he had arrived in Weimar unannounced purely, it seems, to meet Liszt, and a friendship had developed. The Baron and his wife invited him to dinner on Wednesday evening and persuaded him to play the piano, a treat for his dinner guests that the general public were now rarely offered.

The next day, Thursday, Liszt ran errands to Mainz to see the publisher Schott and to Wiesbaden to see the kapellmeister Ludwig Schindelmeisser, who had just put on *Lohengrin* there (the second city to mount it after Weimar) and was about to move to Darmstadt. He and Schindelmeisser sent Wagner a 'Lohengrin snuffbox' as a memento, which Minna forwarded to Wagner in St Moritz. Wagner was delighted and displayed it on his writing table. Liszt needed to arrange with Schindelmeisser the participation of Darmstadt's musicians for the Karlsruhe Festival. He spent the night in Wiesbaden, then back to Frankfurt to pick up his mail, then at 5 p.m. on the Friday left for Weimar. This was a ten-hour overnight trip which delivered him home at 3 a.m. on Saturday 16th.

Now that the principal German cities were connected by train, all these journeys were easy, if neither quick nor comfortable. No musician except possibly Paganini had ever covered as much ground as Liszt had in the previous fifteen years, most of it by coach and boat when he was touring and giving concerts in every corner of Europe. No musician had as much reason as he to be thankful for the coming of the railways even though he had now opted for a more settled life in Weimar and was no longer touring as a star pianist. Weimar's railway in fact had opened at exactly the point when Liszt decided to reside there. It is a mark of his exceptional energy that his copious correspondence rarely complains of discomfort or exhaustion; he always had time to write long letters to the Princess Carolyne, Wagner, Berlioz or others as soon as he reached his destination.

His mother was still there, treating her painful foot with a distillation made of ants, and Reményi was there too; the Princess and her daughter had been gone for a week, taking the waters in Carlsbad and anxious that Liszt should join them as soon as he could. Even after his arduous night journey he needed only a short nap before settling down to read his mail, including a long letter from Berlioz recounting the disastrous reception of *Benvenuto Cellini* in London. The three letters from Carolyne that awaited him took him 'several hours' to read; she surpassed even Wagner in logorrhea and covered page upon page with thoughts about their love, her family, and above all the deity. Focused on eternity, she had nothing to say about her daily doings. Liszt on the other hand always replied with ample details of the people he had met and the places he had visited, as well as with tender thoughts directed at her.

His first duties were to pay his respects to Weimar's ducal family, now in heavy mourning. In the summer months the family divided their time between the Schloss Belvedere, on the southern edge of the city, where the late Grand Duke had died, and the Schloss Ettersburg, a hunting lodge a few miles north. On the day of his return, doubtless short of sleep, Liszt made a condolatory call on the

27 Grand Duke Carl Alexander of Sachsen-Weimar-Eisenach

Dowager Grand Duchess in the Schloss Belvedere. She vigorously supported Liszt, especially in his promotion of Berlioz's music, and was rewarded by the dedication of *Benvenuto Cellini* when it was published in 1856. Her plan now was to visit her brother the Tsar in St Petersburg. The next day, Sunday, in the evening, Liszt had to make a similar call on the new Grand Duke and his wife Sophie who were at Ettersburg. He travelled with Reményi and the French ambassador in Weimar (the son of the great diplomat Talleyrand) and an aide. When they arrived Liszt was directed by a gamekeeper to find the Grand Duke, who was taking a walk in the park. 'Words will now become deeds' was one of the Grand Duke's first remarks, referring to his intention to rebuild Weimar's cultural standing after the decline of his father's reign. The choice of 28 August – Goethe's birthday – for his ceremonial installation was significant. They sat under a tree while the Grand Duke read a letter from Wagner Liszt had brought and Berlioz's letter to Liszt about the London débâcle. Having been there himself, the Grand Duke was able to confirm Berlioz's account. 'Write to Berlioz for me,' he said, 'tell him that all that booing was a good sign and that *Cellini* was a real success.' Liszt was invited to stay for dinner. He was enchanted by the Grand Duchess Sophie's naturalness, but he took little part in the conversation between the various diplomats present talking about 'London, the Caucasus, and exotic races'. On his departure at 10 p.m. the Grand Duke asked him to compose a march for the forthcoming installation, and as he rode back to town in the carriage his mind started to work out the principal theme.

The timing was good since he was desperate to get back to composing. 'I have a real need to write down notes to keep myself in balance,' he wrote. 'I feel all dried up when I spend a few days without music paper in front of me. My brain feels blocked and I can't enjoy things around me. Music is the breath of my soul: it is both my prayer and my work.' Since Liszt was a lifelong reviser of his own music, it is rarely clear which piece he was working on at any given moment. Many works were sketched, drafted, completed, revised and revised again before being published or performed, and even then were often subject to more revision. His output of original compositions and transcriptions of various kinds being so vast, it is likely that his mind, if not his desk, was a traffic-jam of complete and incomplete pieces at all times. At this point in his career he was clearly pressing his claims as a conductor while still developing the series of masterpieces that include the B minor Sonata, recently completed, and the *Faust Symphony*, about to come into being. In July 1853 his most recent work was the *Scherzo und Marsch* for piano completed in May. He set to work now on a *Huldigungsmarsch* for the Grand Duke, and it was finished within four days. He wrote it in piano score, leaving the orchestration of the military band version to the bandmaster and of the normal orchestra version to Raff, who had often served Liszt in this capacity before.

Despite the Princess's urging he was unable to leave Weimar for ten days since the elaborate dance of court etiquette required him to pay visits on a succession of barons and freiherrs and ambassadors and intendants. He was subservient to all these officials (and their wives) and behaved with impeccable civility to all of them, graciously ignoring the fact that his fame already outstripped theirs. In the hierarchy of the court a musician was still only a superior servant, a position against which Liszt never protested with any vehemence, unlike Wagner in his Dresden days. His father's position in the household of the Esterházy family was possibly the root of his acceptance of this old-fashioned patronage. His present position was all the more delicate in that the Princess, although a true aristocrat herself, was cold-shouldered by certain members of Weimar society as a married woman living more or less openly with him.

Liszt was always glad to see Princess Augusta of Prussia, who had arrived with her brother-in-law King Friedrich Wilhelm IV from Berlin to pay homage to her mother, the dowager Grand Duchess, their second visit in two months. Like her mother she was fond not just of music in general, but of the newest music, that of Berlioz and Liszt in particular. When not observing official duties, Liszt worked quietly in the 'blue room' at the Altenburg, the study where he and Carolyne liked to work. He was giving lessons to Mason, Pruckner and Klindworth, and he worked a little with Reményi, but it was a quiet season, and he had time to ponder his plans for new works and to tidy up some old ones. He wrote to Carolyne daily. He paid a quick trip to the city of Jena, not far away, to meet the distinguished art historian Hermann Hettner, recently appointed professor at the university there, but he did not reveal his reason for the visit.

He finally left Weimar on Wednesday 27 July. He stopped in Leipzig to see Brendel, editor of the *Neue Zeitschrift für Musik* and a standard-bearer for the New German School, as it was soon to be known. Brendel liked to know everything he could about Liszt's and Wagner's doings. Liszt then went on to the Hôtel de Rome in Dresden for a night or two. Since Carlsbad was in the Austrian dominions, a passport had to be acquired at the Austrian embassy in Dresden. In Dresden he also visited the publisher Meser and Wagner's friends the Ritters, mother and son. He had promised the Princess that he would be in Carlsbad by Friday, but it was Sunday before he left Dresden and took the train south-west across the border to Bodenbach in Bohemia, and from there by coach to Carlsbad.

CARLSBAD (later Karlsbad, now Karlovy Vary), Teplitz (now Teplice) and Marienbad (now Mariánské Lázně) were the three most favoured spas in the western hills of Bohemia, which are rich in mineral springs of many kinds. Carlsbad lies about eighty miles west of Prague and about the same distance east of Bayreuth. So long as Bohemia was a province of the Austrian empire, its official language was German, and if it drew fewer international visitors than Baden-Baden, it was reliably patronised by well-to-do Germans and enjoyed a high reputation as a place where the sick were well cared for and the healthy had a good time, although the town had no casino. The town's shape was dictated by the angular course of its river, the Tepl, which flows north into the Eger (now the Ohře) and from there into the Elbe, and by the steep hills which enclose it. Many springs flow or burst out of fissures in the granite, chief of which is the Sprudel, gushing up in forty to sixty jets

28 The Sprudel, Carlsbad

a minute and varying from six to ten feet in height. An English visitor wrote of it in 1839:

> The sudden view of the violent, lofty, constant, and prodigal uppourings of hot water out of the bowels of the earth, foaming in the midst of its clouds of vapour, within 45° of the boiling point, on the very margin of a cold, placid, and sluggish stream, the Teple, – rivetted me to the spot for some moments.

During the season (April to October) the Sprudel, standing centrally in its iron and glass pavilion, was attended by local girls from 5 a.m. throughout the day, handing beakers of hot water to crowds of elegant guests, some of whom were at pains to disguise the unpleasant taste. The fact that many of the great and glorious had frequented Carlsbad was enough to sustain its position as one of Germany's leading spas. The springs were 'discovered' by Charles IV, Holy Roman Emperor and King of Bohemia, in 1347. As founder of Prague University and builder of the great Charles Bridge across the Vltava in Prague, he deserves whatever credit may be attached to his name. Emperors and statesmen followed, including Tsar Peter the Great, who went there twice. Carlsbad was important to Bach, who also went twice, in 1718 and 1720, to accompany his patron Prince Leopold of Anhalt-Cöthen. For about a month on each visit he and his fellow musicians performed for an audience of the Prince's guests. Goethe spent thirteen summers in Carlsbad, where in 1812 he passed a couple of days in the company of Beethoven. This was not quite the only or the first meeting of the two giants, since they had both been in Teplitz a week or two earlier, both neurotically anxious about their ailments. Beethoven see-sawed between the three spas Teplitz, Franzensbad and Carlsbad that summer, obsessed by thoughts of the Immortal Beloved, Antonie von Brentano, who spent over a month in Carlsbad with her husband and child. For a week at least Beethoven was staying in the same hotel as they. (In 1853 she was still living in Frankfurt.) Wagner went to Carlsbad in July 1835 looking for singers for his opera troupe in Magdeburg; if he had stayed a couple of weeks longer he might have run into Chopin, who went there not for musical reasons but to visit his parents taking the cure. Wagner was then twenty-two and had probably never heard of Chopin.

Liszt's Carolyne suffered from chronic ill-health and was a devotee of water-cures. With her daughter Marie she spent five weeks in Carlsbad this summer of 1853, earnestly following the prescribed regime, and joined by Liszt on Saturday 30 July. He preferred to stay and work at their hotel, the White Lion, while the ladies submitted to the Sprudel. His robust constitution was in no need of a cure. Watching people outside his window forcing the water down their throats he thanked heaven he neither needed nor desired to try it. The first weekend in Carlsbad he composed a short *Domine salvum fac* for tenor solo and men's choir which he sent back to Raff in Weimar with instructions to orchestrate the piano part for wind and timpani. This was intended for the Grand Duke's inauguration if there was need for another piece beside Raff's own *Te Deum*, which was already programmed for the event. Liszt had a choral setting of Schiller's 'An die Künstler' to write for the Karlsruhe Festival, and he was also working on Raff's opera *König Alfred*. This had been staged in Weimar in 1851 but now needed revision with a view to revival in the autumn. He was reading *Melodie der Sprache* by Louis Köhler, the

29 Princess Carolyne Sayn-Wittgenstein

young composer and pedagogue based in Königsberg on the Baltic coast who had recently travelled to Weimar out of a passionate desire to get to know Wagner's music. Wagner himself was impatient with the book since its rather complex arguments about the relationship between melody and speech did not accord with his own. Liszt, on the other hand, was flattered by its analysis of some of his songs and was quite prepared to send him more of his music and help Köhler find a publisher for his works, as he did for so many of his younger colleagues.

Entertainment in Carlsbad included a 'Divan-Soirée' offered by an Arab family, a performance by a Chinese group, and *Macbeth* and *Othello* played by the black American actor Ira Aldridge, known as the 'African Roscius'. The Viennese pianist Constance Geiger, who played marches and polkas on a dreadful piano in the interval, would have been horrified if she knew the great Liszt was in the audience (perhaps she did). He heard the local dance orchestra under its celebrated conductor Josef Labitsky; he heard and admired a string quartet by the Bohemian composer Wenzel Veit. His own orchestra leader from Weimar, Ferdinand Laub, was giving concerts, and the other musicians in Carlsbad included the pianists Alexander Dreyschock (in his native Bohemia) and Heinrich Willmers (a pupil of Hummel) and a violinist from Stuttgart named Edmund Singer whom he so much admired that he persuaded him to move to Weimar the following year. He narrowly missed hearing the Polish violinist Henri Wieniawski, still only eighteen years of age and on the brink of a great career. He and his sixteen-year-old pianist brother Josef had recently spent a month in Weimar, so Liszt knew them well. There never was any likelihood that Liszt would perform in public in Carlsbad himself.

The poet Emanuel Geibel, whose poems were set by Schumann, Brahms, Wolf and others, was there. As the librettist of Mendelssohn's opera *Die Loreley* he would be better known to musicians if the composer's death had not left it unfinished, while Max Bruch's setting of the libretto has all but vanished from the repertoire. In Carlsbad he was invited to spend the evening with Liszt and the Princess. He told his wife:

> The conversation was exceedingly lively. We talked about Aldridge's *Othello*, which we'd all seen, then about Shakespeare generally, *Midsummer Night's Dream*, Mendelssohn's music for it, then *The Tempest*. We agreed this would be a great subject for music. We went through the main themes of the magical play, and the Bard had us more and more in thrall the more we immersed ourselves in his world. Liszt jumped up and went to the piano. I've always enjoyed his improvising but yesterday it was more marvellous than ever. Everything we'd been talking about came to life in very moving musical form. The storm at sea, the shipwreck, fear, love, Caliban's beastliness, Stephano's drunkenness, and then, as if descending from the sky, Ariel's silver bell, and over it all Prospero's commands, as he brings calm to the elements and draws wisdom from human passions. I cannot possibly give you a true impression of it; you would need to have been there yourself. Liszt felt

he had surpassed himself. We discussed the idea of music for *The Tempest*, and he finally suggested putting the idea to Dingelstedt, to see if he would stage it in Munich. He thinks he could have the music ready in a couple of months.

Geibel went back home to Munich and presented the idea to the court theatre director Dingelstedt, who was on friendly terms with Liszt, having worked several times with him in Weimar. He liked it very much. He had been thinking about *The Tempest* for some time and had even had his designer prepare a model for the first act with a ship that founders 'before one's very eyes'. But he and Liszt were never able to get together to push the idea forward, and no music for *The Tempest* was ever written. Liszt was later to support Dingelstedt's appointment as intendant in Weimar, only to discover that he was an impossible colleague, entrenched against Liszt's progressive plans. It was Dingelstedt's subversive action against the staging of Cornelius's brilliant opera *Der Barbier von Bagdad* in December 1858 that eventually brought Liszt's tenure in Weimar to an unhappy end.

The aristocracy were in Carlsbad in strength, especially from Vienna, the imperial capital, but Liszt had no obligation to pay court to any of them. He seems to have treated his time in Carlsbad as a break from the complications of Weimar politics and an opportunity to compose in peace. Perhaps he was already sketching more symphonic poems or thinking about the *Faust Symphony* which was to be worked out in detail the following year. He was much preoccupied with plans for the Karlsruhe Festival, scheduled for the end of September. He was in no hurry to return to Weimar and seems to have deliberately stayed away long enough to miss the inauguration of the Grand Duke on 28 August; he left it to the last minute to send his apologies, and in turn the Grand Duke had later to apologise to Liszt that the *Huldigungsmarsch* was not in fact played at the inauguration: it was thought it might jar with his mother's mourning and was cancelled.

After two and a half weeks in Carlsbad, without waiting for his brilliant pupil Hans von Bülow, who arrived in Carlsbad from Budapest a day later, he moved on with the Princess and her daughter (and their servants Alexandra and Henri) on the 16th to try a different water cure at Teplitz, seventy miles to the north-east. They lodged at the Hôtel de Londres in the Market Square. Smaller than Carlsbad, Teplitz was equally dominated by steep hills and had the same concentration of bathing facilities and cure-salons in the centre of the town, as well as a busy programme of concerts and entertainments. The pianists Dreyschock and Willmers, who seem to have performed in some kind of double act, had moved on to Teplitz ahead of Liszt.

On Thursday 18th Liszt and Carolyne walked down the (not very long!) Lange Gasse to the Schloss, seat of Prince Edmund Clary-Aldringen, a member of the Bohemian nobility, who was giving a ball in honour of the Emperor. 'Liszt's hair is longer than ever', noted the Prince. Two days later Liszt declined an invitation to play in the Prince's Garten-Salon, where a piano had been installed. Willmers took his place, and the following day it was Dreyschock who played, including what the Prince thought was a clever imitation of Liszt.

Liszt did eventually play, on Friday 26th, to a company that included Countess Schlick, at whose house in Prague he had played in 1840, and the composer Veit, who too had moved on from Carlsbad. The local organist, Anton Mayer, was invited too. He arrived without any idea that the great Liszt was in town and was flabbergasted to be introduced to him, Dreyschock and Willmers in turn. Relieved not to be asked to play himself, he agreed to play the organ for Liszt at Mass on Sunday in the church just next to the Schloss. When the day came the church was full but he could not see Liszt anywhere. 'I had just breathed a sigh of relief,' he reported,

> when at the Sanctus Liszt was at my side. He pushed me gently from the bench and himself sat down to play. A storm of harmonies flowed through the church. Long after the Mass was over, groups of townspeople stood in the square saying they had never heard such playing in their lives.

Probably during his first days in Teplitz the decision was reached to delay the Karlsruhe Festival from mid-September to the beginning of October. Liszt seems then to have put the brakes on all his plans. Having originally told Raff he would be back in Weimar by 24 August, that was extended to the 28th, then the 30th. In fact he did not return until 17 September. On 1 September he went to Herrnskretschen (now Hřensko) to watch a shoot arranged by the Prince for his guests. He told Raff that a number of encounters in Teplitz had opened up important issues for his future and that he had not been able to compose for a week. The most pressing issue remained the question of the Princess's divorce, but whether this was his concern in Teplitz or not is unclear.

He had business to conduct in Dresden and Leipzig. During their Dresden stay he and the two ladies were invited by Count Lüttichau, intendant of the court theatre in Dresden and Wagner's former employer, to an evening in his riverside villa in Pillnitz, a little way outside the city up the Elbe, where the King of Saxony had a splendid Chinese-style palace. The reception was half indoors and half out. The sixty-four-year-old painter and scientist Carl Gustav Carus, a friend of Goethe (as so many exceptional men of his generation were), was especially impressed to see Liszt again and also the Princess, whose presence was something of an embarrassment to members of the Saxon royal family also attending the party. Frau von Lüttichau asked Carus to see that Carolyne was not left out in the cold, a task which he was glad to take on in view of her strong personality and attractive daughter. A quartet of male voices sang Liszt's setting of Goethe's 'Über allen Gipfel ist Ruh', which Carus found rather forced and eccentric. Carus met them again next day at their hotel, the Hôtel de Saxe, where he found the Princess wreathed in smoke from her cigars, and he also invited them to his own house where he showed them his collection of skulls.

They stayed in Dresden long enough to hear Hans von Bülow's concert on Monday 12th in the city theatre, von Bülow having come directly to Dresden after two weeks in Carlsbad. He played Weber's *Polonaise brillante* with Liszt's orchestral arrangement, and Liszt's *Fantaisie hongroise* also for piano and orchestra.

After a few days in Leipzig largely devoted to discussing the theatre's proposed staging of *Lohengrin*, Liszt and von Bülow returned to Weimar at 11 a.m. on Saturday 17 September while the Princess and her daughter went from Teplitz to Regensburg (in Bavaria) and Munich. Despite the travelling, this had been a rare period of a month in which Liszt was able to recover his strength and think deeply about the present and the future, the nearest he ever came to a holiday.

CHAPTER 8

Wagner in St Moritz and La Spezia

JULY – SEPTEMBER

WAGNER saw Liszt off from the Zurich coach-stop on Sunday 10 July. It had been, as he described it, a 'wild week', but now, with Liszt gone, everything was bleak and desolate. He felt he had got to know Liszt better than ever before and was nudged several steps nearer to his giant musical undertaking by the inspiration of Liszt's playing and the modernity of his style. He was more than ever conscious of the wretchedness of his exile and the dreariness (as he saw it) of life in Zurich. His plans were now to take a four-week cure in St Moritz, which he felt, on his doctor's advice, to be necessary before going on to Italy, where he proposed to begin the task of writing music. He had stocked up with music paper and was confident that the first of the four operas, *Das Rheingold*, would be sketched by the end of the year. Looking three or four years ahead, he and Liszt planned to mount the *Ring* for the first time in Zurich, in a newly built theatre.

He was anxious to get away. But he had to stay on a few days since on the Wednesday evening a group of singers and instrumentalists who had performed in his concerts three weeks earlier staged a torchlight concert in front of his house on Zeltweg. They built a temporary platform, played and sang from it, including the sailors' chorus from *Der fliegende Holländer*, and delivered speeches, all supremely flattering to their hero Wagner. He was made an honorary member of their groups and given a diploma. In his speech acknowledging the honour Wagner promised he would give the citizens of Zurich 'something extraordinary', although few of them could have imagined quite how extraordinary that something was going to be.

The following morning he set off with Georg Herwegh for St Moritz, over a hundred miles to the south-east of Zurich in the Engadine valley. Some citizens who had serenaded him the night before were travelling with them. Part of their journey was taken by steamer along Lake Zurich and part along the Walensee, a narrow lake which had been the subject of one of Liszt's great piano pieces, *Au Lac de Wallenstadt*, although Wagner might not have known it. A Swiss professor named Fröhlich observed the two friends on the boat. Wagner was silent and unfriendly, which was probably just as well, since Fröhlich disliked his music, having heard the complete *Der fliegende Holländer* in Zurich, as well as the recent all-Wagner concerts. The icy silence was maintained throughout the weeks that professor and composer were both taking the waters in St Moritz.

It was raining so hard in Chur, some thirty miles short of their destination, that the travellers had to stop, and they then found the next day's diligence fully booked. After a second night in the Hotel Steinbock they reached St Moritz on Saturday 16th. Coming over the Julier Pass into the town, at over 7,000 feet, Wagner

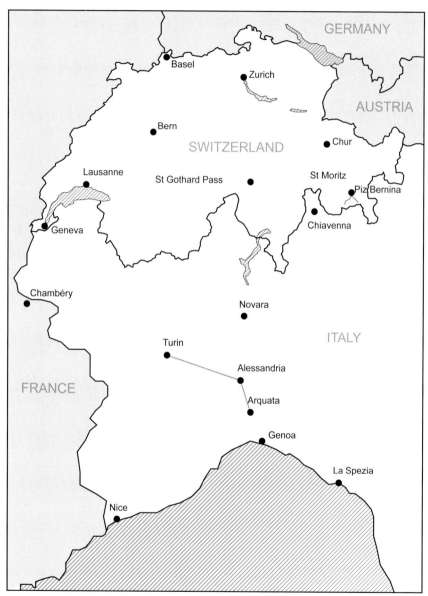

Map 3 Switzerland and Northern Italy

identified the spot with the 'open space on a mountain summit' he had imagined for the second scene of *Das Rheingold*, where Fricka and Wotan contemplate Valhalla for the first time.

Well known today as a winter skiing resort, St Moritz was then, like the German spas, famous for its mineral springs and visited exclusively in the summer when its strikingly barren landscape is more easily observed. Wagner and Herwegh spent over three weeks there. Not being there for the cure, Herwegh found the Pension Faller (later transformed into the grand Kulm Hotel) less than comfortable, but Wagner assiduously followed the prescribed regime, believing the concentration of iron in the water to be invigorating. Before he left, nevertheless, he concluded that none of it seemed to do much good, a conclusion he had also come to after an extended stay at the Swiss resort of Albisbrunn in 1851. He was permanently troubled by his bowels and felt convinced that water treatments would eventually effect a remedy.

It is hard to imagine Wagner ever not working. Previous visits to spas, such as to Teplitz in 1843 and Marienbad in 1845, had been highly productive of new projects, but this time he was in no need of new ideas and was, as he admitted, afraid of composing. He was leaving that task to the Italian journey. This was an *Erholungsreise*, a convalescent holiday devoted to the cure, to some energetic mountain hikes, and to reading, with, of course, interminable discussion and argument with Herwegh. If Herwegh recapitulated the story of how he became fatally enmeshed in the Herzen household, Wagner might have caught the scent of danger with respect to the Wesendoncks. But then he had similar experiences of his own to recount, namely the entanglement with Jessie Laussot three years before and its collapse under his wife's and her husband's angry threats.

He was rereading Goethe: the great collection of poetry, the *West-östliche Divan*, followed by the novel *Die Wahlverwandtschaften* (*Elective Affinities*) which the two passionate intellectuals debated at length, especially the character of Charlotte and her infidelity. Like Liszt he was reading Louis Köhler's *Melodie der Sprache*, prompting a long letter to the author which was not quite so critical as the response he sent privately to Liszt.

The pair's first expedition was a two-hour walk down the Engadine valley as far as Zuoz, allowing Wagner to admire the Swiss neatness of the houses. On the 21st they went further in a grimly bumpy carriage across the Maloja Pass down into Italy, where the town of Chiavenna offered the first breath of warm Italian air. Two days later they went on an eleven-hour hike with a local guide south to the Piz Bernina, the highest peak in the region, and along the Rosegg glacier, near the Italian border. Wagner was obviously in much better physical shape than Herwegh, who kept falling behind and was a nervous climber. He was interested in geology, chipping at rocks with a little hammer while Wagner strode ahead, and he clearly did not share Wagner's awareness of the sublime beauty of their surroundings.

Every morning at six o'clock Wagner attended the Kurhaus to drink the waters, and often to submerge himself in them too. With the exception of a two-day trip on

30 Georg Herwegh

31 July and 1 August over the Bernina Pass to Poschiavo in the very south-eastern-most part of Switzerland, he and Herwegh abandoned mountain expeditions after the first week, while Wagner dedicated himself to the treatment. He was writing long letters of course, but he still had time on his hands that can only have been spent contemplating the next phase of his life, which he must have known was going to be intensively filled with a creative effort that no one had ever attempted before. He was feeling optimistic about money, and optimistic about performances of his operas in Germany, always in the light of what the future was about to witness from his hand.

Herwegh was content to work intensively and quietly, intertwining radical politics with poetry. He was teaching himself Persian and Sanskrit, and tiring of Wagner's ceaseless hypochondria. Wagner eventually felt that the spa treatment was making little difference, in fact it seemed to be the cause of constipation grave enough to merit a mention in his autobiography written many years later. He had sent his wife Minna constant reports of his dutiful water-taking, and of his eating and his sleeping, interspersed with anxious enquiries about *her* health. He apologised for opening a letter addressed to her but sent to him – from Mathilde Wesendonck. He asked constantly after the dog Peps. With his encouragement Minna was meanwhile off for a brief cure of her own in a town inevitably named Baden fifteen miles north of Zurich on the Limmat river. Before the full four weeks of treatment were completed, Wagner was thoroughly disenchanted with it all. 'I'm not a cure person,' he told Liszt. He could think only of getting away to Italy, to Genoa, Corsica and Nice (all then part of Italian territory). He and Herwegh left St Moritz on Tuesday 9 August, stopped the night once again in Chur, and arrived home in Zurich on the 10th. A welcome he particularly looked forward to was the sight of Peps, panting with excitement.

B ACK in Zurich for two weeks, he felt his old impatience with the city and its people and was eagerly anticipating the trip to Italy. His correspondence was much concerned with keeping track of performances of *Tannhäuser* in Kassel, Posen, Darmstadt, Hamburg, Königsberg, Ballenstedt and Cologne, and urging Devrient to mount it in Karlsruhe. *Lohengrin* performances were still scarce, so the prospect of it being played soon in Leipzig exercised him greatly. He was also attempting to extract money from any theatre that would play these operas. After his meeting in Leipzig with Brendel, editor of the *Neue Zeitschrift für Musik*, Liszt asked Wagner to contribute a polemical article on the nature of the *Gesamtkunstwerk* of a kind which he had so often produced in the past. There can be no clearer sign that Wagner was now committed to writing music, not prose, than his adamant refusal to entertain such an idea. He claimed that he had said all he had to say on the subject (which could never have been true) and that he no longer wanted to stir up his old enemies (which might have been true). He already regretted putting into circulation the notion of the *Gesamtkunstwerk* when it was obvious to him that the arts were to be blended in his new music-drama not as a balanced union but under the musician's forceful leadership. The optimism had in any case faded. He was suffering anew from his recurrent depression. 'How can one say "It's just one of those days" when those days occur every day? Wouldn't it be the right thing to put an end to this dreadful existence?' He had talked about suicide a year earlier, but like Beethoven and Berlioz before him contemplating such a fateful step, he knew his creative calling required him to live. His doctor suggested giving up snuff, which he duly did, with an air of pained martyrdom.

Wagner finally left for Italy on Wednesday 24 August, the day of Berlioz's second concert in Frankfurt and of Brahms setting off from Mainz. He anticipated quite a long stay, at least six weeks for the work he was hoping to do, to be followed by a visit to Paris with Liszt. It was all made possible by a line of credit opened on his behalf by the faithful Otto Wesendonck, who was now on a business trip to the United States with his wife. Wagner had already travelled along most of Switzerland's main routes, so the mountain passes were now familiar to him, and he rarely complained about cranky springs on rough roads; wild scenic grandeur moved him strongly enough to imagine it as the setting of most of the *Ring*, and he drank it in eagerly. The first stop was Bern, where he had to call on the French ambassador to get a visa to pass through France. His record as a revolutionary still clung to him, even in France, and his association with the unrepentant Herwegh was no help, so he also pressed Liszt to get Talleyrand, the French envoy in Weimar, and the Grand Duke himself to write on his behalf. Warn Berlioz too, he urged, that the French authorities might question him about his, Wagner's, intentions. Berlioz is a crazy eccentric, he added, but a fine noble spirit.

The next evening the night coach left Bern at nine o'clock and arrived in the early morning in Lausanne, where he took the steamer along Lake Geneva. On the steamer he fell into conversation with Baron Beaulieu-Marconnay, intendant of the Weimar theatre and therefore intimately concerned with Liszt's enterprises there. The rest of Wagner's journey to Genoa turned into an adventure. The Geneva hotel he had notified, the Écu de Genève (now a well-known restaurant) was full, but he found another where, despite the noise from the street, he had a good night's sleep. Next day he bought a birthday present for Minna and sent it to his friend Baumgartner in Zurich with instructions to deliver it to her on 5 September, her forty-fourth birthday. Herwegh was supposed to have booked his passage from Geneva to Turin, but it didn't work out, and the next stage proved very frustrating. He had no choice but to take another night coach, leaving Geneva at nine and reaching Chambéry, sixty miles away, in the early morning. It was a vile ride, and in Chambéry he learned that all scheduled coaches to Turin were booked for a week. He was forced to hire a private carrier. Having found two other travellers to share the cost, it transpired that all the horses were booked. They only got away by bribing a postillion who could magically produce some horses. Like all coach travellers, he had to get used to the ubiquitous smell of horses on journeys such as this.

A consolation for a second night on the road was the magnificent night crossing of the Alps in perfect weather. Since the tunnel beneath the Col de Mont Cénis pass was not opened until 1871, Wagner was taking the loftier route earlier travelled by Charlemagne, Napoleon and perhaps Hannibal too. It was not Wagner's first visit to Italy: he had crossed the border to Chiavenna a few weeks before, and the previous year he had travelled more extensively to Lugano and Lake Maggiore. But it was his first visit to the Po valley and he was particularly excited about seeing the Mediterranean. The coach reached Turin on the Monday afternoon. It was an impressive, well laid-out city, reminding him of Paris, but he had no intention of staying there long. He checked into the Hôtel de l'Europe opposite the Castello Valentino and near the river. He was not too tired to go to the theatre that evening, where he saw a 'wretched' *opera buffa* (which he did not name) superbly played and sung. The following day he went to the opera again, and saw *Il barbiere di Siviglia*, an opera he had known since his days in Würzburg twenty years before, and enjoyed it a lot. In Turin he ran into Sigismond Thalberg, the virtuoso pianist who yielded to Liszt the crown of pianism, but whose popular success never dimmed.

Of the hundred miles between Turin and Genoa Wagner was able to cover the first seventy by train in three hours and forty minutes, hauled by locomotives specially built by Robert Stephenson in Newcastle to deal with the steep gradients. Begun in 1844, the line was opened stage by stage, with the most recent section terminating at Arquate. By the end of the year the huge tunnel under the northern tip of the Apennines would be complete, but on 31 August the final lap was still served only by horse-drawn carriage. On the train Wagner struck up a conversation with the Russian ambassador to the Holy See, named Skaryatin, perhaps the Colonel Skaryatin who had led a Russian force that attempted (and failed) to suppress the Hungarian rebellion in 1848. Wagner proudly told him how because of his own role in those events he was not allowed into the Papal States.

It took him exactly a week to get from Zurich to Genoa. His hotel, the Pensione Svizzera, occupied the upper floors of two renaissance palaces, the Palazzo Grimaldi and the Palazzo Fieschi, on the narrow Nuova Strada (now the Via Garibaldi). He was delighted with the mosaic floors and marble staircase. He sat in a café, had an ice cream, coffee and a cigar, then slept superbly. Next morning he opened the shutters of his room on the sixth floor and found himself gazing at the Mediterranean for the first time: the harbour, the masts and sails of ships, and the blue of the sea. His previous experience of the sea, travelling from Riga to London and across the Channel in 1839, left the impression of a rough and stormy element (magnificently portrayed in *Der fliegende Holländer*), but now the effect of sunshine, warmth and fragrant air aroused in him a sense of excitement he had been looking forward to for weeks, if not months. Here at last was somewhere he could settle down to composing in peace. He decided he would stay two weeks in Genoa and then move on for a longer spell to La Spezia, down the coast, then to Paris. Next year, he told Minna, we must all (you, me and the dog) come here for your birthday. Despite the unbroken sunshine it was not too hot. He decided to go for a swim in the sea.

The next day was quite different. He began to feel homesick. When a dog kept him company during a meal, he felt lonely and sorry for himself. He also felt unwell with an upset stomach, blaming the abrupt change of diet, especially the ice cream. The steamer to La Spezia, it turned out, went only every Saturday, so he decided to take it next day, after only three nights in Genoa. By then his homesickness was even worse and he resolved not to stay away from home too long, however lovely Italy turned out to be. The overnight sea voyage would cure him, he thought, even if he was seasick.

Why Wagner picked La Spezia, fifty miles down the coast from Genoa, as the place to visit is a mystery. Perhaps someone had recommended it. It had some renaissance churches and palaces, but nothing on the scale of Genoa or Pisa. It had not yet been developed as a naval base and was still a relatively small city. He arrived on Sunday morning, 4 September, after a rough voyage. Seasickness had not helped, in fact the diarrhoea that attacked him in Genoa continued to lay him low on board. He took a room in the Albergo Nazionale in the Via del Prione, the narrow street that divides the old town in two named after the *pietrone*, the large stone from which public proclamations were made.

Feeling better, he went for a walk in the afternoon that took him into the hills and also along the shore. He was amazed at the richness and beauty of the country. Back at the hotel he swore never to go travelling again alone. Conversation was his lifeblood. He spoke little Italian and was in no mood or condition to accost strangers. He felt so anxious while attempting to sleep that he enquired about a doctor (though none evidently came). He eventually had a peaceful night, but giddiness and his upset stomach returned in the morning (Monday). He wrote a long letter to Minna describing his dreadful condition and unhappy state of mind. He felt miserable and helpless and had decided to return to Genoa immediately. If he didn't get better there, he'd head straight for Zurich and home. If things improved, he'd go to Nice and perhaps stay there until it was time to go to Paris. At the end of the day he boarded the coach back to Genoa.

The ill-fated expedition to La Spezia might not be of special interest were it not for the fact that Wagner later invested it with the character of a myth by identifying it as the place where his mind was suddenly filled with the music of the *Ring*. In some notes jotted down in 1868 he wrote:

> Steamship to Spezia. Dreadful accommodation. Ill. 2nd day efforts. Walk. Pine woods. Afternoon sleep on a couch. Woke up with the conception of the orchestral introduction to *Das Rheingold* (E flat triad). Sinking in a rush of water. Immediate turnaround and decision to start work.

In *Mein Leben*, written the following year, the account reads as follows:

> By the time I reached Spezia I could hardly take a single step and went to the best hotel, which to my dismay was situated in a narrow and noisy alley. After a sleepless and feverish night, I forced myself to undertake a long walk the following day among the pine-covered hills of the surroundings. Everything seemed to me to be bleak and bare, and I asked myself why I had come. Returning that afternoon, I stretched out dead-tired on a hard couch, awaiting the long-desired onset of sleep. It did not come; instead, I sank into a kind of somnambulistic state, in which I suddenly had the feeling of being immersed in rapidly flowing water. Its rushing soon resolved itself for me into the musical sound of the chord of E flat major, resounding in persistent broken chords; these in turn transformed themselves into melodic figurations of increasing motion, yet the E flat major triad never changed, and seemed by its continuance to impart infinite significance to the element in which I was sinking. I awoke in sudden terror from this trance, feeling as though the waves were crashing high above my head. I recognised at once that the orchestral prelude to *Das Rheingold*, long dormant within me but up to that moment inchoate, had at last been revealed; and I also saw

immediately precisely how it was with me: the vital flood would come from within me, and not from without.

I immediately decided to return to Zurich and begin setting my vast poem to music.

This famous passage has been subjected to relentless scrutiny with much doubt cast upon its veracity, largely because the letter he wrote to Minna that Monday contains no mention of the dreamlike vision of an E flat chord. This can be explained by the fact that Wagner never shared his musical thoughts with Minna, who would not be able to grasp their import. But then he said almost nothing about it in a letter to Liszt either:

> I went to La Spezia; my illness got worse; there was no prospect of enjoying anything, so I came back home to breathe my last or to compose. One or the other, there's no other choice. That's the complete story of my trip.

Yet there is no reason why it should not be a perfectly true account. In one detail it can be shown to be wrong, namely Wagner's statement that he slept a night in La Spezia before the long walk and the dreamlike trance. The letter to Minna makes it clear that the walk and the sleepless exhaustion that followed occurred on the Sunday, the day he arrived in town. His decision to leave and the letter to Minna belong to the Monday.

That Sunday evening he obviously attempted to sleep, which eluded him even though he was exhausted from a bad night on the boat and an energetic walk in the afternoon. He thought about calling a doctor, but none came. Eventually he fell asleep. He had been thinking about this music for five years; he had written the text of *Das Rheingold* nearly a year earlier; he had gone to Italy specifically to embark on the huge score; inevitably the opening scene, in the depths of the Rhine, would have presented him with a challenge that he could not have avoided thinking about. Many operas had watery subjects, and even watery overtures, but it needed an especially radical idea to match the immensity of his conception. That idea was the single note, E flat, and the single chord, E flat major, which would be sustained unbroken for over five minutes. The idea could have come to him at any time, and that time was in fact in the evening of 4 September 1853, on a hard couch in La Spezia. Like so many inspirations, it was born in a confused consciousness already troubled by illness and exhaustion. The clarity of it was nonetheless overwhelming.

(Strange to think of Wagner's mind awash with the music of the Rhine on a day when Brahms was perhaps twice crossing the river itself.)

Wagner never claimed that this was the first music he wrote for the *Ring*. The five years since 1848 may have been barren of finished compositions, but he made sketches from time to time. In 1850, when the plan still consisted only of *Siegfrieds Tod* (eventually *Götterdämmerung*), he drafted the opening scene for the Norns continuing into the first part of the scene for Siegfried and Brünnhilde. In 1852 he wrote out the dragon's motive as an albumleaf for William Mason and elsewhere jotted down a theme for the Valkyries themselves, eventually to become the best known of all the *Ring*'s themes:

Ex. 2 Wagner, *The Ride of the Valkyries,* preliminary sketch

There is also a sketch that shows the wide-spread arpeggio theme with which the horns build up the opening pages of *Das Rheingold.* But these preliminary efforts do not mean that Wagner did not hear in his head, on that evening in La Spezia, the extraordinary texture of the Rhine itself as he portrayed it in his eventual score. The sonority was unique and completely new, beginning with the double basses in their lowest range (E flat is lower than the conventional tuning of the bottom string), with lower strings, bassoons, and horns. Perhaps he heard the extraordinary effect of *eight* horns overlapping one by one like waves in a continually rising flood, with the strings surging up from the depths and the brass endlessly reaching up out of their lowest register, while the chord of E flat remains unchanged. The modern orchestra at that time had four horns. Only massed military bands (and Berlioz in his *Requiem*) ever required more. Yet at a stroke Wagner conceived the sound of an opera orchestra in which the number of horns was doubled, leading to the inevitable step of calling for twice the normal strength of woodwind, five trumpets, extra trombones and tubas, and a completely new conception of the orchestra. With this giant resource the immensity of his monumental dramatic idea had at last found its musical counterpart. Wotan's wrath, Siegfried's heroics, Hagen's black soul, Brünnhilde's apotheosis – all these could now become reality in sound.

The significance of the moment is not to be underestimated. Wagner never doubted, even if others did, that he would compose the music-drama eventually. But the impetus to start work had been missing for several months, partly because he had been away from composing for so long and was nervous of the mental adjustment it would need, partly because he was distracted – or distracted himself – giving concerts, dealing with his health, taking long hikes, or simply procrastinating, as we all do in the face of major undertakings. From La Spezia on, there was no turning back. He little suspected that the work would take over twenty years to complete. He was forty years old and in dubious health, but the Rubicon was crossed. The most potent force in music since Beethoven was about to be unleashed in all its unimaginable splendour. Not only the *Ring,* but *Tristan und Isolde, Die Meistersinger* and *Parsifal* would emerge from that seething brain, and he would never leave off composing for so long again. The entire culture of the *fin-de-siècle* would have been different without Wagner's colossal shadow falling across it. Thank you, La Spezia!

THE big decision was to write music, the small one to turn back. He left La Spezia on the Monday evening by coach along the coast road back to Genoa. The journey continued through the following day, when Wagner, obviously feeling better, delighted in the blue of the sea and the sky, the green of the pine trees and the white cattle in the fields. In Genoa he briefly toyed with his old idea of taking the coast road to Nice which clearly appealed to him, but the demon diarrhoea attacked him again and he dropped the plan. With hindsight he could say that he knew that composing was more important than savouring the delights of Italy. He left Genoa on the Wednesday and took the direct route back to Zurich. North of Genoa he passed through Alessandria and Novara and took the boat for forty miles the length of Lake Maggiore, which he had visited only a year earlier. From there he had to cross the St Gothard pass at 7,000 feet, and then directly north to Zurich. Arriving home on Saturday 10th, he found Minna still away at Baden and he still felt unwell.

The Italian journey had been a failure in the sense that the travelling arrangements were unsatisfactory and his health was disastrous. His need for companionship seriously disturbed him and he did not find the tranquillity he needed to compose. If he arrived home with nothing written down, just a bundle of blank music paper, his capacious head was full of music and a start had been made. He wanted to set to work as soon as he got home, but because the planned meeting with Liszt in Paris (not due to happen for a month) would interrupt the flow he decided to wait. Or was that just an excuse?

Instead of composing he occupied himself with answering the correspondence that had chased him around Italy and taking regular trips to Baden an der Limmat to visit Minna, who was taking the cure, but not, evidently, being cured of whatever it was she suffered from. He wrote to old Spohr after a gap of many years. In the week after his return he went down to the Kornhaus to see a famous Dutch menagerie on display to the public. There was an elephant, Miss Baba, doing tricks, and a mongrel that spoke the words *papa, mama* and *grossmama*. The animal-lover Wagner bought a parrot for Minna to replace the deceased ex-parrot Papo and to make up for his pending (and perhaps also recent) absence, also for the absence of her daughter Natalie who was working in a hotel somewhere in Switzerland. Minna named the parrot Jacquot and taught it to say 'Richard Wagner is a naughty man.'

Otherwise his time was devoted to the eternal efforts to get his works performed in Germany. Liszt was, as usual, called in to help. Hans von Bülow had the idea of presenting the same concerts in Berlin as Wagner had given in Zurich, but with Liszt conducting. All their minds were now concentrated on the forthcoming Karlsruhe Festival, when Liszt was going to present some of Wagner's and Berlioz's works. Wagner, of course, would not be able to attend, but the prospect of Liszt coming to see him afterwards in Basel and the two of them then going to Paris together was a source of huge excitement to Wagner, enough to keep him a little longer from the desk where the pile of ruled fourteen-stave music paper awaited him.

CHAPTER 9

Liszt in Karlsruhe

SEPTEMBER – OCTOBER

For all alert German musicians the Karlsruhe Festival of October 1853 was one of the biggest events of the year. In July the *Neue Zeitschrift für Musik* already predicted that this would be an epoch-making event, and the build-up that followed was a model of effective public relations.

Unlike most European cities, which have grown up on a river around a core of winding mediaeval streets with a central church and market, Karlsruhe was created in an empty space in 1715, not unlike the foundation of the cities of St Petersburg and Washington, DC. Indeed, the layout of the latter city may owe something to Karlsruhe, whose plan was familiar to Pierre L'Enfant, its designer. The Margrave's palace of Karlsruhe was set at the centre of thirty-two radiating streets connected by concentric ring streets, many of which survive today, despite a rectangular grid of streets superimposed on the southern part of the original plan when the city expanded rapidly in the nineteenth century.

Until 1715 the seat of the Margraves of Baden-Durlach was at Durlach, a town twenty miles north of Baden-Baden and about five miles east of the Rhine. But when he succeeded his father as Margrave in 1709, the battle-scarred, tulip-loving Carl Wilhelm decided to build a new palace on a grand scale a mile or two to the west of the town and take his entire court with him. From the tower in the centre of the palace he could watch his subjects in all thirty-two directions, or perhaps imagine them watching him. The overwhelmingly focal layout of the city is in the grandest baroque manner, although the palace itself is somewhat understated by the standards of the age.

The Margrave's court included a kapelle of musicians, augmented in 1771 by the kapelle from Baden-Baden as Karlsruhe grew steadily to overshadow both Durlach and Baden-Baden in importance and wealth. In 1806 the margravate became a grand duchy, and a new theatre was built. This burnt down with the loss of sixty-three lives in 1847, and a second theatre opened its doors in 1853 under the patronage of the Prince Regent of Baden, later Grand Duke Friedrich I. His kapellmeister was Joseph Strauss, whom we met in Chapter 5 assisting Berlioz in his August concerts in Baden-Baden. Strauss had succeeded Franz Danzi in 1824 and built up a strong if undistinguished musical culture in the capital. Much more significant was the theatre director Eduard Devrient, whose appointment in 1852 set the stage for some ambitious plans, the first of which was to be a grand festival under the direction of Liszt. Anxious to show off his burgeoning city to the world, the Prince Regent was firmly behind this far-sighted boost to the city's culture. The railway came to Karlsruhe in 1843, and by 1853 the population was close to 25,000.

Liszt's first impressions of the city were good, but he thought in the long run he preferred the random, winding streets of Weimar. The neat pavements and gas lighting reminded him of London.

Coming from a family with wide connections in opera and the theatre, Devrient's first career was as a singer. He had sung the part of Christ in Mendelssohn's famous revival of the *St Matthew Passion* in Berlin in 1829. When his singing voice deserted him soon after, he turned to his gifts as writer, actor and director. He wrote some successful librettos, including *Hans Heiling* for Marschner, and was appointed to an ill-defined position in Dresden in 1844 which gave him limited oversight of opera and theatre. In this role he became a close friend of his colleague Wagner, and was drawn into the circle of Wagner's admirers. Although he resigned his position in 1846, he remained in Dresden at least through the revolutionary days in 1849, working as an actor and writer. He had strong views on the need for theatre reform not unlike those of Wagner, naturally enough.

His appointment to the direction of the Karlsruhe theatre in 1852 was a bold move on the part of the court and it provided him, now in his early fifties, with the opportunity for putting some of his innovative ideas into effect by instituting both a drama school and an opera school in the city. He had met Liszt briefly in Weimar but could not be classed as a close friend; he knew at least that with his production of *Lohengrin* and two other Wagner operas in Weimar Liszt shared an admiration for his former Dresden friend. After the celebrations in Bonn in 1845 for the inauguration of a statue of Beethoven, all under Liszt's energetic command, and a music festival in Ballenstedt-am-Harz in 1852, Liszt would have been seen as the

31 Prince Regent Friedrich of Baden-Baden

ideal figure to lead another festival. Inviting him as the main attraction was sure to be a strong draw, and in addition the Prince Regent's marshall Count Leiningen was on close terms with Liszt since he was courting one of Princess Carolyne's husband's Sayn-Wittgenstein nieces. They called him 'Linange'. Further strong support for the Festival came from Hermann Krönlein, editor of the local newspaper, the *Karlsruher Zeitung*, and a fervent Wagnerian.

The original invitation, sent in December 1852, envisaged a festival that would open in May 1853 with a new opera and a new play, to be followed by some concerts at the beginning of June. Liszt was asked to keep the plan to himself for fear of offending old Strauss, as Devrient referred to him (he was sixty). The dates quickly proved to be unworkable, so the Festival was put off first until the middle of August and then to 20 and 21 September. During the Weimar festivities in May, when Brahms and Reményi were visiting, Liszt was planning a visit to Wagner in Zurich with a detour to Karlsruhe to discuss the logistics of the plan. This council of war took place at the end of June when Liszt spent two days in Karlsruhe working with Devrient and Count Leiningen. He had audiences with both the Prince Regent and his mother the Dowager Grand Duchess, formerly a Swedish princess. Perhaps Strauss was also in on the deliberations at this stage, even if there was no conducting for him in the plan. Liszt told Princess Carolyne that there was considerable local opposition to the Festival, but Strauss worked energetically for the success of every event. His junior was a young pianist and composer Wilhelm Kalliwoda, son of a famous father, who assisted Liszt in preparing the performances.

Both Darmstadt and Mannheim were to unite their orchestras and choruses with those of Karlsruhe and Baden-Baden in order to assemble a body of nearly 200 players and a larger number of singers. How could such numbers be accommodated in the theatre? Liszt never hesitated in his plan to include music by Wagner, Berlioz and himself, with a performance of Beethoven's Ninth Symphony as the principal event and homages to Meyerbeer and Schumann also included. He discussed the possibility of giving the first performance of Berlioz's *Te Deum*, already four years old but still unheard. The severe choral demands of this work, with its six-part chorus singing almost constantly throughout, probably eliminated it from the running. The next idea was to include some extracts from *Benvenuto Cellini*, including the Goldsmiths' Chorus, but this needed a tenor like Tamberlik, as Berlioz was quick to point out, which Karlsruhe didn't have. In the end Liszt settled for some selections from *Roméo et Juliette*, at least one movement of which was familiar to the musicians who had played it recently under the composer's direction in Baden-Baden.

The Wagner pieces were to be the Prelude to *Tannhäuser* and some movements from *Lohengrin*. Although this music had been performed in Weimar, Liszt was determined to use the revised and adapted versions as played by Wagner in Zurich in May, and for this he needed the parts Wagner had himself prepared. Wagner needed constant badgering to remind him to sort out the parts and send them to Devrient. A major part of the plan was to feature the two most brilliant young instrumentalists in Germany, both Liszt's protégés: twenty-three-year-old Hans von Bülow was to play Liszt's *Fantasy on Themes from Beethoven's 'Ruins of Athens'* for piano and orchestra, of which he had recently given the first performance in Pest; and twenty-two-year-old Joseph Joachim was to give the first performance of his own new violin concerto. The two concerts would include overtures by Meyerbeer and Schumann respectively, with a leavening of vocal pieces.

When, in August, the Festival was once again postponed from September to the begining of October, Liszt was able to stay a little longer in Teplitz and Dresden and relax a few more days. After von Bülow's concert in Dresden, he and Liszt travelled back together through Leipzig to Weimar on Saturday 17 September. Liszt just had time to attend to some of Raff's problems (trying to get him a job in Munich and advising him about his debts), write to the Princess, who was in Regensburg, and repack his bags, skipping a performance of *Fidelio* that evening. He and von Bülow, assisted as always by the faithful Hermann, left that same night at 1 a.m., arriving in Frankfurt for a stop for Sunday lunch with Liszt's American pupil William Mason, then on to Karlsruhe where they were lodging at the Erbprinz Hotel on Rheinstrasse (curiously the same name of hotel as Liszt's official address in Weimar). First order of business on Monday morning was a conference with Devrient and Leiningen to decide the final dates, fixed now for 3 and 5 October. Concert and opera announcements at that time were never given out more than a week in advance, and often less. For something as important as a festival, an exception had to be made so that the press could give the public at least a week to plan their visit. He had allowed a generous two weeks to prepare the Festival programme, knowing that he would need to go several times to Darmstadt, Mannheim and Baden-Baden to work with their musicians.

Liszt wanted all his flock of pupils and fans to come for the Festival, and the roll-call of those who came was impressive. Pruckner was already there when Liszt and von Bülow arrived. Despite claiming a migraine from travel exhaustion, von Bülow went on Monday with Pruckner to Baden-Baden to rehearse the soprano soloist Kathinka Heinefetter in her two operatic arias. She was a replacement for Sophie Cruvelli who had evidently, diva-like, cancelled. On Saturday at the end of the week von Bülow read in the newspaper of his father's death at the age of forty-nine at his home in Switzerland. It was a harsh blow, especially since his parents had divorced five years before. He had been close to his father, who was a well-known writer and editor in Leipzig and Dresden and a strong supporter of the 1848–9 revolution. In 1849 he married a cousin and went to live in a castle in Switzerland. Liszt had heard the news from Hans's mother two days earlier but had inexplicably not told him, going off to Baden for two days with the letter in his pocket. Von Bülow spent the second week not rehearsing with Liszt but in mourning with his step-mother in the small town of Oetlishausen, near Lake Constance. A Rhine steamer took him nearly all the way there and back.

Liszt moved back and forth on the train between Darmstadt, Mannheim and Baden-Baden. In the latter city he had the benefit of the Countess Kalergis's hospitality at the Hôtel de l'Angleterre in the company of a group of Russian diplomats and notables. The English and French embassies were located there too, so both received him in his efforts to promote the Festival. Liszt moved effortlessly in this high society. He also saw Ernst and the lovely young Amélie, and thought wistfully that he might bring Ernst to Weimar one day. In Liszt's absence from Karlsruhe Kalliwoda took the rehearsals. Von Bülow observed that Kalliwoda, the orchestra leader Will and the chorus master Krug were having some difficulty with the strangeness of the music, being steeped in what he called *Mendelssohnianismus*. Karlsruhe was not familiar with the music of Berlioz and Wagner, and even the Ninth Symphony was virgin territory. Their current repertoire, said von Bülow with the hint of a sneer, was Gluck's *Armide*. Joachim heard Cherubini's opera *Der Wasserträger* one evening and was bored. With the first concert due on Monday 3 October, the whole weekend of 1–2 October was taken up with final rehearsals.

Krönlein, in the *Karlsruher Zeitung*, prepared his readers with five long, impassioned articles about 'The Latest Directions in Music', which acknowledged that the music of the previous thirty years was rich and interesting. But just as political and social conditions had changed powerfully in recent years, especially as a result of the 1848–9 upheavals, so too music was on the verge of reaching out into new territory. The message is that the composers represented in the coming concerts are the pioneers leading us in these new directions. His 'Neueste Richtungen' inevitably invites comparison with Schumann's 'Neue Bahnen'.

By that time the 'young eagles' had assembled. Joachim arrived at the Erbprinz from Düsseldorf on the 24th or 25th, looking forward to another noisy reunion with his Weimar friends, and to working with Liszt; von Bülow came back from Switzerland; Pruckner and Mason had been there some time; Cornelius came from Mainz; Reményi came from Weimar. A new member of the group was Richard Pohl, a twenty-seven-year-old critic from Dresden, who had known Schumann well and who was a firm adherent of Liszt and Wagner. He admired Berlioz also and later wrote his biography. In his favour too was the fact that his wife Johanna was an excellent harpist, particularly in demand for the scores of progressive composers such as Berlioz and Liszt. (She was born in Karlsruhe.) As an assistant to Brendel on the *Neue Zeitschrift für Musik* his job was to report the festival in full. He happened also to be a friend of Kalliwoda's. He put up at the Roman Emperor Hotel.

Kapellmeisters Schindelmeisser and Mangold from Darmstadt were visiting in support of their own troops, the great double bassist August Müller among them, but Theodor Lachner, director of Mannheim's music, was kept at home by an attack of jaundice. The bass clarinet player came from Wiesbaden. Liszt's Weimar cellist Cossmann was summoned by Joachim from the south of France where he was holidaying. As observers and audience Isaac Strauss (no relation), Napoleon III's ballroom conductor, came from Paris, Ernst and Ehrlich came up from Baden-Baden, Julius Benedict was there from London, Arnold Wehner and his wife came from Göttingen. Musicians came in from Freiburg, Stuttgart, Bern, Basel, Mulhouse, Strasbourg, Heidelberg, Kaiserslautern, Constance and elsewhere: there can have

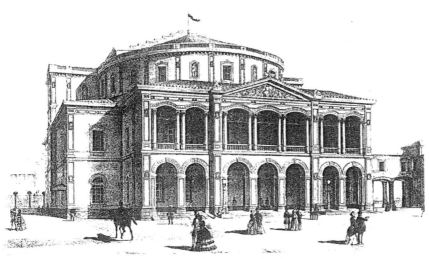

32 The Hoftheater, Karlsruhe

been few occasions in those years when so many musicians of all ranks gathered in the same place. Two German diplomats, Angelrodt and Ade, were there, although their postings were in the United States, in St Louis and Cincinnati respectively. A mystery resides in the identity of the Fräulein Laussot who arrived at the Zähringer Hotel on the 5th and described as a singer from the Paris Opéra. Since there was no such singer at the Paris Opéra, it would be a delightful fancy to think that Wagner's flame from 1850, Jessie Laussot, was discreetly there to hear some of his music.

Last but not least, Princess Carolyne and Marie arrived to join Liszt in the Erbprinz Hotel just before the concerts, having done a wide circuit of southern Germany after their summer cure at Carlsbad and Teplitz. They were taking in art museums and galleries in the company of their cousin Eugène, himself a painter, sculptor and minor composer. Liszt was impressed that in Munich they had had an audience with King Ludwig I of Bavaria. They were friendly with Count Leiningen, who was betrothed to Eugène's sister. The last stage of their journey, from Stuttgart, was on a railway line which had opened for the first time that very weekend. 'Times are changing,' observed Liszt. Whereas the journey from Stuttgart previously took eight or nine hours, the opening of the railway now reduced the time to three and a half hours.

Liszt hoped Berlioz would be there to hear *Roméo et Juliette*; the Prince Regent invited him, along with Meyerbeer and Schumann. None of the three came. Meyerbeer sent his apologies, being busy in Paris rehearsing his new opera *L'Étoile du nord*. Berlioz pleaded that he didn't have time, but the real reason was that he never enjoyed other people's performances of his music. Despite his close friendship with Liszt, the experience of *Benvenuto Cellini* in Weimar had taught him not to trust Liszt on the podium. Liszt, Joachim and Cossmann entreated Bettina

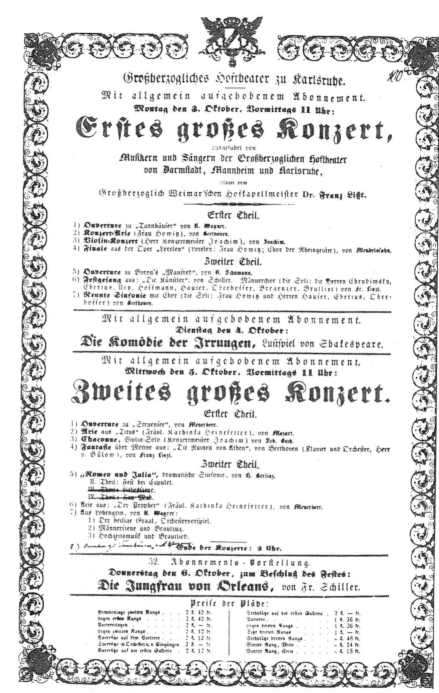

33 The Karlsruhe Festival, 3–6 October 1853

von Arnim to come from Cologne, but she wouldn't or couldn't. Klindworth and Raff were not there. The most obvious absentee was of course Wagner himself, although he gave Liszt precise instructions how to rehearse his pieces and followed rehearsals intently by letter.

The Festival ran for the four days from Monday to Thursday 3–6 October and comprised two concerts and two new productions of old plays. They all took place in Heinrich Hübsch's handsome new theatre, which stood just to the left of the ducal palace until felled by a bomb in 1944. Two floors of colonnaded archways fronted a semicircular auditorium beneath a flat conical dome, not unlike Semper's 1841 opera house in Dresden. The interior adopted the conventional parterre seating below with four ranks of boxes above in a horseshoe layout with plenty of gilded statuary. The ducal box directly faced the stage. The Dowager Grand Duchess was in mourning for a Swedish cousin and could not attend, but the Prince Regent occupied the box with any sufficiently grand nobility who came in from nearby cities. The Grand Duke and Duchess of Hesse-Darmstadt, attending in support of their musician subjects, the Margrave of Baden with princesses, the Prince of Fürstenberg and family – these were some of the grandees proudly mentioned in the press. Count Leiningen with a group of Sayn-Wittgensteins sat in an adjoining box.

The first concert was given at 11 a.m. on the Monday morning. The huge orchestra tuned up off-stage; when the curtain rose they were revealed in their places on stage ready to play with Liszt standing on the podium, baton raised. No wonder he was accused of theatricality by envious rivals! The programme opened with the overture to *Tannhäuser*, followed by a Beethoven concert aria (probably 'Ah! perfido') sung by Clementine Howitz-Steinau, a recent acquisition by the Karlsruhe opera. Then Joachim played the solo part in his own one-movement Violin Concerto in G minor which he had been working on all summer, and the first half closed with the finale from Mendelssohn's unfinished opera *Loreley* with Howitz-Steinau singing the title role. The second half comprised Schumann's overture to *Manfred*, then *An die Künstler* for men's chorus and wind ensemble by Liszt on a text by Schiller; this was its first performance, although the handbill did not say so. Finally came Beethoven's Ninth Symphony.

A three-hour programme such as this was not out of place in a festival, yet there can have been no lunch for anyone until at least 2.30. On the Tuesday and Wednesday afternoons the Schlossplatz and the Marktplatz were turned into a fairground with all kinds of popular fun and games. A 'climbing-tree' was set up, there were hot-air balloons, archery, clog races, sack races, wurst-chopping contests, a 'shaking beam', a magician named Wiljalba Frikell, a carousel, punch-and-judy, refreshment stalls and of course bands playing. The weather was perfect.

On Tuesday evening Devrient's new production of Shakespeare's *A Comedy of Errors* was put on, with the second concert on Wednesday morning, again at 11 a.m. Meyerbeer's overture to *Struensee* opened the first half, with the aria 'Parto, parto' (with a prominent clarinet solo) from Mozart's *La clemenza di Tito* to follow, sung by Kathinka Heinefetter from Baden-Baden. Then Joachim played the Bach *Chaconne*, not with Mendelssohn's accompaniment which was then widely done, but in its original unaccompanied version. He declined to play an encore even though the audience was clamouring for some Paganini. The first half closed with von Bülow playing Liszt's *Fantasy on Themes from Beethoven's 'Ruins of Athens'*, an exercise in hair-raising virtuosity. The second half was supposed to begin with three movements from Berlioz's *Roméo et Juliette*, but in all probability the delicate, speedy *Reine Mab* scherzo would have been unworkable with three orchestras playing at once, so only one movement was played, the *Roméo seul – Tristesse* leading into the *Fête chez Capulet*. Miss Heinefetter then sang Fidès's aria from the last act of Meyerbeer's *Le Prophète*, and finally three excerpts from *Lohengrin*: the Prelude, the Men's Scene and Bridal March, and the Wedding Music and Bridal Song from Act III. The *Lohengrin* pieces had the same function in the second concert as the Beethoven symphony in the first: to provide a stirring much-anticipated climax, placed unusually for those days at the end of the programme.

Since two of the Berlioz movements had been dropped, the *Tannhäuser* overture, which had been wildly applauded at the first concert, was repeated to close the concert (or perhaps cause and effect were the other way round). The audience emerged from another long concert this time to be confronted by the clog-dancers and wurst-choppers on the Schlossplatz. There were fireworks that evening and the Festival closed on Thursday evening with a torchlight procession through flag-bedecked streets and a new production of Schiller's play *The Maid of Orleans*. Three other plays were running in repertoire on other days. The local infantry regiment and fire brigade also put on displays.

The press enjoyed linking the progressive flavour of the concerts with the *völkisch* traditionalism of the outdoor amusements. Somehow they all seemed to reflect well on the regime of their monarch, the Prince Regent of Baden-Baden, and the prosperity of the city, as well as on German pride in a broader sense. They were delighted to see trainloads of visitors arriving at the station (they had free return tickets during the period of the Festival).

34 Karlsruhe Station

The *Karlsruher Zeitung* naturally reported the concerts enthusiastically. Both generated storms of applause, the second even more than the first, which was marred by an incident, of which more later ... Krönlein's prose takes wing:

> It was impressive to follow these immense forces now boiling like storm-lashed ocean waves, now whispering like the west wind in the leaves, now locked in apparently chaotic conflict, now coming together in a perfect, enchanting unison, now stirring in passionate movement, now in silent transfiguration, but always controlled and temperate, driven by artistic inspiration.

Joachim's Bach electrified both the audience and an admiring orchestra, and von Bülow was equally applauded. The Wagner scenes and the repeat of the *Tannhäuser* overture all had the audience in wild acclamation, with no sign of incomprehension or hostility. Krönlein also commented on Liszt's singular style of conducting, but he was by no means the last to do so.

Pohl's first report appeared in the *Neue Zeitschrift* on 7 October. As he pointed out at the start, music criticism did not yet get sent to its editorial office by telegram, although it surely soon would. So he started with a preview of events. The rest of his long report appeared in the issues of the 14, 21, 28 October (the issue that also offered Schumann's 'Neue Bahnen' on its front page) and 11 November. He proclaimed the Festival the 'Entry of Modern Art into South Germany'. Never before, he claimed, had such a range of difficulties to be overcome, the three main ones being the co-ordination of three sets of orchestra and chorus from different cities, the players' and singers' unfamiliarity with all the music they had to perform, and the innate prejudice against new music and new ideas that both audiences and performers too readily feel. It was to Liszt's enormous credit that all these problems were overcome and that prejudice was scattered to the winds. The virtuosity of von Bülow and Joachim was beyond praise; in fact Pohl was reduced to quoting Krönlein in praising the latter:

> Such profound artistry, such warmth and depth of feeling is not often [Pohl would have preferred 'never'] encountered in the world of the virtuoso. This artist no longer has any issue with difficulties; he overcomes them effortlessly so that they seem nothing other than necessary moments in the full, deeply felt presentation of the work, with a fundamental respect for the music.

In the case of von Bülow, Pohl had heard his recent recital in Dresden and was now confirmed in attributing world-class status to him.

When it came to the Berlioz, Pohl's neighbour, a gentleman from Heidelberg said: 'I'm very glad that some of the Berlioz has been dropped.'

'Why, if I may ask?' replied Pohl indignantly, conscious of many Berlioz-haters in the musical world.

'Because that way we get to hear more Wagner. I came here to get to know his music better.' Hearing the Bridal March from *Lohengrin* one day in Wiesbaden had whetted his appetite for Wagner. 'When you do *Lohengrin* again in Weimar, I'll be there to hear it!'

But the thrilling sounds of the *Fête chez Capulet* brought the Heidelberger to his feet with excitement, to Pohl's great satisfaction, since he saw Berlioz as one of the most original voices in contemporary music, full of poetry and imagination, in spite of what most Germans viewed as his un-German style of writing harmony. To follow this with the aria from *Le Prophète* could only show up Meyerbeer in the weakest light, especially since the glorious Prelude to *Lohengrin* came next.

In Pohl's view the problems faced by Liszt were responsible for the inaccuracies and mistakes that marred the first concert, the second concert being in this respect much more satisfactory. Liszt's cantata was too difficult for the men's chorus and the Ninth Symphony was especially accident-prone. The players should be blamed, he thought, not Liszt. There were mistakes and missed entries that passed more or less without notice, but the start of the 6/8 B flat section of the finale had to be played twice since the bassoon player came in wrong and the performance fell apart. Liszt's enemies in the audience (there were inevitably some) booed. Such miserable people, observed Pohl, have never conducted anything in their lives, let alone a long difficult piece on only two full rehearsals; they were just waiting for something to go wrong.

At issue was not simply a natural resistance to artistic progress, of which Liszt was an outspoken champion, but a problem with the nature of conducting itself. It was still a young art. Spohr and Mendelssohn were perceived as pioneers in using a baton rather than a violin bow with which to lead the orchestra. Conductors differed over whether they should face the players or face the audience, for example. One of Schumann's manifest disadvantages as a conductor was his lack of experience of instruments other than the piano; he simply didn't know how an orchestra works from the inside. Liszt was similarly inexperienced with orchestras, and when he started to conduct in the early 1840s there was no handbook on how to do it. Yet by 1853 there was one, written, by a curious irony, by Kalliwoda's predecessor as assistant kapellmeister in Karlsruhe and published in Karlsruhe in 1844. This was *Dirigent und Ripienist* by Ferdinand Gassner. If Gassner had been alive to watch Liszt conducting the Ninth Symphony, he would have known exactly what the trouble was. But he died in 1851, and his book is so little known even today that it is most unlikely that Liszt had seen it.

For Liszt developed a conducting technique that owed nothing to Gassner's methodical approach but was related to his performances as a piano soloist. He always derided the steady beat as beneath contempt: the conductor was there to illustrate the music and to bring out its essential elements; his job was to represent the music, to *be* the music, and thus to inspire his players and singers, and, not least, convey the essence of the music to the audience as well. Little wonder that Berlioz was impatient with Liszt's exhibitionist conducting. He had taught himself to conduct from his absorption in orchestral instruments and the way in which they contribute to the orchestral ensemble like cogs in a machine. He saw conducting as a device for getting the players to play together and in the right spirit. This division between conductors who serve the orchestra and those who serve the audience is with us still today, perhaps in a more acute form even than in Liszt's time. At all events, the problem in the Ninth Symphony was Beethoven's unhelpful beginning of the passage in question on the off-beat:

Ex. 3 Beethoven, Ninth Symphony, Finale

The conductor's essential duty here is to show the silent first beat of the passage so that the bassoon, contrabassoon and bass drum can enter on the second beat. Liszt's instinct led him not to give the main beat but to give the entry itself. Any player that took that to be the first beat would therefore come in a beat late. If Liszt gave no more beats until the third bar of the passage, the misunderstanding would be compounded. Mason, like Pohl, thought it was not Liszt's fault that the players came in wrong.

Pohl was a perceptive analyst of the polarisation that was gradually seizing the whole territory of German music, even though he was far from an impartial observer: his own loyalties to Liszt and Wagner were barely concealed. In general he was appalled at the way certain critics clung to their prejudices; he devoted his final article to a broad debunking of the petty minds that lay in wait for Liszt to make a mistake, or who could not bring themselves to accept the steady advance of modern music. The minds of such people were made up before they even arrived, he claimed, and complaining voices irked him dreadfully. The Frankfurt paper *Didaskalia* wondered why Liszt was invited to conduct, not Lachner or Schindelmeisser. Why not a Schwabian conductor, asked the *Schwäbischer Merkur*? Why did Liszt have to play *Lohengrin* and not a Handel oratorio? asked another. The concerts fell short of expectations, some said. According to the *Dresdener Journal* the *Tannhäuser* overture came apart after twenty bars. How can the writer say that, asked Pohl, when that was the best performed piece in the programme and when the critic wasn't even there? They'll make up these stories just to make a partisan point! Joachim said he'd never heard it better performed than then. Pohl's series of articles was later printed in book form, and he followed it up with a long series on Berlioz in the *Neue Zeitschrift für Musik* which later formed the foundation of a full-length book on the composer.

But some of the criticism was less frivolous; some darts carried a sting. The new Cologne music journal, the *Niederrheinische Musik-Zeitung,* edited by Ludwig Bischoff, which had just published Schindler's withering account of Berlioz's concerts in Frankfurt, had nailed its colours to the mast of Liszt's enemies. In its review on 29 October it made a great point of blaming the breakdown in the Beethoven on Liszt's inadequacy as a conductor. Their report of the concert was signed with the initial 'H', usually assumed to conceal the identity of Ferdinand Hiller, although that is probably wrong. No one seems to have recorded his presence in Karlsruhe; in fact Joachim wrote to him not long after, hoping he would not believe some of the untruths that were circulating. Joachim had led the orchestra in Düsseldorf only a few months before in the Lower Rhine Music Festival when Hiller, it will be remembered, had himself conducted the Ninth. The article reads:

> After the Karlsruhe Festival it is universally agreed that Liszt is not qualified to wield the baton, at least not in front of large forces. It's not just that he generally gives no beat (in the simplest meaning of the word such as it has been understood hitherto from the example of the greatest masters), his strange vivacity constantly causes the most severe vacillation in the orchestra. On the podium he does nothing but shift the baton from his right hand to his left, sometimes putting it down altogether, then swapping it from one to the other or even clutching it with both hands, giving signals in the air in accordance with his earlier instruction to the players 'not to take too much notice of his beat' (these were Liszt's very words at rehearsal). Is it any wonder that not a single piece went smoothly and correctly? Should the players not receive our deepest condolence for having risked their high vocation as professional artists and expert orchestral players? Is it any wonder (without going into the complete colourlessness of the performance) that gross mistakes happened, such as in the finale of the Ninth Symphony where Liszt, in the face of complete breakdown, had to give audible instructions to begin the movement again from the beginning?

Stung by this criticism, Liszt later (after his return to Weimar from Paris) wrote to Pohl what amounts to a manifesto about his attitude to conducting:

> In the various accounts of the Karlsruhe festival I have read there is one point on which all seem to be agreed, namely the *inadequacy* of my conducting. [...] In my opinion, the works that spring from Beethoven's late style demand of their performers and orchestras a sense of progress, [...] in accentuation, rhythm, phrasing, and declamation, and in the art of bringing out the light and shade – in a word progress in performance style. Between the players and the conductor there must be a bond other than that created by rigid time-beating. In many passages the crude regularity of beating each bar $\underline{1}$–2–3–4, $\underline{1}$–2–3–4, jars with the sense and the expression. There and elsewhere the letter killeth the spirit, and to this I will never subscribe however specious in their hypocritical impartiality the attacks to which I am exposed.
>
> For the works of Beethoven, Berlioz, Wagner, etc., I see less purpose than elsewhere for the conductor to act like a windmill and sweat copiously in order to infuse his musicians with some heat. When it comes to understanding and feeling, to entering into the meaning of the music, to embracing all hearts in a sort of communion of beauty, of great art, of

artistic and poetic truth, *adequacy* and the old routine of normal conductors is *inadequate* and is even hostile to the dignity and sublime freedom of art. Whatever my critics may say, I will in future stick to my *inadequacy* on principle and out of conviction. [...] The conductor's true task, I believe, is to make himself almost unnecessary. *Nous sommes pilotes, et non manœuvres* – we are helmsmen, not oarsmen.

'Helmsmen, not oarsmen': if the conductor feels the music sufficiently deeply, Liszt argues, he does not need to bother with the niceties of direction. He became more convinced, not less, that time-beating was a superfluous art. The Karlsruhe experience seemed to harden his resolve never to be a mere time-beater on the rostrum. He found it particularly irritating that the controversy about his conducting had overshadowed what was meant to be a banner proclamation of the best in modern music. Krönlein, Pohl and others echoed this message in long, glorious tributes to Berlioz, Liszt, Wagner and the great future of music, but yet the Karlsruhe Festival has come down to us in the literature as a misstep by Liszt which drew attention to what many saw as his exhibitionism. Although his own music was included in the programmes, there is no doubt that in Liszt's mind the single important aim of the Festival, as it had been also of the Ballenstedt-am-Harz Festival in 1852, was to draw attention to the greatness of Wagner as the true heir to Beethoven's Ninth Symphony. Having spent a week with him in Zurich three months earlier, Liszt was the only person in Karlsruhe that week who had any inkling of the real achievement on which Wagner was now ready to embark.

CHAPTER 10

Schumann and Brahms in Düsseldorf

SEPTEMBER – OCTOBER

S CHUMANN'S journal entry for Friday 30 September 1853 includes the following: 'Hr. Brahms a. Hamburg', 'Mr Brahms from Hamburg'. Schumann was actually not there to meet him that day, but the following day's entry is: 'Brahms zum Besuch (ein Genius)', 'a visit from Brahms, a genius'. It took only one day's acquaintance for Schumann to reach this conclusion and to apply to his visitor a term which in all his years as a music critic he had used only very rarely. If Brahms had suffered any anxiety about his reception in the Schumann household, it was immediately laid to rest.

When he arrived in Düsseldorf off the train from Cologne, perhaps a day before he called on Schumann, he took a room in the Roman Emperor Hotel on what was then part of Steinstrasse but is now Stresemannstrasse, no. 26. The building was greatly refurbished in 1903 and is now a bank. It was about ten minutes' walk past the army barracks to the house in Bilkerstrasse where the Schumanns lived. He had introductions from Joachim, Wasielewski, and the Deichmanns, so he was well armed. He also had a portfolio of compositions which appealed immediately to Schumann and his wife, and the personal magnetism that quickly developed between the three of them was not only of immense benefit to Brahms's career, it gave Schumann a vital charge at a point in his life when his professional standing was in serious trouble and his health was rapidly deteriorating.

Since the Lower Rhine Music Festival in May, when Joachim had played the Beethoven Violin Concerto, the Schumanns had not left Düsseldorf except for a brief trip to Bonn at the end of July. The summer months were usually free of civic concerns, so Robert was able to compose with increasing fertility. Seven short pieces designed as fughettas were written in June, followed by three piano sonatas for children, op. 118. Pianists familiar with the *Kinderszenen* and the *Album für die Jugend* are often unaware of these charming and highly accessible pieces, each one dedicated to one of his daughters. He was rereading the immense œuvre of his favourite author, Jean-Paul, the source of much in Schumann's imaginative world. He had not seen Wagner's *Ring* libretto, but he had instead been asked to read a libretto about the Nibelungs by Luise Otto intended for the Danish composer Niels Gade, one of Schumann's friends from his Leipzig days. Clara was composing again too, after a break of some years.

In August a new intense spell of composition began. He wrote an overture for the long gestating *Faustszenen*, followed by an *Introduction and Allegro* for piano and orchestra. In his journal he kept reporting his happy state of mind, even if he sometimes felt unwell. When Joachim arrived on 28 August, fresh from Göttingen

35　The Schumanns' house on Bilkerstrasse, Düsseldorf

with more excited talk about Brahms, he was received with open arms. The music-making was *wundervoll*, and when he left on 1 September Schumann immediately began to compose a *Phantasie* for violin and orchestra, completed four days later. This was followed by a full violin concerto, begun on 21 September and finished two weeks later. In between the two violin works he composed the delightful *Kinderball*, six pieces for piano duet.

Two incidents might be regarded as warning signs. On the visit to Bonn at the end of July to hear his choral work *Der Königssohn* conducted by Wasielewski, he suffered on the following morning what he took to be a rheumatic attack. Wasielewski thought it was a stroke, but the doctor thought otherwise and sent him home a day later on the boat to Düsseldorf but with clear apprehensiveness about his underlying condition. Then during Joachim's visit Schumann recorded a 'strange vocal weakness' which hinted at troubles yet to come. After working a few hours alone in his study, he sometimes found it difficult to speak. Conscious of his delicate state, Clara adopted a strongly protective attitude to her husband, often discouraging visitors from speaking to him. One evening he did not recognise one of his own songs that had just been sung.

12 September, the day following that last incident, was the Schumanns' thirteenth wedding anniversary, always an important celebration in the light of the battles they had fought to be allowed to marry, with Clara's diary recording her deep thankfulness for their current happiness and wellbeing. The following day was Clara's thirty-fourth birthday. Robert told her first thing in the morning that

the post had failed to deliver her present, so she would have to be patient. At noon they drove by carriage to Benrath, about five miles south of Düsseldorf, with its magnificent baroque palace and park. Champagne was drunk. When they returned to Bilkerstrasse at five o'clock Clara found a new piano in the middle of the music room covered in flowers. At the piano sat Fräulein Then, one of Clara's pupils, and behind it stood two ladies and two gentlemen who proceeded to sing a part-song with piano accompaniment 'Die Orange und Myrthe hier', whose poem Robert had written in 1840 when he had given her an earlier piano. The new piece was a present along with the flowers and the piano, made by the Düsseldorf firm of Klems, as well as the collection of works that Robert had been composing without her knowledge in the previous month or two. 'Am I not truly the happiest wife in the world?' she wrote in her diary.

Next morning Schumann wrote to Joachim enclosing the *Phantasie* with a request to check the violin writing and advise him what works best. A week later Joachim arrived unexpectedly in Düsseldorf bringing the piece back to its composer duly checked. That evening Joachim played the new *Phantasie* three times, as well as Schumann's Violin Sonata in A minor, op. 105, the same piece he had played there in May, accompanied by Clara now playing her new piano. Perhaps before he had to leave on his way all the way up the Rhine to Karlsruhe for the Festival (perhaps by steamer) Joachim was allowed to see the violin concerto taking shape on Schumann's desk.

So Schumann was thoroughly well briefed about Brahms before the latter arrived on 30 September. When the doorbell rang, twelve-year-old Marie, the eldest of the Schumanns' six children, ran to open the door. She saw a 'wonderfully handsome young man with long fair hair' asking to see her father.

'My parents are not in,' she told him.

'What time should I call back?'

'Tomorrow at eleven o'clock,' she replied. 'My parents usually go out at noon.'

Brahms returned next morning, 1 October, at eleven, when the children were at school. Schumann invited him in and after a brief exchange Brahms took a seat at the piano and started to play his sonata in C, op. 1. Before he had played very much Schumann interrupted him and said, 'Excuse me a moment. I must go and get my wife.' Clara joined them; Brahms played some more, and then left; the children came home for lunch. 'I shall never forget that lunch,' wrote Marie later, 'with my parents thrilled and deeply moved, going over and over the visit they had received that morning.' On that basis alone Schumann entered the word 'genius' in his diary.

The month that followed was immensely stimulating for all three of them. Brahms's name appears in their diaries almost every day and both men were busy composing. Schumann finished the draft of his Violin Concerto on the very day of his first meeting with Brahms. The following day, Sunday 2nd, Brahms played them his F sharp minor sonata, op. 2, a work that puts the full range of his talents on display. A big forceful first movement, already revealing his command of tight structure; an Andante rich in harmonic nuance leading into a typically skittish scherzo with a Schubertian trio; and a finale that was solemn, serious and grand, not the playful fireworks that virtuoso pianists were turning out in great quantities. 'Veiled symphonies' Schumann called the three early sonatas. As yet, of course, there is no sign of Schumann's influence, but neither is there any trace of Mendelssohn. It already has Beethoven's depth, but reconceived for the modern piano and the modern pianist.

Schumann found he had nothing he could tell him which could improve the work. Clara was most moved to see him at the piano, watching his expressive face and beautiful hands, and admiring his fluent technique. 'Here is one,' she wrote, 'who comes as if sent straight from God.'

Albert Dietrich, one of the young men that Schumann would classify as an apostle, was invited that evening for dinner with Brahms, who played some of his Reményi-inspired Hungarian pieces. Dietrich was particularly struck by this 'unusual-looking young musician, seemingly little more than a boy in his short grey summer jacket, with his high voice and long fair hair. Especially fine were his energetic, characteristic mouth and the earnest deep gaze in which his gifted nature was clearly revealed.' Brahms and Dietrich quickly became friends, taking breakfast regularly together at an outdoor restaurant in the Hofgarten.

Things were moving fast. On 3 October Schumann finished orchestrating the Violin Concerto and learnt that, for the eighth time, Clara was pregnant (one child had died very young). On the 4th Brahms played a *Phantasie* for piano trio, a 'very youthful, wild piece' according to Clara, although no such work by him has survived. Louise Japha, a Hamburg friend of Brahms who was now living in Düsseldorf, was present that evening. She was a pianist and composer who was studying with Clara. She reported that after the *Phantasie* Brahms turned to her.

'What shall I play?' he asked her.

'The Scherzo,' she suggested. 'Schumann has heard your two sonatas; choose something short this time.'

After playing it to the company Brahms scolded Louise: 'Why did you give me that advice? Liszt didn't care for the Scherzo and now Schumann doesn't like it.'

He was wrong, since Schumann continued to be deeply impressed by everything he heard. Some songs were sung, perhaps the group Brahms had been composing in Göttingen. Always fiercely self-critical, Brahms destroyed a number of works that dissatisfied him, and that was the probable fate both of the *Phantasie* and of the violin sonata in A which the Schumanns heard on the 5th. The violinist was probably Ruppert Becker, Wasielewski's successor as leader of the Düsseldorf orchestra. Two days later a string quartet by Brahms was played, and of that too no trace survives. Clara played one or some of Robert's fugues on the name BACH originally for pedal-piano, and then, with Robert, the new duets entitled *Kinderball*. On the 8th she played Robert's F minor sonata (better known as the *Concert sans orchestre*, op. 14) for Brahms.

At this point Schumann wrote to Joachim in Karlsruhe comparing Brahms to a

36 Drawings by J.-J.-B. Laurens: (*top left*) Schumann; (*top right*) Brahms; (*bottom left*) Hiller; (*bottom right*) self-portrait

young eagle that had suddenly flown down from the Alps to land in Düsseldorf, and to a cataract like Niagara that falls from a great height with rainbows glistening in the spray, butterflies fluttering on the bank and nightingales singing on high. (Schumann could never resist the image of butterflies and nightingales.) 'Johannes is the true apostle that the Pharisees will never understand in a hundred years ... only the other apostles will understand him ... even Judas Iscariot perhaps ... This is only for the eyes of the apostle Joseph!'

Brahms too wrote to Joachim: 'I don't need to tell you how infinitely happy the Schumanns' reception, friendly beyond all expectation, has made me.' Through Dietrich he made other music-loving friends in Düsseldorf, such as a group of painters including Carl Sohn (who was painting Clara's portrait), Carl Lessing, Hans Gude (a Norwegian landscape painter) and Johann Schirmer (professor at the Düsseldorf Art Academy). His lifelong devotion to painters and painting flowered brightly here in Düsseldorf. He was invited to musical soirées at the house of the blind pianist Rosalie Leser, a friend of Clara's, and by Joseph Euler, a lawyer living near the barracks. At the Eulers' house he played Bach's Toccata in F and his own Scherzo, 'bending his head down over the keys and, as was his habit, humming the melody aloud as he played'. Torrential applause followed these brilliant performances. In his social life he managed, says Dietrich, to overcome his objection to the company of women, and he found that parties from which girls were not excluded were not as bad as he thought. One day he and Dietrich were part of a group that went on an excursion to Grafenberg (now a leafy eastern suburb of the city). Dietrich spotted him pulling turnips from the field, cleaning them, and facetiously offering them to the girls as refreshment. That day they spent the evening at Professor Sohn's house, where a group of Swedish student artists sang part-songs. Brahms replied by singing his own 'O versenk' and a song called 'Nachwirkung', again to enthusiastic applause. At this or some other such occasion Brahms played Schubert's Fantasia in G and more extracts from his own sonatas. Dietrich's summary is unusually vivid:

> The young musician had a strong physique. The severest mental work hardly seemed an exertion to him. He could sleep soundly at any hour of the day, if he so wished. With his friends he was lively, often exuberant, occasionally blunt, and full of pranks. With the boisterousness of youth he would run up my stairs, knock on the door with both fists and burst into the room without waiting for a reply. He tried to lower his strikingly high voice by speaking hoarsely, but that made an unpleasant sound.

He made regular visits to Louise Japha and her sister Minna, a painter, despite the latter being in quarantine for measles. He borrowed E. T. A. Hoffmann's stories from Schumann's library and read it with Louise, the book open in front of them.

Not only were the Schumanns the most important and the most admiring audience for his music, they encouraged him to pursue his star. Did he ever even mention the rejection of his manuscripts in Hamburg many years before? During these weeks in Düsseldorf he practised a great deal, fired, as Schumann thought, by Clara's example. He also composed the rest of the next piano sonata, eventually to be op. 5. Two of the movements were already done, as we have seen, but the three that remained to be composed were substantial pieces that framed the whole work and added up to the most solid and impressive piece he had yet written.

Schumann was composing too. The four *Märchenerzählungen* for clarinet, viola and piano were finished on the 11th, in parallel with some prose. He was now moved to make a public declaration of his admiration, so he began to draft an article for the *Neue Zeitschrift für Musik*, the Leipzig journal he had himself founded in 1834 and which was now, under Brendel's editorship, leaning more and more to the progressive school. It was currently serialising eight long articles about Wagner. Schumann's name still carried immense weight with the journal's readers and he knew that anything he wrote would be presented seriously in its pages. It is quite a short article, but it took him three or four days to write. Brahms at this point was quite unaware of the plan.

On the 11th the Schumanns and Brahms spent the evening with the landscape painter Schirmer, whose other guest was the French artist Jean-Joseph-Bonaventure Laurens. Laurens was employed in the medical faculty at Montpellier but his passions were painting and music. He had known Mendelssohn and had already corresponded with Schumann the year before. During the next week he visited the Schumanns almost every day. He would arrive at five when Schumann was ready to stop work and walk with him to a nearby brewery for a pint or two. (On one such occasion when having a drink with the violinist Becker Schumann threw down the newspaper he was reading and said, 'I can't read any more: I hear a constant A', an aural delusion to which he was occasionally subject.)

Schumann struck Laurens as friendly but unusually taciturn. He made four drawings of Schumann, one of which he gave to Clara, and a beautiful aquarelle of Clara herself. The drawings met with their sitters' approval, although Laurens, who knew a bit about medical matters, mentioned to Clara his concern that the pupils of Schumann's eyes were abnormally enlarged. She too was troubled by that. Laurens also drew two charming portraits of Brahms, looking no more than a boy, which Schumann hung over his work desk. He even asked for one of the portraits after his confinement to the asylum in Endenich, where it is still housed.

On the afternoon of the 12th Clara again played her husband's F minor sonata. She then bravely, we might think, played Brahms's E flat minor scherzo to its composer, and this was followed by Robert's Piano Trio no. 3 composed two years earlier, and now played by Becker and the cellist Robert Bockmühl. Laurens brought his family to listen and they enjoyed the music enormously.

The next day Schumann finished his article about Brahms while Clara had a concert engagement with her friend the soprano Mathilde Hartmann in Barmen, now a part of Wuppertal. The 14th brought another surprise visit from Joachim, this time on his way back from Karlsruhe, with many tales to tell about the festival and about his visit to Basel and the time he had spent with Wagner. The Schumanns knew Wagner well from their years together in Dresden, but although Robert admired his gifts as a composer for the stage he could never bring himself to see Wagner as a great musician in the broader sense. Wagner's conversational torrents used only to aggravate Schumann's taciturnity, and Clara's opinion of him was far from favourable. During Joachim's brief visit the Laurens family came in, Brahms and Dietrich too, and music was played: Schumann's D minor Violin Sonata and his Piano Trio no. 1, also in D minor. Clara played the piano in the chamber music while Brahms played some of his own pieces. At nine o'clock the whole party walked over to the Breidenbacher Hof on Alleestrasse (now Heinrich-Heine-Allee) for a merry supper. (The hotel still exists, but in a different location.)

Joachim had to leave for Hanover next morning, but Laurens had still one more visit to enjoy. String players were assembled and Schumann's Piano Quartet was played as well as his Piano Trio no. 2. Robert gave Laurens some sketches of his Piano Quintet and while he was about it gave Brahms some sketches of his string quartets. Joachim's departure prompted Schumann to dream up the idea of a violin sonata to be composed jointly by Brahms, Dietrich and himself, and offered to Joachim as a testimonial from his admirers. The sonata would enshrine the letters F, A and E to reflect Joachim's motto 'Frei aber einsam' ('free but solitary'), a somewhat baffling motto for someone who so clearly thrived on congenial company. Dietrich was assigned the first movement, Brahms the scherzo, while Schumann himself undertook the slow movement and the finale. First he had to finish a few more piano pieces, collected as *Gesänge der Frühe*, and some harmonisations of Paganini, but the slow movement, 'Intermezzo', was done on the 22nd and the finale just one day later. The theme is shown early on in Dietrich's movement:

Ex. 4 Albert Dietrich, Sonata 'FAE', first movement bars 19–21

The three-note theme appears clearly stated in both of Schumann's movements too, but it is missing from Brahms's scherzo. This is doubtless because he had already inserted it into the finale of the piano sonata he was writing at the time, the F minor sonata, op. 5; indeed, it may well have been this that gave Schumann the idea of doing the same thing throughout a violin sonata.

The plan was to present the new work to Joachim when he made yet another visit to Düsseldorf for a concert in one of the city's subscription concerts on Thursday 27

October. This was to be the last concert Schumann conducted in Düsseldorf. The programme included a performance of Joachim's *Hamlet* overture (revised since its play-through under Liszt in Weimar in May), the Beethoven Violin Concerto, a bass aria from Mendelssohn's *St Paul*, the first performance of Schumann's new *Phantasie* for violin and orchestra, and Mendelssohn's choral cantata *Die erste Walpurgisnacht*.

The following day three visitors came to call. Two of these were Bettina von Arnim, aged sixty-eight, sister of the poet Clemens Brentano, and her twenty-six-year-old daughter Gisela. Bettina was one of the foremost figures in the complicated panorama of German Romantic literature; there was no major figure in German intellectual life with whom she had not been close, including Goethe and Beethoven, both of whom she knew well. Her literary output, though less than that of her husband Achim von Arnim, was extensive, and she was a leading figure in the liberal politics of her time. She was also a modest composer. Visiting Weimar the year before with Gisela, she had befriended Liszt, while Joachim had fallen for her daughter, a relationship which blew hot and cold in the coming years, probably hotter on Joachim's side than on Gisela's. Since they were travelling from Bonn, where another daughter lived, their arrival in Düsseldorf was certainly timed to hear Joachim play.

The third visitor was Liszt's disciple the poet and composer Peter Cornelius, who knew Bettina and Gisela from their time in Weimar. From his parents' home in Mainz he had attended the Karlsruhe Festival, visited Wagner in Basel, and then returned to Mainz, where he spoke of his 'Wandercharakter'. On a visit the next week to Bettina von Arnim in Bonn, she evidently persuaded Cornelius to go with them to see Schumann, whom he had always admired, though there had never been any contact between them. This was the only occasion on which the two men met. Cornelius had not been in Weimar during Brahms's visit, so this was their first encounter too. If Cornelius had hoped to spend some time with Schumann and talk about his own work, he chose the worst moment to come, since all attention was focussed on Joachim and Brahms.

The three visitors were thus present with Dietrich, Brahms and a considerable group of local friends when Joachim received the surprise gift of the FAE sonata. Gisela, in peasant costume, presented him with a basket of flowers. He and Clara read the work through and Joachim was challenged to identify the composer of each movement, a challenge which he met without the slightest difficulty.

Next day, in a public recital with Clara in a hotel on Bergerstrasse managed by Jakob Cürten, Joachim played Beethoven's Kreutzer Sonata, Schumann's Sonata no. 1 and the Paganini caprices (nos. 1 and 24) to which Schumann had recently added a piano accompaniment. After that he had to return to Hanover where he was expecting a visit from Berlioz. He left the FAE sonata with Dietrich for some revision, but he never played it again and it remained unseen until after the death of two of its composers. At the end of his life, in 1906 (Dietrich was still alive), Joachim allowed the Berlin Brahms-Gesellschaft to publish Brahms's movement, the scherzo, but the full work was not published until 1935. Schumann meanwhile, even before Joachim had left, began two more movements to complete what he then classified as his Violin Sonata no. 3. This too remained invisible, proscribed by the critical Clara, and was not published until 1956. A similar fate befell the Violin Concerto, which Schumann had finished on 1 October. Both Clara and Joachim felt it to be unworthy of the master, perhaps even tainted by incipient dementia, and suppressed it. It was not performed and published until 1937, and is still an unhappy stepsister to the great violin concertos of Beethoven, Mendelssohn and Brahms. Worse still was Clara's condemnation of five *Romanzen* for cello and piano which Schumann wrote immediately after Joachim and Brahms had left: she destroyed them some forty years later.

On the day after Joachim's concert with the orchestra Schumann's article about Brahms, headed 'Neue Bahnen' ('New Paths') appeared in the *Neue Zeitschrift für Musik*. Published in Leipzig, it took a day or two to reach Düsseldorf where a plan was hatched to keep Brahms from seeing it. Joachim had already seen it in manuscript. Of all Schumann's many writings for that journal this is the most celebrated and the one that had the most far-reaching effect. It is not very long: it is almost entirely contained on the journal's front page, but the tone of confident judgment is truly remarkable. He names a dozen young composers whose works have come to his attention in the nearly ten years since he gave up the editorship, including Gade, Franz and Heller. He even names both Joachim and Dietrich in this category. These have all shown ways to inject a new element into music.

> But I thought, as I watched them with the greatest interest, that after such a build-up someone would suddenly appear who would give the most perfect expression to the spirit of the time, and he would display his mastery not in the process of development, but fully formed, like Minerva emerging fully armed from the head of Zeus. He has indeed come, one over whose cradle the graces and heroes kept watch. His name is Johannes Brahms, from Hamburg. [...] He has arrived displaying all the outward signs that proclaim him to be one of the elect. Seated at the piano, he began to reveal wondrous regions of music, drawing us into ever more magical enchantment. His playing is brilliant too; he can make the piano sound like an orchestra of wailing or rejoicing voices.

He lists some of the music Brahms has written and then echoes his letter to Joachim: 'Then it was as though he brought it all together like streams flowing together and crashing over a waterfall into the turbulent waves below, spreading the rainbow of peace and accompanied by butterflies fluttering on the bank and nightingales singing aloft.' No mention of Pharisees this time.

If he embarks on larger choral and orchestral music, Schumann suggests, he will reveal still more glimpses of the secrets of the spirit. Brahms is a mighty warrior. And invoking the image of a closed circle to which only the select few are admitted, recalling the Davidsbündler of his earlier years, Schumann declares that as a member of the elite circle Brahms will be the one to spread truth and light around the world.

The *Neue Zeitschrift für Musik* was the most widely read music journal in Germany, so a Messianic declaration of this kind from its founder and former editor attracted the immediate attention of every musician far and wide. Mason recalled what an impact it made in Weimar.

'Have you seen Schumann's article?' Liszt asked von Bülow.

'I'm not losing any sleep over Mozart–Brahms or Schumann–Brahms,' he replied. 'Only fifteen years ago Schumann spoke in similar terms about the genius of Sterndale Bennett.'

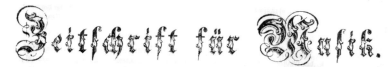

37 Schumann's article 'Neue Bahnen'

Some of the composers Schumann had named took umbrage even though he had intended to present them as members of the elect. Above all it burdened Brahms with the responsibility to live up to well-nigh impossible expectations wherever he chose to appear.

Quite unaware of the fuse about to detonate his sudden worldwide celebrity, Brahms brought his visit to an end since he had promised to follow Joachim to Hanover, and he planned to go back to Bonn for a few days first. Although Joachim was the Schumanns' guest when he came as concert soloist, Brahms had not been staying in their house, which must have been filled to bursting with the six children and their servants; where he was living we don't know. Perhaps not in the Roman Emperor Hotel all these weeks; more likely in lodgings; perhaps he was put up by one of the Schumanns' wide circle of friends.

Joachim left on 1 November and Brahms on the following day. (On the 1st Wagner had just begun to compose *Das Rheingold*.) It had been an extraordinarily eventful month for both of them. Brahms's meeting with Schumann had launched his career in more ways than he could possibly have foreseen. The shy Brahms and the taciturn Schumann seem to have hit it off at once. Brahms's lifelong devotion to Schumann and his music is perfectly evident from his music, which from now on constantly echoes features of the older composer's style in harmony or rhythm. Schumann's fondness for shifting the pulse away from the main beat, for example, is also an unmistakable characteristic of Brahms's music. The latter's delight in chamber music forms such as violin sonata, piano trio and piano quartet may equally be attributed to these October music sessions. In later years Brahms said Schumann only taught him to play chess, but this masks an indebtedness which he would have been the last to deny. Schumann also promoted Brahms's career in a highly practical way by recommending him to Breitkopf & Härtel in Leipzig, the publishers that were soon to accept his first handful of opus numbers and pay him handsomely for them. Liszt, of course, had recommended him to them already. As for Brahms's devotion to Clara, that is an oft-told story that belongs rightly to a later chronicle, although we know that Brahms's playing and his music moved her profoundly from the moment she first heard it. Over him she exercised a spell that remained with him throughout his life, immeasurable in its effect.

All this superb music making and good company contributed to Schumann's remarkably high spirits. But there was serious trouble brewing in the city chambers. In the middle of this same October he conducted a Mass by Moritz Hauptmann in the Maximilian Church. No mention of it is found in either Robert's or Clara's journal because it was a fiasco in which, among other mishaps, he did what conductors only do in bar-room jokes about bad conductors: he kept on beating after the music had stopped. This is hard to believe of a musician of such technical sophistication and such creative fluency, but it was real enough to the chorus who had learned in the previous few years to expect the worst when he was in charge. These members of the Gesangverein refused to perform for him in future. The chairman of the association and another member had words with Schumann a few days later. He viewed their complaints as shameless, but they did have a responsibility to their members and to their audience. Tausch, Schumann's deputy, was put in charge of the Mendelssohn *Die erste Walpurgisnacht* performance on 27 October, but that did not prevent mishaps in the rest of the programme which Schumann did conduct. In a rehearsal of Joachim's *Hamlet*, for example, the horn player had not made an important entry, having received no cue from the conductor. Joachim pointed it out, but at the performance there was still no cue and still no entry.

Two members of the committee discreetly suggested to Clara that her husband should hand over the reins to Tausch, conducting only his own works in future. Clara was outraged, assuming that Tausch was conspiring to unseat him. On 9 November Schumann informed the committee that he considered their suggestion a breach of his contract and that he would not hand in his notice, if at all, until his term was up. But he did not take any part in the next subscription concert, leaving Tausch to do all the conducting. When told that he was the one to be breaking his contract, Schumann drew a heavy line under the whole unhappy history of his employment in Düsseldorf by saying 'After such happenings, we can have nothing to do with one another.'

How much this protracted humiliation contributed to Schumann's approaching decline is impossible to say. His medical condition was a ticking bomb. We simply have to be glad that his mind and body were whole enough throughout the month of October to recognise the genius in Brahms and to have enjoyed some of the finest music-making of his life.

CHAPTER 11

Liszt, Wagner and Berlioz in Paris

OCTOBER

O N the day after the Karlsruhe Festival, Thursday 6 October, Liszt led a party of enthusiastic supporters on an expedition to Basel to visit Wagner. They took the train the 125 miles south into Switzerland and arrived at the Les Trois Rois Hotel in Basel by six o'clock, where Wagner was due to meet them. Still today impressively overlooking the Rhine, the hotel had once housed Napoleon, so perhaps it was up to Wagner's standards of luxury. He had had an uncomfortable overnight journey from Zurich in the diligence and was there ahead of Liszt's party. He was sitting in the hotel dining-room that evening when he heard the trumpet fanfare that announces the King's arrival in *Lohengrin* sung by a handful of vigorous male voices in the lobby. The door opened and Liszt entered with his merry supporters whom he introduced one by one.

There were six young musicians in the group: von Bülow, Joachim, Cornelius, Reményi, Pohl and Pruckner. Mason, who knew Wagner from a visit in Zurich with his parents a year earlier, never much liked Wagner's music and declined to join them. They were all remarkably young. Cornelius at twenty-eight was the oldest, and Pruckner the youngest at nineteen. Von Bülow knew Wagner from his stint as conductor at the Zurich opera two years before under Wagner's tutelage. Joachim, on whom *Lohengrin* had made such a profound impression in 1850, had never met him. He was particularly keen to see Wagner now having cancelled his earlier plan to go with Liszt to Zurich in July. Cornelius, Pohl and Pruckner were also meeting Wagner – so widely talked about and so little seen – for the first time.

Also in the party were Princess Carolyne with her daughter Marie and her nephew Eugène von Sayn-Wittgenstein. Wagner was once again deeply impressed by the Princess's penetrating mind and eager interest in what everyone was doing. Sixteen-year-old Marie fascinated him with her dark pensive eyes, and seemed to be fully alert to everything going on.

The first evening developed into one of those rumbustious affairs, aided by what Wagner called Liszt's 'magnificent unconventionality'. Wagner had been looking forward to his reunion with Liszt for weeks; Liszt was ready to relax after the arduous tensions of the festival; and young men in a group in a strange city need no incitement to enjoy themselves. Noticing at one point that Pohl had disappeared, Wagner went to his room and found him suffering from a splitting headache. Wagner's sympathetic visit (he claims) was all that was needed to produce an instant cure. Pohl jumped out of bed, put on his clothes and rejoined the party, which continued far into the night.

The next day, as Marie later remembered, there was music all day long, everyone playing or singing their own compositions in hoarse and quavery voices. Wagner's gentle speaking voice moved her to tears. Normally, she said, he bubbled with jokes, wild ideas and comic remarks. In the evening Wagner read the text of *Siegfried* to the company, most of whom had probably already read it in Weimar but who were now enthralled by Wagner's energetic delivery. Not to be outdone, Liszt then played Beethoven's mighty *Hammerklavier* sonata.

On Saturday afternoon they all left Basel. Joachim left his glasses behind and Cornelius left his wallet and his passport. Von Bülow punned that too much Piesporter had made him a poor passport-porter. Pruckner took von Bülow's overcoat instead of his own, leaving in the pockets a red silk handkerchief, a hairbrush, comb and mirror, and a pair and a half (!) of black gloves.

Pohl, Pruckner, Cornelius and Reményi returned directly to Germany in various directions while Liszt, Wagner, the Princess, her daughter, Eugène, Joachim and von Bülow took the route through France along the west bank of the Rhine up to

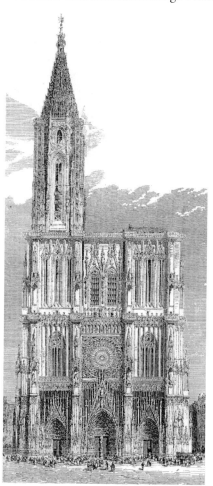

38 Strasbourg Cathedral

Strasbourg. Fortunately Wagner had obtained a French passport at the very last minute. The German party ran into trouble in Baden-Baden by singing the *Lohengrin* fanfare again, not in a hotel but in the street. The police were called and some crafty explanations were required to set the matter straight. The others meanwhile spent the night in Strasbourg, and there the ladies decided not to return to Weimar as planned but to go on with Liszt and Wagner to Paris because Marie wanted to hear Wagner read the rest of his long opera text, which he had not yet had time to do.

Joachim and von Bülow parted from them there and crossed back over the Rhine. Von Bülow headed back to Karlsruhe, having gazed with amazement for the first time at Strasbourg cathedral. Karlsruhe seemed lifeless now that the festival was over. He returned to his previous room in the Erbprinz Hotel expecting his mother to arrive from Switzerland, but they met instead in Stuttgart where he was planning to give a concert; Joachim even promised to see if there was a job for him in Hanover. Liszt was full of plans for the all-Wagner concert he was to give in Berlin. (The Berliners turned it down.) Joachim himself went with von Bülow as far as Karlsruhe and then continued north, reaching Düsseldorf on the 14th. Although Wagner observed a certain aloofness in Joachim, their parting was warm and friendly. Von Bülow told Wagner that Joachim was troubled after reading *Das Judenthum in der Musik*. However affected he may have been by that injudicious pamphlet, Joachim would already have been aware of anti-semitic feeling quite widely entertained in Germany, if not always so brazenly expressed as by Wagner. But aloofness does not preclude admiration. However widely it might be assumed that Joachim was tempted by his friendship with Schumann and Brahms to distance himself from Wagner and however vehemently he later expressed his opposition, the impression Wagner made on Joachim during those two days was strong and positive. He was so impressed by the power of Wagner's *Ring* readings that he promised to lead the orchestra when the work would one day be performed. In turn Wagner later thanked Liszt for bringing Joachim to Basel. After his return to Hanover a fortnight later Joachim wrote to Wehner in Göttingen:

> Wagner is one of those rare people who act as they do because the inner truth (or at any rate what they take to be the inner truth) will not permit them to do otherwise. [...] His every movement and every tone of voice are like heralds proclaiming the integrity and nobility of his soul. When you hear him read his *Siegfried* you realise for the first time that what his writings express in the crudest manner is, when you overlook his disturbing fondness for labyrinthine argument, nothing less than a purely artistic enthusiasm, which ignores custom and recognises only feeling.

He compared Wagner to a hard, solid rock jutting out of the sea, in contrast with ordinary musicians everywhere who were like a broad colourless sandbank.

THE purpose of the trip to Paris is not entirely clear. Liszt went there partly to see his three children, who had lived there all their lives, and his mother, who had returned there after a long stay in Weimar. He also needed to examine a monstrous pedal-piano that was being built for him by the firm of Alexandre and Co. It had three keyboards and a pedal board and was supposed to rival an orchestra in the hands of a nimble player. The manufacturers wanted to call it a 'Liszt-piano'. Berlioz, a good friend of the Alexandres, had supervised its construction and declared it to be all it should be, so it was ready to be shipped to Weimar once Liszt himself had seen it.

In addition, Paris was the city where Liszt grew up and where he enjoyed his first friendships and first successes, so he had a wide circle of friends and connections. Whatever the Germans wanted to believe, Paris was still the world's musical capital in two spheres: in the world of the piano and in grand opera. French opera enjoyed as much currency on German stages as Italian opera, perhaps more. The Opéra itself represented the pinnacle of stage technology and extravagant productions, without a rival. Piano-makers and music-publishers were more numerous in Paris than anywhere else; foreign musicians were drawn to Paris in great numbers, many of them pianists; and the intense interest in musical events, especially opera, displayed by highly cultivated Parisians was endemic to that city and to that culture.

Wagner's attitude to Paris was profoundly ambivalent, since he had been unhappy and unsuccessful during the two and a half years he and Minna spent there from 1839 to 1842, and with the exception of Berlioz he had no very high opinion of French music. On the other hand he knew it was a source of much that was new and enterprising in the world of opera and he still regarded a production at the Paris Opéra as the pinnacle of any composer's ambition. The eventual staging of *Tannhäuser* there in 1861 violently dispelled that notion, but in 1853 he was still ready to make the right political moves to bring this about. He said he was anxious about Paris for fear of displaying his bad French to Berlioz, but his French was sufficiently fluent and useful to serve him in any social situation in Paris. For Liszt, of course, French was the language he always preferred to speak. As we have seen, Wagner had an almost unquenchable thirst for Liszt's company, and this more than anything spurred him to join him on this trip at a time when he equally longed to begin the task of composing that lay ahead. On 29 September, before their meeting in Basel, Wagner told Liszt, 'I have a great desire finally to get to work. My normal life is only bearable when I devote myself entirely to myself. Furthermore I cannot keep silent any more – which I would dearly love to do – unless I compose this music at once.' He envied Liszt's intensely active career and had come to see his own inactivity of the last few months as the worst thing that could befall him. 'Die Ruhe ist mein Tod', he said. The Paris trip meant that a few more weeks would yet pass before his real work began.

The French musical press were quite excited about Liszt's visit, having mentioned the possibility of his coming as early as July, but as usual they were much more excited by the latest goings-on in their opera houses. There was talk of Gounod's *La Nonne sanglante* being ready soon for performance at the Opéra; excitement over Halévy's *Le Nabab* at the Opéra-Comique; a mystery opera at the Théâtre-Lyrique: would it be a Verdi opera for the favoured soprano of the day Mme Ugalde? Would it be Meyerbeer's *Semiramide* (which was over thirty years old)? Is it an unknown Rossini? What was Meyerbeer's new opera at the Opéra-Comique going to be like? There was excitement over a new star, Marie Cabel, whose brilliant début in Adam's *Le Bijou perdu* at the Théâtre-Lyrique on 6 October was the talk of the town. *La France musicale* even announced that Liszt was writing a grand opera for 'one of our theatres', perhaps to be played this coming winter. Where they picked up this piece of gossip is another mystery, since his efforts to compose an opera *Sardanapale* had produced merely a pile of incomplete sketches in 1851. News from abroad was scanty at best: the French never picked up Schumann's promotion of Brahms, in fact they never understood the cauldron of new ideas circulating in German musical discussion, confident that Paris's supremacy as a cultural capital would remain indefinitely unchallenged.

The city was beginning to build on its charm and magnetism and to create its image as the tourist mecca it has been ever since. Plans for creating grand new boulevards were taking shape. Louis-Napoleon had proclaimed himself Emperor Napoleon III the previous December, causing consternation among liberals, some of whom, notably Victor Hugo, preferred self-imposed exile to suffering the regime. Berlioz was probably relieved to have missed the elaborate festivities mounted throughout the city in mid-August to proclaim a message of imperial magnificence to the Emperor's subjects. In order to seem Napoleonic, the old Emperor's nephew was allowing himself to get entangled in the dispute between Russia and Turkey that would soon lead to the Crimean War. Wagner wandered around the city, recalling his stay over a decade before, half pained by what he remembered of his own lack of success, half fascinated by the prosperity all around him and by the Parisian taste for chic. He wondered how he could afford some of the elegant things he saw in the shops.

The five of them (plus Hermann and the Princess's servants) arrived in Paris on Sunday 9 October. They stayed at the Hôtel des Princes at 97 Rue de Richelieu, close to the Opéra in the Rue Le Peletier and the Opéra-Comique just behind the hotel. It was one of Paris's finest hotels with forty rooms. Wagner's bill at the Hôtel des Princes was paid by Liszt, of course.

On their first day in Paris Liszt hastened to see his three children, the offspring of his scandalous liaison with Marie d'Agoult in the 1830s, scandalous because Marie had never been divorced by her husband, the Comte d'Agoult. The affair had come to an acrimonious end in 1844, at which point Liszt was almost continually far from Paris as a touring virtuoso. Under French law he had custody, which allowed him to place the children in the care of his mother and of various boarding schools in Paris and forbid them to see their own mother. He was briefly passing through the city in 1846, but it is not clear if he saw his children then. If not, nearly ten years had passed since he had seen them. Blandine was now seventeen, Cosima fifteen and Daniel fourteen. Since 1850 they had been in the care of two elderly straight-laced French ladies, Madame Patersi and her sister, living on the Rue Casimir-Périer near the Invalides. Madame Patersi had been Carolyne's governess in Russia many years before. To Liszt's annoyance the children had contrived to visit their mother from time to time in her rather grand villa near the Arc de Triomphe, and despite what we would regard as Liszt's inhumane neglect they always felt attached to him and followed with keen interest his life in Weimar and elsewhere. When Liszt walked into the house on 10 October, they were thrilled to see him; it must have been an extraordinary moment of recognition, especially for him to see his children so transformed. Marie Sayn-Wittgenstein was there with her mother, both meeting the children for the first time. Carolyne complimented the children on their good looks and gave them each a small gold watch. Marie described them as somewhat unsophisticated and rather bewildered. Blandine was prettier and plumper than Cosima, and clearly ready to please. Cosima was in the throes of adolescence: tall, angular and fair-skinned with a large mouth and long nose, the very image of her father. She had beautiful long blond hair. Her child's heart seethed with all the fury of a volcano, Marie reported, thinking perhaps of the woman she later became, 'dark passion and boundless vanity pulsated through her veins'.

With hindsight, we know this was a historic moment: Wagner was there too, setting eyes on his second wife for the first time. His autobiography, written under the merciless gaze of Cosima herself, scarcely mentions the meeting. In any case he was almost certainly more than a little taken on this trip by Marie, the same age as Cosima, who was spellbound by his readings of the *Ring* poems and who was, according to the playwright Hebbel, the most wondrous blend of culture and nature he had ever seen. Emanuel Geibel (whom we encountered in Carlsbad) called her a 'fairy-tale flower with a dawning secret in its cup'.

Berlioz joined them at some stage; he had probably not met Liszt's children before. This was also historic for the reason that this, with their breakfast meeting next day, was the only time that Berlioz, Liszt and Wagner were ever all in a room together (unless Wagner attended Liszt's concert in Paris on 20 April 1840; we know that Berlioz was there). They all had a supper, followed by a reading by Wagner of the poem of *Götterdämmerung*. The children knew very little German and Berlioz knew none, so it must have been a strange experience for them. Wagner said Berlioz endured it with admirable patience. After the reading Marie took down from the wall a laurel wreath which Daniel had won at school and placed it on Wagner's head. Cosima later remembered: 'I did nothing but look at the floor; my weak eyes and shy disposition made me unable to do anything but snatch at everything by stealth, as it were.' Present too, although no one ever mentions her, was Liszt's mother Anna.

Berlioz was fortunate to be in Paris when the visitors came. He had planned to be in Hanover by now, giving concerts with Joachim, but King Georg was not back from his summer holidays in Schloss Rotenkirchen and insisted that the concerts be postponed. He was also able to enjoy a quick visit from his son Louis whose ship *Le Corse* had docked at Calais after sailing around the British Isles. After a week in Paris with his father he returned to Calais on the day that Liszt and Wagner came into town.

In the month since his return from Baden-Baden and Frankfurt Berlioz had resumed his regular métier as critic for the *Journal des débats*. He reviewed Halévy's *Le Nabab* and a long forgotten opera by Adolphe Vogel named *La Moissonneuse*. He had attended a performance of Meyerbeer's *Les Huguenots* at the Opéra in the presence of the Emperor and Empress and reviewed that. He saw *Bonsoir, voisin* by Jean-Alexandre Poise at the Théâtre-Lyrique and reviewed that, and when Liszt and Wagner arrived in Paris he had just been to see Adam's *Le Bijou perdu* and had just written his review of that. Barely a note of what he had heard gave him any joy; barely a note of it is ever heard today. The grinding misery of this task struck him eternally as a sign that something was wrong: he knew he should be composing and conducting, but his taste for the former had left him, and his chances of the latter depended entirely on the whim of German and English entrepreneurs. He had German concerts set up in the immediate future and he had also received a promising proposition from London, but that seems to have vanished into thin air. His willingness to cram a number of reviews into a single month may be ascribed to his plans to spend the next two months in Germany. He was also employed as librarian by the Paris Conservatoire, a job to which he gave very little of his time but which required him always to seek the permission of the director, Auber, when he planned to be absent. This month too he had a large pile of proofs to correct for the full score and vocal score of *La Damnation de Faust*, to be published in 1854 with a dedication to Liszt.

He was now due to leave Paris for Brunswick on the Wednesday after Liszt's arrival, so there was little time to meet. Following the Monday evening at Madame Patersi's, Berlioz invited them all to breakfast with him and his Marie in the Rue de Boursault next day, the Tuesday. He already knew Carolyne and her daughter from his visit to Weimar the year before. Afterwards, for Wagner's benefit, Liszt played selections from *Benvenuto Cellini* with Berlioz singing the voice parts.

That evening Wagner went to a play at the Théâtre Français, but he developed a bad headache and had to leave early. Meanwhile Berlioz was obliged to attend one of Meyerbeer's famous dinners at the Café de Paris. These dinners were generally designed to win Paris's leading journalists over to Meyerbeer's cause, in this case to prepare them for the production of his opera *L'Étoile du nord*, which was being intensively rehearsed at the Opéra-Comique, a theatre not accustomed to the weight and scale of a Meyerbeer work. He was more than usually nervous about it. He was in the habit of holding his work back in order to make revisions and improvements, otherwise this one would have been staged earlier. In fact it did not open for another four months. The dinner was small but select, in the view of Jules Janin, a prolific critic and writer and Berlioz's colleague on the *Journal des débats*. The other guests that evening were the Vicomte Daru, a wealthy businessman, the philosopher Victor Cousin, the Bertin brothers, owners of the *Journal des débats*, and the writer Ludovic Vitet. Meyerbeer, who shared with Wagner an obsessive concern with his own health, hosted the dinner after spending all day in bed with a string of unpleasant ailments.

Janin felt sorry for Berlioz having to go all the way to Germany to make a living. 'He would certainly have a fine position now if he had married *une honnête femme* and stayed put where he is' was his absurd comment. For Berlioz, time spent with Liszt and Wagner had undoubtedly increased the rush of business in his preparations for the German tour. He was also exercised by the recent death of George Onslow which had created a vacancy for a musician at the Institut, a prize he very much coveted for the prestige and the stipend it carried. He had already put himself forward twice without success, and he was to be disappointed twice more before finally being elected to membership of the 'immortals' in 1856. Knowing he would be abroad, his submission this time merely took the form of a letter of intent, which he knew was not enough. After a wild day of preparation and packing (and perhaps a visit to his sick wife Harriet in the Rue Blanche) he and Marie left for Brunswick, via Cologne, at eight o'clock on Wednesday evening.

Meyerbeer's diary entry for the Thursday reads: 'Visited Baron James Rothschild who is here with Richard Wagner and who was very concerned to see me at a third place without visiting me. A few hours later he visited me.' This cryptic entry is the only mention of Wagner in his diaries for this period, which leaves the question open whether Meyerbeer and Wagner actually met at this time. Meyerbeer had evidently not read *Das Judenthum in der Musik*, which attacks him only by inference, but he did know about *Oper und Drama*, in which he is both named and vilified, so he might well have been reluctant to speak to him; Wagner likewise had made up his mind that Meyerbeer was a charlatan, so a meeting is unlikely. What connection Wagner might have had with James de Rothschild, head of the French branch of the Rothschild bank and one of the wealthiest men in France, is hard to say, unless Wagner thought he might touch him for a franc or two.

Whatever occupied Wagner on Thursday, Liszt went that day with the Princess, Marie, Eugène Sayn-Wittgenstein and his three children to visit his old friend Janin. Janin wrote to his wife that Liszt

> stormed in like an explosion, talking at the top of his voice, smoking, singing and striking the piano so forcefully that the unfortunate instrument must have thought its last hour had come. [...] Liszt is as good a fellow as ever, boisterous and rowdy, well content with his glory and pretty ignorant of everything that's happened in Paris since he was last here. The Princess is too much!

At one point in the conversation when nothing of particular moment was being said, she fell on her knees at Liszt's feet crying 'Let me worship you!' 'She is a kind woman, rather ugly, with a pointed nose,' Janin went on.

> She smokes cigars like a trooper and has teeth as black as the bottom of a frying-pan. She is evidently a bit mad, and I fear she'll drive the poor fellow crazy with her follies.

On Friday afternoon, after a morning rehearsal at the Opéra-Comique, Meyerbeer paid a call on Liszt and the Princess at their hotel. Wagner was probably out. Meyerbeer knew the hotel well since he had stayed there many times in the past for its convenient proximity to the theatres. He now preferred to stay at the Hôtel du Danube, 11 Rue Richepance, near the Madeleine, opposite the Opéra's scenery storage facility. He did not attend a performance of his own *Robert le diable* at the Opéra that evening, but Liszt, Wagner and the ladies did. Both men knew the theatre well from their earlier sojourns in Paris. Liszt had even had his only opera, *Don Sanche*, performed there in 1825 when he was fourteen. Both men had seen *Robert le diable* there too; in fact it was one of the first operas Wagner worked on in his first job as repetiteur at the theatre in Würzburg in 1833. At that time and during his earlier stay in Paris Wagner admitted to admiring Meyerbeer's

39 Wagner, by Eugène Sayn-Wittgenstein

music, and he learnt much from it. Now he had turned against it, and Liszt too was depressed by the performance, even though he was obviously thrilled to be in that theatre again. The *Revue et gazette musicale* reported that the revival was poor; the production had been in the repertoire for over twenty years and was showing its age.

There is no hint that they attended a much-anticipated première at the Opéra three days later: *Le Maître chanteur* by the Belgian aristocrat Limnander de Nieuwenhove. At the back of Wagner's mind was the outline of an opera about the *Maîtres chanteurs* of Nuremberg, but he need have had no fear that Limnander had stolen his thunder. The new work was a typically contrived story about an emperor in disguise, etc., etc., which was revived in 1856 but otherwise sank without trace. Being out of the country, Berlioz was spared the task of having to finesse his opinion of the music for the *Journal des débats*.

Wagner stayed in his room a good deal when the others were out, suffering from nervous headaches. Eugène made a medallion of his image during the Paris visit. Then as he strolled along the Rue de Richelieu on Saturday 15th he unexpectedly ran into his Zurich friends the Wesendoncks, who were spending a fortnight in Paris on their way back from New York. One can imagine him beaming with pleasure and surprise at seeing Generosity and Beauty arm in arm. He had not seen them since his concerts in May and he made immediate plans to introduce Liszt to them the following afternoon. After that Liszt and the whole party, including his children, were invited to the house of Pierre Erard, head of the firm that made some of the best pianos and harps in the world, and there Liszt played to them all after dinner. Cosima was particularly thrilled to hear her father's brilliant playing, famous all over the world but unfamiliar to her. It was the Erard family that looked after Liszt and his parents when they arrived from Vienna in 1823. Liszt was then twelve and the firm was run by its founder Sébastien. Pierre, his nephew, was now in charge, ready to celebrate the fact that the firm and the virtuoso had both benefited immeasurably from their long interdependence.

On Monday night (while Limnander was playing at the Opéra) they were entertained by the Countess Marie Kalergis, who had moved back to Paris, where she maintained a salon, after her long summer stay in Baden-Baden. She was anxious to see Liszt and Wagner again. Her close connection with her uncle, the Russian Chancellor Nesselrode, who had guided Russia's foreign policy for nearly forty years and was now spearheading the expansion of Russian influence in the Balkans, created some problems with her liberal French friends. Wagner found her alarmingly chilly, especially since he had heard she was on suspiciously close terms both with Cavaignac, the general who had put down the 1848 rebellion in Paris, and with Louis Napoleon, now the Emperor. When the conversation turned to the Emperor, Wagner said he could not understand how anyone could expect great things from a man whom no woman could really love, which created something of an embarrassing silence. After dinner, while Liszt played the piano, Marie Sayn-Wittgenstein noticed that Wagner had moved away from the group; at the same time he seems especially to have noticed *her*. The Countess suggested a second evening together, but once Liszt had left Paris, Wagner was evidently reluctant to return. In later years, though, especially during Wagner's stay in Paris for the 1861 *Tannhäuser* and when *Das Rheingold* and *Die Walküre* were performed in Munich, she became one of his most staunch and most generous supporters.

Wagner's political standing was not irrelevant. There were rumours that he was to be sent back across the border at once, but in fact he received a visit from a French police officer who assured him that he would be allowed to stay a month; he even seemed to be disappointed that Wagner did not intend to spend quite that much time in his city.

On Tuesday evening, the 18th, they were entertained, this time invited by Jules Janin. Wagner, who went with them, found his French very hard to understand. Janin stood in for Berlioz at the Opéra the night before and could therefore tell Liszt and Wagner anything they needed to know about the new Limnander opera. He liked it!

That day a message arrived from Weimar requiring Liszt to return at once to his duties. He had planned to celebrate his forty-second birthday, 22 October, with all his children and friends in Paris, but he had to leave with the two ladies on Wednesday 19th instead. The children were upset to see him go so suddenly. They had not seen as much of him as they would have liked, especially since he seemed to go out with Carolyne and Marie on a few occasions, visiting museums and suchlike, without including them. They did all however have an outing to the Palais Royal one evening for dinner. In future Liszt arranged to see his children at least once a year and to bring them more closely into his own life.

One of the near-misses of history must be chronicled at this point. Following the premières of *Il trovatore* in January and *La traviata* in March, Verdi was enjoying a crescendo of success. He was in correspondence with the management of the Paris Opéra concerning his next work which would eventually be *Les Vêpres siciliennes*, staged in 1855. In order to work at close quarters with his librettist, the eternally recalcitrant Eugène Scribe, Verdi had decided to spend the winter in Paris. He left his farm at Sant' Agata on Saturday 15 October. The journey would have taken anything from three days to a week, in which case he would have arrived between the 18th and the 22nd. Liszt's party left on the 19th; Wagner was there for one more week. Verdi and Giuseppina Strepponi (like Liszt's Princess and Berlioz's Marie, she was now his permanent partner) took an apartment at 4 Rue Richer, close to the Conservatoire and five minutes' walk from Liszt and Wagner's hotel. He probably had no idea that Liszt and Wagner were in Paris; they probably had no idea Verdi was coming. His arrival was not reported in the musical press until the 30th, by which time Wagner too had left. In any case, while Liszt knew some of Verdi's music, having conducted *Ernani* in Weimar and composed paraphrases on *Ernani* and *I Lombardi*, Wagner had never heard a note of it (*Ernani* was played in German in Zurich earlier that year, but there's no sign that he heard it) and had no notion that this man might be the other great musical dramatist of the century. Verdi knew nothing of Wagner other than his reputation and was never particularly curious to know more. They never met. Nor did Liszt and Verdi, although both attended the same performance of Massenet's *Le Cid* at the Opéra on 27 March 1886.

Wagner had arranged for Minna to join him, disappointed that she missed Liszt by one day, but relieved perhaps not to confront the formidable Carolyne; Wagner may not have wanted her to observe his interest in Marie. The Wagners had to leave the Hôtel des Princes and move to the Hôtel des Italiens just round the corner in the Boulevard des Italiens and still close to the opera houses and all the best restaurants. They were presumably now having to pay their own bills, for which purpose Wagner had begged his Zurich friend Sulzer to help him out. They sought out two German acquaintances from their stay in Paris many years before. Ernst Benedikt Kietz was a painter who had worked in Paris since 1838 while Gottfried Engelbert Anders had been working at the Bibliothèque Nationale, just along the Rue de Richelieu, for many years. They all got together, including Eugène von Sayn-Wittgenstein, to celebrate Liszt's birthday on 22 October in the honoree's absence. Wagner persuaded Erard to send a piano round to his hotel room so that he could play not Liszt's music but his own: bits of *Tannhäuser* and *Lohengrin* exuberantly sung to his own accompaniment. Wagner arranged for Kietz to paint one or both of the Wesendoncks.

In Paris Wagner had one of those deeply affecting experiences which he acknowledged stayed with him all his life. Before Liszt left they heard the Maurin-Chevillard Quartet give what he called a concert, but since the quartet were giving no public concerts at that time, it was probably a rehearsal or a private performance. This group, consisting of Maurin and Mas (violins), Chevillard (viola) and

40 The Maurin-Chevillard Quartet

Sabatier (cello), had formed the year before for the express purpose of performing the late Beethoven quartets, which were still little known in Paris despite some pioneering performances by Baillot and others. Beginning in December 1852 they inaugurated an annual three-month series of concerts which continued until 1870, playing almost nothing but late Beethoven. Liszt and Wagner heard the E flat quartet, op. 127, and the C sharp minor quartet, op. 131. Wagner had heard both works before, but this, he said, was the first time he had really grasped their full stature, especially op. 131. He compared the effect of this performance with that of the Ninth Symphony which he had heard at the Paris Conservatoire under Habeneck in 1839. 'I was again able to admire the great artistic zeal which the French devote to these musical treasures, still so clumsily performed by German musicians.'

Liszt and Wagner also visited the Rue Saint-George atelier of Adolphe Sax, who displayed his full range of saxophones, saxhorns and saxtubas for his eminent visitors. Large numbers of these instruments were in use in French military bands and at the Opéra for stage music, as for example the eighteen saxhorns employed in

Meyerbeer's *Le Prophète*, which Wagner had seen and heard in Paris in February 1850. If the sound that he heard in his mind in La Spezia required the eight horns so prominent at the beginning of *Das Rheingold*, the visit to Sax might have been the moment when he realised that the extra quartet of horn players could at times be required to play saxhorns, with their darker colour and sombre tone, thus immeasurably enhancing the characteristic tone-colour of so many scenes in the opera on which he was about to set to work. Normally referred to as 'Wagner tubas', these instruments are essentially saxhorns shaped in an oval configuration. Some years later Wagner told King Ludwig of Bavaria that it was in Sax's showroom that he had first come across the instruments he wanted.

In Paris Wagner was introduced to a young German doctor named Lindemann who had been inoculating himself with various poisons in order to show what the effects might be. Wagner inevitably fell for any suggestion that he could correct his troublesome health with a new remedy. Laudanum and valerian were prescribed, but whether Wagner agreed to take these remains uncertain. Neither are actually poisons: laudanum is a narcotic and valerian is now widely used as a relaxant and sedative.

On Thursday 27th the Wagners finally headed back to Zurich. It had been a busy two and a half weeks. He described himself as tired but relaxed, conscious that he had to be in exactly the right frame of mind to start the work that he planned for his return. They stopped the night in Strasbourg, but unlike on his visit *en route* to Paris it was now so foggy that the cathedral's famous single spire was invisible. Minna bought a cauliflower in the market in front of the cathedral, also a lobster and some oysters to take back to Zurich. They were expecting to entertain friends the day after they arrived home, which was Saturday 29th.

On Tuesday 1 November Wagner sat down at his desk and began to compose *Der Ring des Nibelungen.*

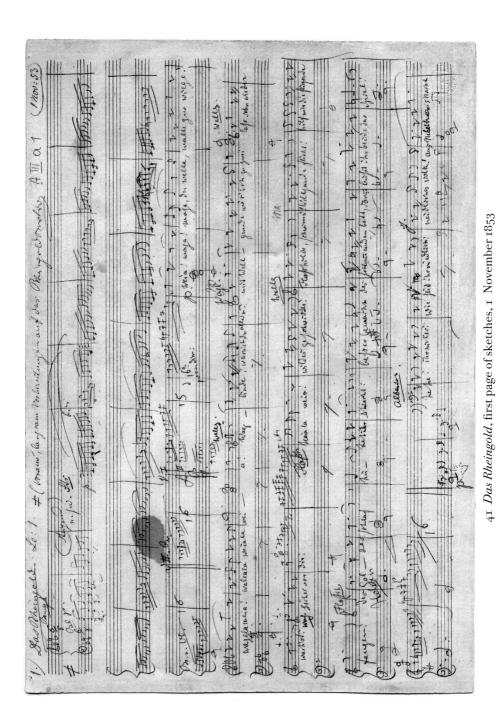

41 *Das Rheingold*, first page of sketches, 1 November 1853

CHAPTER 12

Berlioz, Joachim and Brahms in Hanover

OCTOBER – NOVEMBER

THE idea of a *Hamlet* concert in Frankfurt which Gustav Schmidt had put forward in August came to nothing, so Berlioz had to cross that city off his autumn itinerary. Meanwhile he had invitations from Brunswick and Hanover, with a possible date in Bremen. Munich and Prague remained possibilities. His blood quickened whenever he left Paris behind and headed for German cities where the prospect of conducting well-disciplined orchestras in front of discerning audiences reminded him of what music-making ought to be. He had no orchestra in Paris and no certain support from critics and public. It was seven years since he introduced *La Damnation de Faust* to Paris, and the memory of its lukewarm reception precluded any other ventures of that kind. The only substantial composition in the intervening years had been the *Te Deum*, composed in 1849, and that work still awaited its first performance.

After two extraordinary days in the company of Liszt and Wagner, he and Marie left Paris on Wednesday 12 October and took the train to Cologne and then on to Brunswick. Anxious to present *La Damnation de Faust* in as many places as possible, he had been madly correcting proofs for the publisher Richault, even though the printed scores would not be ready for this trip. He still had to carry with him the trunkful of manuscript orchestral and choral parts that he had taken to Baden-Baden and Frankfurt in the summer.

They reached Brunswick on Friday 14th with a week to prepare two concerts. They stayed at the Deutsches Haus Hotel (which is still in business), and their principal guide was an old friend, Robert Griepenkerl, a teacher of German literature at the Carolineum University in Brunswick (now the Technische Hochschule) and a passionate devotee of modern music. On Berlioz's first visit, ten years before, Griepenkerl had stood out as a critic prepared to dispute the querulous reviews of Berlioz's music which had appeared in the *Neue Zeitschrift für Musik* and to go so far as to publish a pamphlet, almost a book, called *Ritter Berlioz in Braunschweig*, which unhesitatingly aligned the 'knight' Berlioz with Beethoven and Shakespeare. Such supporters were not to be underestimated. The single concert Berlioz had conducted in Brunswick in 1843 had been one of the most satisfying of that earlier tour, and he remembered Brunswick's musicians with affection and admiration, especially the numerous Müller brothers. Four of them (Carl, Georg, Theodor and August) made up the renowned Müller String Quartet, while Georg was also the city's kapellmeister. Four of Carl's sons were later to form a second Müller Quartet.

Joseph Adolf Leibrock, cellist and harpist, was still there too. He had played in the first German performance of *Le Roi Lear* overture in Brunswick in 1839, before

42 Robert Griepenkerl

Berlioz's first visit, which inspired him to publish a piano-duet arrangement of it the following year. His brother Eduard ran a music publishing business, which in 1853 had been taken over by Henry Litolff, a virtuoso pianist of English birth. Litolff discussed with Berlioz the possibility of publishing some scores or perhaps a German translation of *Les Soirées de l'orchestre*, but the only publication that did eventually come out of Brunswick was not discussed at this time, namely the first vocal score of *Benvenuto Cellini*.

Brunswick was a small Duchy whose Duke Wilhelm, unlike the sovereigns in Hanover and Baden, showed no interest in music. That did not matter if the musicians and the public could make up for it in commitment and enthusiasm, as they certainly did. Some of the Duke's ministers attended the second concert.

The first concert took place on Saturday 22 October in the ducal theatre on Hagenmarkt, and the second three days later. Both were sold out. The orchestra was 'prodigious' in Berlioz's opinion, and they would have needed to be to tackle the programmes he chose. The first concert consisted entirely of his own music, with much the same programme as he had given in Frankfurt: extracts from *La Damnation de Faust*, including Marguerite's *Romance*; the *Repos de la Sainte Famille*; and the three instrumental movements from *Roméo et Juliette*. He had Gustav Schmidt's German version for the tenor soloist, Friedrich Schmetzer. Griepenkerl was thrilled.

On the day of the first concert a stranger sitting next to Berlioz at lunch told him that he had come the seventy miles from Detmold in order to hear the extracts from *Roméo et Juliette*. He had evidently been listening to a rehearsal. It was George

Wilhelm Henry, Baron von Donop, chamberlain at the court of Lippe-Detmold. He had heard Berlioz's concert in Baden-Baden in August but they had not met then. 'You should write an opera on this subject,' he said. 'From the way you have treated it as a symphony and from the way you understand Shakespeare, you would do something quite new and wonderful.' Berlioz replied in the pessimistic tone which all suggestions for new works elicited from him at that time, explaining that the effort would kill him. During the interval of the concert itself the Baron mentioned his idea to a neighbour, who remained silent an instant and then exclaimed, 'All right, let him die – but let him write the opera!'

A couple of weeks later Berlioz wrote the Baron a letter which sets out his feelings with particular clarity:

> I cannot start up again those agonising efforts that I made in Paris ten or fifteen years ago. A culture of mediocrity has grown up there which closes off avenues, bricks up walls, whispers in the corridors of power, and keeps me away from any chance of presenting my works. It's like the way marine insects in Polynesian islands build coral into reefs on which ships run aground. I feel I should devote what energy I have to making those scores that already exist better known than to leave them to the whim of the musical world and give them sisters whose first steps I cannot guarantee.

43 Baron von Donop

Herzogliches Hof-Theater.
Braunschweig, Dienstag, den 25. October 1853.
Benefiz zu einer von Herzogl. Hof-Capelle speciell zu gründenden Wittwen-Casse.
Grosses Vocal- und Instrumental-Concert
gegeben und dirigirt von
Herrn Hector Berlioz.

Erste Abtheilung.

1. Ouverture zu König Lear, von H. Berlioz.
2. Beschwörung der Irrlichter, Fragment aus Faust, von H. Berlioz.
3. Concert und Ballet der Sylphen mit Faust und Mephistopheles.
4. Concert für Violine, componirt und vorgetragen von Herrn Concertmeister Joseph Joachim.
5. Die Königin Mab, oder die Fee der Träume, ein Scherzo von H. Berlioz.
6. Ungarischer Marsch, Fragment aus Faust.

Zweite Abtheilung.

1. Harold, Sinfonie in 4 Abtheilungen mit obligater Bratsche, von H. Berlioz.
(Das Bratschen-Solo vorgetragen von Herrn Concertmeister Müller.)
1. Harold auf den Bergen, Scenen des Glücks und der Freude.
2. Pilger-Marsch.
3. Serenade eines Bergbewohners der Abbruzen.
4. Erinnerung an die früheren Scenen. Orgie der Räuber.

Dritte Abtheilung.

1. Ruhestelle der heiligen Familie, aus dem Oratorium im alten Styl „Die Flucht aus Egypten", von H. Berlioz.
2. Caprice für Violine von Paganini, instrumentirt und vorgetragen von Herrn Concertmeister Jos. Joachim.

Zum Beschluß, auf Allseitiges Verlangen:
Das Fest bei Capulet. Fragment aus der Sinfonie „Romeo und Julie" von H. Berlioz.

Preise der Plätze: Parterre 10 Ggr. Sperrsitz 16 Ggr. Parterre-Loge 14 Ggr. Erster Rang (Fremdenloge) 1 Thlr. Erster Rang 20 Ggr. Zweiter Rang 8 Ggr. Dritter Rang 4 Ggr. Gallerie 3 Ggr.
Das Theater-Büreau befindet sich im Hause № 1877 auf der Wilhelmsstraße, und ist von Morgens 10 bis Mittags 1 Uhr geöffnet.

Anfang: halb 7 Uhr; Ende: nach 9 Uhr.
Die Kasse wird um halb 6 Uhr geöffnet.
(210)
Druck der Hofbuchdruckerei von Eduard Krampe.

44 Berlioz's concert, 25 October 1853

Baron von Donop remained a staunch friend to Berlioz and a particular admirer of *Roméo et Juliette*. A month after their encounter in Brunswick he arranged for the Detmold chorus and orchestra to perform the entire symphony, supported by his employer the Prince of Lippe-Detmold who himself sang the part of Père Laurence while other members of the royal family sang in the chorus. Berlioz himself was by that time in Leipzig and could not attend. When he eventually embarked on the composition of *Les Troyens* three years later he wrote the Baron the plain words, 'I have finally followed your advice.'

For the second concert Berlioz included the *Roi Lear* overture and some of the same extracts from his own works. As a special feature he had persuaded Joachim to come the forty miles from Hanover and play his own G minor violin concerto, first heard in Karlsruhe at the beginning of the month, and one of the Paganini caprices (repeated in Düsseldorf four days later) to which he had added an orchestral accompaniment. Between these two pieces he laid down his violin and played the viola solo in the complete *Harold en Italie*, which he had never played before. Joachim first met Berlioz at the age of eighteen when he played in one of Berlioz's concerts in Paris in February 1850, and in the summer of 1852 they had got to know each other well during a season of concerts in London, leading to considerable mutual admiration. Joachim's appearance in Brunswick was evidently a favour to Berlioz, but equally a favour to Joachim to give him a prominent platform in a city close to his new home where he had never played before. With characteristic energy he returned to Hanover on the 26th and then went straight on to Düsseldorf to play in Schumann's subscription concert on the 27th and to give a recital with Clara on the 29th.

Profits from the second Brunswick concert went to a new fund for musicians' widows and orphans to be named the 'Berlioz Fund'. Georg Müller presented him with a silver-gilt baton on behalf of all the musicians, and afterwards a lady came up to him, kissed his hand and said 'It's not love, it's admiration!', which Berlioz took to be not an entirely flattering compliment. Then he was given a dinner with a hundred guests at his hotel.

A newspaper later rebuked the citizens of Brunswick for attaching a foreigner's name to a charity on behalf of German widows, but another paper, from Hamburg, stood nobly behind the deed, declaring that art observes no frontiers. Others felt vaguely that Berlioz contributed nothing to the legacy of Mozart, Beethoven and Weber, despite the enthusiasm of the audience. They were simply unaccustomed to the intrusion of French music in the symphonic repertoire: in opera, yes, French music had its place, but in the shadow of Beethoven it was holy writ in Germany that the symphony was a national possession – an attitude that would continue to gather momentum in the coming years.

On the Sunday afternoon between the two concerts Berlioz went to a popular concert given in the Hall of the Weisses Ross, part of a public garden, on Cellerstrasse where an audience of 1,200 heard an orchestra playing the *Carnaval romain* overture. The performance of this difficult piece was surprisingly good and was encored. When some of the players spotted Berlioz in the audience there were waves and shouts of recognition.

Before moving on to Hanover he and Marie had a few days to kill, so they took the train thirty miles south to Bad Harzburg on the edge of the Harz mountains. Berlioz was not often drawn to the wide open spaces, but in this case the lure was the setting for the witches' sabbath in Goethe's *Faust* on the Brocken, at 3,700 feet the highest mountain in north Germany, lying a mile or two outside the town. Mendelssohn's *Die erste Walpurgisnacht*, which he much admired, evoked the same place. On the 28th he went for a hike towards, perhaps even up, the mountain, and later that day copied out the splendid words he wrote for Faust's big solo in *La Damnation de Faust*:

> Nature immense, impénétrable et fière!

including the line

> Forêts, rochers, torrents, je vous adore!

which he echoed in a letter to his close-but-distant friend Humbert Ferrand, once a fellow-Romantic-in-arms: 'Those forests! Those torrents! Those rocks! They are the ruins of a whole world. I looked for you, I missed you amid those poetic heights. I confess I was breathless from emotion.'

They reached Hanover on 30 October and installed themselves at the British Hotel where they had stayed on their previous visit ten years before. Built in 1750, it stood on the corner of Georgstrasse and Kleine Packhofstrasse, although it did not survive the Second World War. He had less than a week to rehearse his first concert, aided by Joachim, who returned from Düsseldorf in time to help. The old opera house where he had performed before had recently been replaced by a splendid new theatre with a grand classical facade, occupying at the time the largest footprint of any theatre in Germany and still standing majestically on Georgstrasse, clear evidence of Hanover's kings' passion for the arts. Beginning on Friday the 4th he had a hard series of rehearsals with, as usual, a tough programme to learn. But as he told Janin, he never felt better than when working hard with a sympathetic chorus and orchestra, no matter how tiring rehearsals might be. He truly felt he was, as he put it, a fish in water. With the King and Joachim firmly behind him, the performers were much more enthusiastic than Griepenkerl said they would be. There were a number of new young members of the orchestra, probably drawn by Joachim's appointment as konzertmeister. At the first rehearsal he was greeted with applause and a trumpet fanfare, and a laurel wreath had been placed over his scores on the podium. He addressed them in French with a few words of English: 'I don't know how they understand,' he wrote. Marschner, chief conductor of the opera house, rehearsed the singers in advance, but was long past showing any interest in Berlioz himself.

At the end of the first day of rehearsals a musical celebrity arrived in Hanover in the person of Brahms, who appeared at Joachim's window on the Friday night.

After leaving Düsseldorf he had made a quick visit to the Deichmanns in Bonn, and then come on to Hanover. Perhaps he was still unaware of Schumann's 'Neue Bahnen' article, which had appeared a week earlier; the matter is not clear. Albert Dietrich wrote to Joachim on 6 November (Sunday), sending him the manuscript of the FAE sonata, with pictures, probably engravings, of the two Schumanns, and a copy of the *Neue Zeitschrift*. Joachim had seen a manuscript draft of the article in Düsseldorf, but Dietrich must have thought Joachim (and therefore Brahms) had not seen it. Brahms would then have seen it for the first time on the 7th, the day before Berlioz's first concert. What his reaction to it was we do not know, but he saw clearly enough that he was now famous throughout Germany as a young composer whose works hardly anyone besides Schumann and Joachim had ever heard. Joachim and Brahms must have pored over the article together wondering how to handle this new-found fame and perhaps thinking about many years of fruitful music-making ahead. Brahms's letter of thanks to Schumann was not written until the 16th, the day before he left Hanover. Perhaps he found it a difficult letter to write. He found *all* letters difficult to write.

On the morning after Brahms's arrival Joachim took him to Berlioz's 9.30 a.m. rehearsal. Brahms had heard about Berlioz from Joachim (very positive), Schumann (non-committal) and Clara (negative), and had certainly heard his name mentioned in Weimar. Unless he attended Berlioz's concert in Hamburg at the age of nine, he had never heard any of his music. The two composers met for the first time at that rehearsal, all four hours of which Brahms listened to while Joachim led the orchestra. The two younger men then went off to find Brahms's lodgings at 4 Papenstieg, just outside the old city gate, the Aegidientor. Joachim then had to finish marking the violin part of Schumann's *Phantasie*, which he sent back to Düsseldorf. He also wrote to Wehner in Göttingen urging him to come to Hanover for Berlioz's concert. 'All the Karlsruhe crowd *must* be there,' he insisted, with Brahms's signature appended for extra force. 'The orchestra is gigantic!' Joachim added.

All four hours of the Monday morning rehearsal were attended also by the King and Queen, both of them committed admirers of his music who had been somewhat embarrassed by the reception of *Benvenuto Cellini* in London in their presence. For the Hanover programme Berlioz had hoped to give a complete performance of *La Damnation de Faust*, the first since 1847, when he conducted it in Berlin. He particularly wanted Joachim to hear the full work. That plan was abandoned and a mixed programme like those heard in Frankfurt and Brunswick was put together instead. The concert took place at 7 p.m. on Tuesday 8th, divided into three parts: Part I: overture *Le Roi Lear*, *Le Repos de la Sainte Famille* sung by the tenor Carl Bernard, then the first part of *La Damnation de Faust*. Part II was the second part of *La Damnation de Faust*. Part III opened with Marguerite's *Romance* from the last part of *La Damnation de Faust*, followed by three movements from *Roméo et Juliette* (the *Scène d'amour*, the *Reine Mab* scherzo, and the *Fête chez Capulet*). Berlioz included Marguerite's *Romance* since Hanover had a fine mezzo, Madeleine Nottes, whom the King valued so much that he added 50 per cent to her salary when she threatened to move to Vienna. The *Faust* soloists were Eduard Sowade (Faust), Louis Böttcher (Mephistopheles) and Jakob Haas (Brander), all members of Hanover's opera troupe.

The success of this concert was particularly gratifying since his concert in Hanover in 1843, unlike the Brunswick concerts that year, had not been well received by the audience. A notable exception then was the Crown Prince, who now, as King, summoned Berlioz to an audience next morning. Amid showers of compliments he asked him to repeat the concert on the following Tuesday. 'How well you conduct!' he said. 'I don't see you, but I can feel it. I am deeply grateful to Providence for granting me a feeling for music to make up for what I have lost.' Berlioz was next due to give a concert in Bremen, but that plan still allowed time to repeat the concert in Hanover.

A snag arose in Hanover with payments to musicians, since the intendant had been informed incorrectly that Berlioz's terms were half of the net receipts after expenses had been paid, when in fact they were half of the gross receipts. Since these concerts were not part of the subscription series, the orchestra was due to be paid for them, enormously increasing the expenses. The orchestra, as a mark of respect to Berlioz, agreed to waive their fees for the first concert, while Berlioz agreed to accept half of net receipts for the second. The second concert was less well attended but more rapturously received than the first. The French ambassador told Berlioz afterwards: 'You have brought corpses to life. Hanover audiences are the coldest on earth, they only applaud anyone twice a year at most.' The ambassador was accompanied by two ladies who were reduced to what Berlioz called a 'weeping-duet' by the music. A curiosity of this concert was an unannounced performance during the interval by the pianist Oscar La Cinna from Pest as a preview for his full recital the following day.

A few days before his second concert Berlioz received a visit from Bettina von Arnim, who had been in Düsseldorf the week before, when Joachim read through the FAE sonata. She was with her daughter Gisela, anxious to spend more time in Joachim's company, and in Brahms's too. Berlioz first met them the previous November in Weimar, having known Bettina by repute from reading about Goethe and Beethoven. She came to his hotel not to *see* Berlioz, she told him, but to *look at* him – whatever that may have meant. They stayed in Hanover until the 21st and then went to Weimar.

The pianist Ehrlich seems to have been absent throughout this period; his contract as court pianist required him to reside in Hanover only one month of the year.

How Berlioz and Marie passed the time between concerts can only be guessed. Operas playing those weeks included *Il barbiere di Siviglia*, Boieldieu's *La Dame blanche*, Flotow's *Indra*, Lortzing's *Undine*, and Donizetti's *Lucia di Lammermoor*. None of these would have passed the test of worthiness set out in his book *Les Soirées de l'orchestre*, where only great operas are treated with respect, so it is unlikely they attended any of them. Despite Baron von Donop's urging, he was not composing.

A question mark hangs over the relations of Berlioz and Brahms during the twelve days that they were simultaneously in Hanover. Scarcely a biography of either composer mentions their proximity. Having heard a full rehearsal Brahms would surely have attended the first concert on the 8th, if not the second on the 15th. But direct exchanges were problematic, since Berlioz spoke no German, and Brahms, even though he had learnt some French at school, had never had an opportunity to use it. Joachim's French was good, so he would have had to act as interpreter, and he must have brought them together more than once during those days. Brahms no doubt preferred to keep a low profile now that his name was known to all alert musicians. Despite Schumann's insistence that he should go on at once to Leipzig, he was vaguely planning to stay in Hanover several weeks, shielded by Joachim from an enquiring world and applying the perfectionist's polish to his collection of unpublished works. He was debating with Joachim and himself which pieces he should offer for publication, beset by doubts that certain works might not live up to his own standards or the expectations of the public. He had a *Phantasie* in D minor for piano trio which he had played with Joachim and a cellist either in Göttingen or Düsseldorf, tentatively marked down to be his Opus 1, and he still had work to do on the third piano sonata which he was working on in Düsseldorf. He was glad of the seclusion afforded by his lodgings on Papenstieg (still a quiet residential street today). The house had been built as a single-storey retreat for members of the court, located between the city and some orchards and hidden from view by trees. It was reached by a hidden path leading to what appeared to be an Egyptian temple with a tiny balcony supported on columns with lotus-shaped capitals. The next-door house was occupied by a well-known sculptor, Heinrich Hesemann.

If Brahms was curious about Berlioz the composer, one could scarcely choose a more satisfying selection from his best music that he might hear. But what did he think of it? He had never heard anything like it; in fact, orchestral music was largely outside his experience, but alas he left no hint of his feelings in his correspondence. The work by Berlioz that we know he later valued most was *Le Repos de la Sainte Famille*, in preference to *La Damnation de Faust*; he preferred the work with the least colourful orchestration and the most sober tone. His mind was in any case working in the quite different worlds of piano music, chamber music and songs, while Berlioz, probably unaware of the significance or even of the existence of 'Neue Bahnen', would have had little reason to show interest in yet another brilliant young pianist, even one recommended by Joachim. *En revanche*, Joachim's passionate interest in Berlioz seems to have fallen on deaf ears.

On Thursday 17 November Brahms moved on to Leipzig, and on the following day Berlioz and Marie left by train for Bremen, seventy-five miles to the north-west. They stayed at Hillmanns Hotel, on what is now Hillmannplatz, not far from the old city centre. He had not been to Bremen before and he knew none of the city's musicians. His visit had been arranged in advance by Griepenkerl in Brunswick, who put him in touch with Gustav Wilhelm Eggers, the secretary of Bremen's music society, the Gesellschaft für Privatconcerte. Being an independent republic like Hamburg and Lübeck, Bremen lacked the paraphernalia of court life but none-theless sustained concerts and opera on a level to match other cities of comparable importance.

The programme of the concert, which took place on Tuesday 22 November, featured a local tenor, Wilhelm Hagen, who sang an aria from Mendelssohn's *Elijah* and songs by the Viennese composer Gottfried Preyer and the north German composer Friedrich Fesca. His contribution to Berlioz's part was *Le Repos de la Sainte Famille*, once again. A pianist named Georg Mertel played Mendelssohn's D minor concerto. Two movements from *Roméo et Juliette* closed the concert, yet the highlight was definitely the first three movements of *Harold en Italie* since the faithful Joachim came over from Hanover (despite a fearful cold) to play the viola solo once again. The concert was rapturously received by the audience.

Next day Joachim accompanied the Berliozes back on the train to Hanover. Early that morning they received a visit from Hanover's Consul-General in Bremen, Baron A. W. L. Brauer, bearing a bracelet as a gift for Marie from King Georg. It was made by W. Lameyer and was inset with the initials GR in diamonds. Sovereigns habitually gave artists presents such as this, even when the money they cost might have been more welcome instead, but in this case Berlioz was sincerely in the King's debt and genuinely convinced of his admiration. Two years later Berlioz was awarded the Order of the Guelphs by the same King Georg. After Marie's death in 1862 Berlioz passed the bracelet to his niece Josephine.

Several member of Bremen's Musical Society went to the railway station to see them off. As Berlioz was stepping on to the train, an old man grabbed his arm with one hand and raised his hat with the other: 'Monsieur! Monsieur! Grand componist, Monsieur, grand componist!' he stammered in the best French he could muster. Berlioz was also introduced by a professor of composition to one of his students. The professor took the student's hand and rubbed it along Berlioz's sleeve. 'This young man must never forget,' he explained, 'that he has touched the arm of Berlioz!'

In Hanover Joachim left the train while Berlioz and Marie carried on to Leipzig. When the train halted in Brunswick he had arranged to say a quick hello to Griepenkerl to urge him to come to Leipzig to hear his concerts there (which he did). When they reached Leipzig that evening they had covered over 300 miles of bumpy train tracks in a day. Their beds in the Hôtel de Bavière must have been more than usually welcome.

CHAPTER 13

Brahms, Berlioz and Liszt in Leipzig

NOVEMBER – DECEMBER

B RAHMS left Hanover on 17 November and headed for Leipzig. It had always
been one of the main goals of his many months of travel; at last he felt ready
to present himself to a city full of professional musicians who had had a few weeks
to digest Schumann's proclamation of his genius. Leipzig was in all but name the
capital of German music. Since the death of Beethoven and Schubert – or more
properly since the start of Metternich's long era as guardian of imperial policy –
Vienna had barely maintained its former glory in the domain of music and opera.
Otto Nicolai, one of the best conductors of his time, did much for the city's music,
but he died tragically early at the age of thirty-eight in 1849, two months after his
finest work, *Die lustigen Weiber von Windsor*, was first staged there. Berlin's music
was well staffed but so full of intrigue and discontent that Mendelssohn turned
down good offers to work there, his home city, and chose to move to Leipzig instead.

The old city walls of Leipzig formed a relatively small rectangle within which
the main buildings were located, with new suburbs stretching to the south and east.
The railway station, made up of a series of parallel terminals where each of the
independent lines arrived, stood just outside the north-eastern city limits and was
already handling considerable traffic. The line to Dresden, completed in 1839, was
the first inter-city main line in Germany. Berlioz rode the length of it and back in a
single day in 1843, astonished that such a thing was even possible.

Leipzig had a strong liberal tradition and an active commercial life, and although
it lay within the King of Saxony's domain, the court was in Dresden, leaving
Leipzig to manage its own affairs. Bach, during his years as Cantor at St Thomas's
church, was beholden to the city council, not to a court. In fact the figure of Bach
was beginning to embody the depth of Leipzig's musical culture, with the Bach-
Gesellschaft inaugurating its monumental series of scores in 1851. The University
was one of the oldest in Germany (Joachim called Leipzig the 'town of bookshops'),
and the city's long tradition of concert-giving, to which both Telemann and Bach
made important contributions, was now at a peak thanks to the institution of
the Gewandhaus concerts. The building dated from 1781, and the orchestra was
renowned throughout Europe thanks largely to Mendelssohn's efforts between
1835 and his death in 1847. During that period he introduced works by Bach and
Schubert that had not been heard before, and new music by Schumann, himself and
others. He had two gifted assistants in Ferdinand Hiller and the Dane Niels Gade,
and his outstanding konzertmeister was the violinist Ferdinand David, a pupil
of Spohr. In 1843 Mendelssohn, with help from Schumann and David, founded
the Leipzig Conservatoire, soon to become the leading conservatoire in Europe.

45 Ferdinand David

David's pupils included Joachim, Wasielewski, and a whole generation of first-class violinists. Mendelssohn was succeeded at the Gewandhaus by Julius Rietz, who was already in charge of the city's opera and whose response to new music such as Liszt's was unfortunately less than lukewarm. Yet he had been persuaded to set in motion a production of *Lohengrin*, only the third staging in Germany after Weimar and Wiesbaden, which was even now almost ready for opening night.

Since the eighteenth century Leipzig had also been the centre of music publishing, expanding to the point where by the end of the nineteenth century there were at least sixty music publishers there, including such names as Breitkopf & Härtel, C. F. Peters, Hofmeister, Senff and Kistner. Music engraving and printing in Leipzig was developed to a high point of excellence at this time. Its leading music journals were the *Neue Zeitschrift für Musik*, founded by Schumann in 1834 and now in 1853 edited by Franz Brendel, and the *Signale für die musikalische Welt*, which offered a comprehensive coverage of musical affairs at home and abroad, not surprisingly free to take a different view of Wagner to that of Brendel when its writers so wished.

Eventually Leipzig became a bastion of musical conservatism whose supporters were always on the look-out for dangerously modern trends, but in 1853 it was still a place where music was composed, performed, printed and discussed with a greater variety, intensity and seriousness than in any other city in Germany. Otto Jahn was there, writing the first big biography of Mozart with an eye to the 1856 centenary; Schumann said there was no better place for a young musician to be; Wagner was proud to have been born there.

Brahms's host in Leipzig was Heinrich von Sahr, a young composer trained in Dresden who had spent much of 1852 in Düsseldorf. As soon as he read the 'Neue Bahnen' article he got in touch with Albert Dietrich to find out more. Now living in Leipzig, Sahr took it upon himself to take Brahms away from the hotel where he spent his first night and offer him the hospitality of his home. He was determined too to introduce him to as many of Leipzig's notables as possible. First in priority were the brothers Raymund and Hermann Härtel, in charge of the publishers Breitkopf & Härtel, already well on the way to establishing themselves as the leading music publishers in the world; their range may be grasped from the fact that they were simultaneously publishers of the *Bach-Gesellschaft* and of *Lohengrin*. Brahms had already written to them on 8 November offering a group of compositions (unnamed) and besides Schumann's public encomium in the *Neue Zeitschrift*, he had letters of introduction to the Härtels from both Schumann and Liszt. He now decided to offer them his first four opus numbers:

op. 1 Piano sonata in C major
op. 2 Piano sonata in F sharp minor
op. 3 Six songs
op. 4 Scherzo in E flat minor

Although the Scherzo was the first of these works to be composed, Brahms felt that the two grandly conceived piano sonatas, manifestly in Beethoven's lineage, would strike the public as a stronger banner proclamation of his talents and his ambition. On Saturday evening 19 November the Härtels heard him perform op. 1 and op. 4, and an unnamed lady sang some of his songs. They immediately accepted the four works. They paid Brahms the handsome sum of thirty-six *louis d'or* and put the music into immediate production. With Härtel's signature Brahms could now face his parents, having promised them he would come home only when he had found a publisher for his music. The timing was good, since Christmas was approaching and his mother had set her heart on seeing her son again then.

The question of dedications was a delicate matter which he resolved as follows:

op. 1 to Joachim
op. 2 to Clara Schumann
op. 3 to Bettina von Arnim
op. 4 to Ernst Ferdinand Wenzel

This last name is surprising, especially since Schumann himself is not one of the dedicatees. If he planned to dedicate something more substantial to him as a worthy gesture, he never did so. Wenzel was a good friend of the Schumanns, a pupil of Clara's father Friedrich Wieck and Mendelssohn's choice as professor of piano at the Leipzig Conservatoire. He was also a regular contributor to the *Neue Zeitschrift*, but there is no evidence that Brahms knew him before his arrival in Leipzig.

Sahr also introduced Brahms to the elderly composer Isaak Ignaz Moscheles, whose eventful career as a touring pianist led him after a long stay in England to the Leipzig Conservatoire as a piano teacher alongside Wenzel. He also met Clara's father Wieck, who has never been forgiven by history for his unflagging efforts to prevent his daughter marrying Schumann; her sister Marie Wieck, Ferdinand David and Julius Rietz were also among the prominent musicians he was introduced to in that busy week. Another new friend was Julius Otto Grimm, still a student at the Conservatoire, but later to succeed Arnold Wehner as director of Göttingen's university music and to remain a lifelong friend. The three new acquantances Sahr, Wenzel and Grimm went walking with Brahms, doubtless showing off the sights of Leipzig, including the Thomaskirche and Nicolaikirche where Bach presided over the music, the school building where Bach lived and taught, the Gewandhaus and the handsome Rathaus. No doubt they ended up in Auerbach's Cellar, imagining that Faust and Mephistopheles might suddenly appear.

Introductions from Joachim led him also to the houses of Friedrich Hermann, violinist in the Gewandhaus orchestra and two members of the extensive Klengel family of musicians, Moritz, a violinist, and his son Julius (father of two more famous Klengels, Julius and Paul). The density of fine musicians in Leipzig reminded Joachim of how much he missed in Hanover's comparatively underfurnished musical milieu.

46 The Gewandhaus, Leipzig

One morning David visited Sahr's house and played Brahms's A minor violin sonata with its composer; he then listened while Brahms played the C major piano sonata. He was struck dumb with astonishment. Perhaps in pursuit of a policy of hedging his bets, Brahms approached a different publisher, Bartholf Senff, with the violin sonata along with a second collection of six songs. Senff was also the publisher of the *Signale für die musikalische Welt*. He took the songs (op. 6) but declined the sonata on the grounds that he did not publish violin music. Brahms offered him the new piano sonata in F minor instead, which Senff accepted and published as op. 5. The violin sonata, which Reményi, Joachim, David and Wasielewski had all played, subsequently suffered the fate of so many of Brahms's works which did not meet his exacting standards. It was destroyed by the composer, although Wasielewski was said to have retained a copy of the violin part. The string quartet in B minor, played in Düsseldorf, disappeared too; a Hamburg friend of Brahms once said that the first published quartet, op. 51, was preceded by twenty others, all condemned. The *Phantasie* for violin, cello and piano was another victim of that pitilessly self-critical eye.

Leipzig offered Brahms a very different atmosphere from the sheltered and studious weeks in Hanover. After a week being noisily fêted and closely watched, he went back to Hanover on 25 November to spend a few more days with Joachim. It is far from clear whether this was a planned move or whether he was impulsively fleeing from too much attention. Everyone recognised his shyness. He knew he would have to come back to perform to the Leipzig public at some stage, which had yet to be arranged, and he was expecting to correct the proofs of his first publications, but he also needed to consult his friend about the next stage of his dealings with publishers and to confirm his choice of dedicatees.

Or was he troubled by the arrival of Berlioz on 23 November? Berlioz was loudly greeted by the press in advance of his two orchestral concerts to be given in the Gewandhaus. The Gewandhaus concerts were officially in the hands of Rietz, but this year they were being managed by David, who invited Berlioz to conduct one of the regular subscription concerts on the 1st and an extra concert on the 10th. Once again Berlioz was in a city he had first visited ten years before, when he had found both Mendelssohn and David superbly friendly and helpful, both speaking excellent French. Berlioz was more satisfied with his concerts there than the press, who exhibited even then Leipzig's marked resistance to music that seemed to cross permissible frontiers, and he was accused of trying to be original at the expense of all else. Mendelssohn himself was always reserved about his music no matter how friendly he was in person.

This second visit in 1853 was bound to stir up once more the hurrahs and boos of criticism, especially since Brahms was also a centre of attention and *Lohengrin* was in rehearsal at the opera. One could scarcely imagine a more critical convergence of different kinds of music at the same time in the same place in a city that thrived on debate and *parti pris*. Berlioz, relying as usual on French and a few words of English, was exhilarated by the rehearsals since he had really fine players in the orchestra and an expert choir made up of members of the Singakademie and the Pauliner Sängverein, a choir based at the university church, the Paulinerkirche. He also had the boys from Bach's church, the Thomaskirche, making a total of over 150 singers. To play the harp he had Johanna Pohl brought over from Dresden. The Gewandhaus was just a few yards down the narrow Preussergässchen from his hotel, the Hôtel de Bavière (which traded under the French version of its name), and David proved to be an admirable host. Berlioz's reputation as a conductor was such that word soon got around that his rehearsals were worth sitting in on, so that at the final rehearsal on Wednesday 30 November the hall was half full of interested eavesdroppers. One of them was a young blind man who had taken the train from Dresden and who later called on Berlioz in his hotel: 'I speak such bad French, forgive me, Monsieur,' he stammered, 'your hand ... allow me to ... I know your partiturs by heart. I am so happy. Goodbye, Monsieur, excuse me.' Then he left.

These rehearsals carry immense significance because Berlioz had programmed the first complete performance of *La Fuite en Égypte*, the little biblical cantata he had composed in 1850. The central chorus, *L'Adieu des bergers*, had been performed at that time, and the final section, *Le Repos de la Sainte Famille*, after its première in London in May, had been heard recently in several German cities. But the overture had never yet been played. The work was almost a symbol of Berlioz's retreat from his role as composer. He had composed nothing since and he had neglected to perform it except piece by piece. In addition it was scored for a small orchestra and was written in an archaic style, including modal inflexions, that confounded those who expected his music to be noisy and brilliant.

It was not the fact of its first complete performance that is significant: it is the impression this work made on his admirers in the orchestra. For almost casually, in a letter to his sister written between the last rehearsal and the concert, he reported that everyone thought he had captured exactly the right tone for his 'biblical legend'. 'They are urging me to extend it with *La Sainte Famille en Égypte*,' he added, 'and I will.' After years of revulsion at any suggestion that he ought to be composing, after insisting that he had no future as a composer, that his music had no audience, that he could not afford the effort and expense, even after telling the Baron von Donop that he could never possibly write an opera, after all that – he mutters, like a blushing bride, 'I will.' It was a momentous turning point, falling a mere thirty days after Wagner too had become a composer again. Berlioz knew what his next piece would be; he knew what reading he would need to do before he could begin; and he knew to whom the work would be dedicated (the Leipzig chorus). Scales had fallen from his eyes.

The concert, at 6.30 p.m. on Thursday 1 December, opened with a performance of Beethoven's Eighth Symphony, a work he knew well but had never conducted before. The rest of the music was his own, beginning with the complete *La Fuite en Égypte*. The tenor soloist was Carl Schneider, who also sang the song *Le Jeune Pâtre breton*. This orchestral song had always previously been sung by women, one of whom was Marie Recio. She would inevitably have recalled singing it in the very same hall in 1843 in the days when she was still singing and still thought by Schumann and others to be 'apparently more than Berlioz's concert singer'.

David exchanged his violin for a viola in order to play the solo part in the first three movements of *Harold en Italie*, just as Joachim had done in Bremen the week before. The second movement featured Johanna Pohl's harp playing, as did the *Reine Mab* scherzo from *Roméo et Juliette*. The programme continued with the Elbe scene from Part II of *La Damnation de Faust*, Schneider singing Faust and Heinrich Behr singing Mephistopheles, and the rousing *Carnaval romain* overture closed the concert.

Berlioz was delighted with the excellent performances but disappointed at the audience's reception, which had none of the fiery enthusiasm he had experienced in Brunswick, Hanover and Bremen. He confided to Hedwig Salomon, the daughter of a Leipzig banker, in a tone of deep melancholy, 'On ne me veut plus', which hardly accords with his confident tone of the day before. Meeting him for the first time she was struck by his muscular fingers and by the softness of his eyes in contrast to his Roman nose and firmly set mouth. A French composer now resident in Germany, Théodore Gouvy, was staying in the same hotel as Berlioz in preparation for a performance of one of his symphonies in the coming January. They had met two years before but were not particularly close. Gouvy agreed that the performance and the conducting were excellent and that it was simply the Leipzigers' resistance to what they regarded as eccentricities that lay behind their coolness and occasional boos. Another factor, according to Gouvy, was the presence in the audience of none other than Liszt, surrounded by nine or ten of his disciples: Raff, Cornelius, Laub, Cossmann, Reményi, Klindworth, Pruckner, perhaps more, who had caught the train from Weimar at 3 a.m. in icy cold weather with a change of trains in Halle to be there. Their noisy support at the concert evidently had the opposite of the desired result. The two most gifted members of that circle were absent: Joachim, committed to his duties in Hanover, and von Bülow giving spectacularly successful concerts in Berlin.

After the concert they all went off to one of Leipzig's best restaurants, Kitzing & Helbig's at 22 Schlossgasse at the south-west corner of the inner city. The Härtel brothers were their hosts. David was leading a group of musicians, which included Senff, Wenzel and Sahr. Liszt and Berlioz were always glad to see each other, and the Weimar gang were all committed Berliozians as a result of Liszt's energetic promotion of his music, including performances of *Benvenuto Cellini* in Weimar in 1852 which Berlioz had attended. Cornelius had not met Berlioz before, but he had been enthusiastically studying his scores (which left a clear mark on his own); nor had Reményi, whose Hungarian origins clearly intrigued Berlioz. Liszt greeted Gouvy heartily, and told him he'd been playing one of his symphonies in a piano duet arrangement in Karlsruhe. Berlioz was in low spirits and it took all Liszt's inexhaustible energy and positive mood to pull him out of it.

They were soon joined, to everyone's surprise, by Brahms, whom they all (except Cornelius) knew from his visit to Weimar in June and who arrived by

47 Peter Cornelius

train from Hanover after the concert was over. Brahms was clearly not expecting to see the Weimar people there and was embarrassed to find himself face to face with Reményi again. He knew they had all passed 'Neue Bahnen' around. He was simply too young to know how to handle such a situation, even though in musical matters he had an iron determination and will. Hedwig Salomon observed that he was clearly uncomfortable, remarking that the poor boy could hardly help it if Schumann's intemperate praise had made him a target for all kinds of envy and malicious gossip.

But things improved for everyone in the next few days. Against Sahr's vehement advice Brahms paid a call on Liszt at the Hôtel de Bavière. He was very warmly received by Liszt, and by Reményi too. Their earlier differences were not even mentioned and Brahms found that Reményi had changed for the better. Liszt returned the visit, bringing Cornelius and others from the group, and the atmosphere was clearly easier than the evening before. Brahms's modesty and unassuming manner helped, especially since they recognised his high musical gifts and underlying self-confidence. That evening a large group attended a soirée given by David and his wife Sophie at his home at 1670 Weststrasse (now Friedrich-Ebert-Strasse). Liszt, Berlioz and Brahms were all there. Berlioz was profoundly grateful to David throughout his stay in Leipzig for his friendliness, his high artistry and his social accomplishments. Liszt performed for the company his amalgamation of two solemn tunes from *Benvenuto Cellini* under the title *Bénédiction et serment*, grand in conception but, Liszt being Liszt, not without leaping octaves for both hands.

Before returning to Weimar Liszt had some business to conduct with Härtel on Wagner's behalf, Wagner being as usual ferociously concerned with every detail of publications of *Lohengrin* that the new production might engender. In this case Härtel was unwilling to publish five piano arrangements from the opera since they had been prepared by von Bülow who was regarded with alarm by Härtel's less adventurous advisers for having displayed excessive fervour for advanced music (i.e. Berlioz and Wagner) in some recent articles in the *Neue Zeitschrift*. Liszt as usual had a lot of smoothing out to do, but the piano pieces were not published. Härtel was issuing nine extracts for solo voice and piano, and they came out soon after the production opened.

Cornelius meanwhile, under the overwhelming impact of Berlioz's music, wrote a new German translation of the *Adieu des bergers* which had just been sung for the first time in German in an unattributed translation printed in the concert programme. Berlioz's three six-line verses are rhymed in an ABABAB pattern, the A rhyme being a feminine ending. This is particularly challenging for a translator, yet the version the chorus had just sung included no rhymes at all. Cornelius, like the poet he was, respected the rhyme scheme in his version and sent it to Berlioz.

Il s'en va loin de la terre,	Du entfliehst der Heimat Hainen,
Où dans l'étable il vit le jour;	Entfliehst der dunklen Krippe Hut;
De son père et de sa mère	Mag der Eltern Lieb' sich einen
Qu'il reste le constant amour !	Zu schirmen dich mit frommen Muth.
Qu'il grandisse, qu'il prospère,	Wachse, blühe! Sei den Deinen
Et qu'il soit bon père à son tour !	Vater einst auch du, mild und gut.

Thinking of the endless trouble he had had with German translations in the past, Berlioz was delighted with Cornelius's offer to do the same for *Le Repos de la Sainte Famille*, the German of which, it will be recalled, was hurriedly prepared by Gustav Schmidt in Frankfurt in August. Although *La Fuite en Égypte* had already been published in Paris, Berlioz and Cornelius arranged with the Leipzig publisher Julius Kistner to put out a new full score, vocal score and choral parts with a new translation by Cornelius. Since *La Damnation de Faust* was already in proof, Berlioz asked Cornelius to review it, and when *L'Enfance du Christ* was completed a year later, the translation was made by Cornelius; before *Benvenuto Cellini* was revived again in Weimar and published in Brunswick, Cornelius made a new translation of that too; and finally in his will Berlioz expressed the wish that Cornelius would translate *Les Troyens*, although that was never done. This particular skill, as well as Cornelius's passionate advocacy of his music, was something Berlioz greatly prized. It was in a report written for the Berlin *Echo*'s first issue of 1854 that Cornelius suggested Berlioz as the third B in a triumvir with Bach and Beethoven, a notion later stolen by von Bülow in naming Brahms, not Berlioz, in that honoured place.

48 Brahms in Leipzig, 1853

On Saturday 3 December reviews of the concert started to appear in the press. Ferdinand Gleich in the *Leipziger Tageblatt und Anzeiger* discussed each work in the programme as the work of a musical genius, whose presence was a historic moment for the city of Leipzig. The *Leipziger Zeitung* offered the usual admiration for Berlioz's daring instrumentation, but cautiously suggested that rules are rules. If they are sometimes broken, 'German souls will have to get used to that. Whether it leads anywhere, we will have to see.' The writer in the *Signale* was Johann Christian Lobe, a critic who had long before declared his allegiance to Berlioz as man and musician and had recently invited him to write a kind of manifesto for a different journal which he edited, the *Fliegende Blätter für Musik*. Lobe's understanding of Berlioz was profound, dismissing the eternal *canards* about his music being technically crude and upholding its right to be sympathetically imbued with literary images and subjects. Berlioz was immensely pleased with this fine article, which was later published in Paris in French. Brendel in the *Neue Zeitschrift*, as might be expected, upbraided the Leipzig public for their stuffiness.

The *Tageblatt* soon resounded with controversy, since a writer who signed himself H.Œ. argued that original was not the same as great. He saw Berlioz as a commercial traveller who displayed trinkets for sale: 'we heard several pieces of beautiful music but not many beautiful pieces of music.' Gleich responded with the plain declaration that Berlioz was the greatest musician of the century, at which point the editor declared the controversy closed. In sum, though, it was widely agreed that Berlioz had won the battle of opinion, and that the nay-sayers were in retreat. Preparing for his second concert, he took heart that the booers heard at the first concert might this time hold their peace.

On Sunday afternoon (4th) there was another party, this time hosted by Franz Brendel at his home at 4 Mittelstrasse (now Hans-Poeche-Strasse) east of the city near the station. Brendel asked the writer Arnold Schloenbach to report it for the *Neue Zeitschrift*, from whose purple prose we learn that the guests included, besides Berlioz and Brahms, musicians, poets, critics, journalists, booksellers and their attendant ladies, even priests. Brahms described the guests as 'literary nobility – or should I say nullity?'. Johanna Pohl played the harp to immense applause and a warm double handshake from Berlioz. Berlioz stood there, said Schloenbach, victorious! He had conquered all his enemies, he was 'so simple, so modest, so calm'. Schloenbach saw great depth of feeling in his nobly sculptured face and the bright eyes under greying hair, watched by the 'fiery glance of his beloved wife'.

There followed some Schumann songs and some extracts from *Tannhäuser*, *Lohengrin* and *Benvenuto Cellini* with piano accompaniment, all sending Schloenbach into ecstatic rhapsodies. The climax of the evening came when Brahms stepped to the piano. Since the appearance of 'Neue Bahnen' no musician in Leipzig was free of the desperate need to know if Schumann's extravagant launch of Brahms's genius was tenable, or perhaps the product of a deranged mind or even a hoax. Since the Weimarians had gone home, there was no one in the room who had ever heard Brahms play before. When the slender, fair-haired young man appeared, his voice still high-pitched, few suspected the genius that lay within that shy, modest nature. He played his Scherzo, op. 4, and an Andante, probably the slow movement from the Sonata, op. 1. Berlioz observed a similarity in Brahms's profile to that of Schiller, and when the music was finished he threw his arms around Brahms in a warm embrace, like a great oak enveloping an oak sapling in its branches, as Schloenbach put it. Berlioz spoke so enthusiastically to him that the others could only echo what he had already said. Writing to Joachim a few days later, Berlioz thanked him for his introduction to this young, shy, bold musician 'who plans to write new music. He will suffer much.' Joachim reported Berlioz's letter to Brahms a few days later, only omitting the last four words.

Brahms was not yet done for the day. He was invited that evening, through Sahr's agency, to visit Hedwig Salomon at the house of her sister Elizabeth von Seebach. Hedwig, who was thirty-two, had a soft spot for young composers: she had been linked with Gade for a while and she eventually married another composer, Franz von Holstein. Brahms clearly caught her eye. She had scarcely got to know him at the restaurant, so this was a chance she made the most of. They had friends in common, such as Joachim and the Wehners, and when they talked at length about literature Brahms enthused about Schiller's *Kabale und Liebe* and Hoffmann's *Serapionsbrüder*, in fact all Hoffmann's writings on music, hence his nickname for himself, 'Joh. Kreisler'. 'I spend all my money on books,' he told her. When she suggested that his appetite for music might decline when he became a kapellmeister or professor, he firmly answered, 'But I won't take such a position.'

This independence and determination struck everyone, all the more from someone who looked and sounded so young. Hedwig felt that any girl would want to kiss his child's face without having to blush. What most impressed her was the fact that the idolisation of 'Neue Bahnen' had not dented his modesty or his naïveté. Far from the synchronous appearance in Leipzig of Berlioz and Brahms being a contest, it was turning out to be a triumph for both of them, and a moment of real empathy between them.

Two days later yet another soirée was given, this one by Moscheles in his house on Elsterstrasse, not far from where David lived. We know only that Berlioz and Brahms were both there, but who the other guests were and whether any music was played is unreported. Neither had ever met Moscheles before. Moscheles later expressed a guarded admiration for Brahms's music and a thinly veiled distaste for Berlioz's. At fifty-nine he was perhaps not yet old enough to dismiss all new music, yet unbridled enthusiasm for it was a tall order.

Berlioz was having difficulty arranging rehearsals for his next concert, since the musicians were required for rehearsals for *Lohengrin* and they also had another Thursday subscription concert to prepare. Brahms described him as feeling 'horribly squeezed'. Brahms went on the Wednesday evening to see a play, *Der Erbförster* by Otto Ludwig, a leading playwright of the time who had studied composition under Mendelssohn. The play affected him strongly. During the day he was already correcting proofs of his op. 1 and op. 3, delivered by Härtel's speedy engravers.

The regular subscription concert that Thursday was conducted by David. The first half began with Schumann's overture to *Genoveva*, a clarinet concerto and some Mozart and Verdi arias. The main piece was Schubert's Great C major Symphony which Brahms had never heard before. In a sense the work belonged to Leipzig, since it was Schumann who discovered it and Mendelssohn who first performed it in Leipzig in 1839, and it was published by Breitkopf & Härtel. The Gewandhaus orchestra had made it their own. Berlioz heard the first performance in France on 23 November 1851 and described the second movement as a 'marvel', but he evidently did not go to hear it this time. Brahms was bewitched by the piece but disappointed by the performance: the tempos were too fast, the trombones and trumpets too loud, and the horns terrible throughout.

Berlioz's second Gewandhaus concert took place at 6.30 p.m. on Saturday 10 December. It was an 'extra' concert, which meant that regular subscribers would only attend if they were interested in hearing the music. This was much to Berlioz's advantage since many of the people who had disliked his music at the last concert were only there because they were subscribers. In any case the word had now got around that Berlioz's presence was something out of the ordinary, not to be missed by serious musicians, and the circle of his friends had widened considerably during the week. Brahms, for a start, was there, having missed the first concert. Liszt, as loyal as ever, came back from Weimar, not with such a large group as before, only Cossmann and Cornelius.

The programme included a repeat of *La Fuite en Égypte*, framed by larger extracts from Berlioz's largest and finest works, *Roméo et Juliette* and *La Damnation de Faust*. The *Roméo* extracts included the rarely heard Introduction, with the evocation of Capulets and Montagues fighting in the streets of Verona, followed by the choral recitative that sets out the course of the action. The three main instrumental movements followed, with Johanna Pohl still there to play the harp. Elisabeth Dreyschock, wife of David's assistant konzertmeister, sang the mezzo part, and Carl Schneider sang Mercutio's song about Queen Mab. Schneider was again the soloist in *Le Repos de la Sainte Famille.* The second half consisted of the first two parts of *La Damnation de Faust*, with the same soloists as before, plus Herr Cramer as Brander.

After the concert Liszt hosted a reception for which a list of guests was scrawled on the back of a concert poster: Griepenkerl (who had travelled from Brunswick), Lobe, Cornelius, Cossmann, David, Brahms, Wenzel, Senff, Pohl, two Berliozes, Schloenbach, Götze. The concert had been not only well received but also profitable, making a profit of 130–150 thalers, and to Berlioz's utter delight the orchestra agreed not to be paid for the concert, even though it was additional to their obligations. He could have had no better prelude to his fiftieth birthday, which fell next morning, Sunday 11 December. Unlike Wagner and Germans in general, Berlioz rarely made any fuss about birthdays, least of all his own. Yet he must have taken stock on reaching such a landmark and realised that his situation had markedly changed. He still had the problem of knowing that his music was admired and played in Germany while being scorned and neglected in France. He was obliged to live in Paris since his source of income, his journalism, was there. But what had changed was his willingness to be a composer again, the métier which he had neglected for over three years and which he knew to be his true calling. He had Germany in general and Leipzig in particular to thank for that.

He and Marie left Leipzig on Monday 12 December on the long journey back to Paris. He had firm offers to return for concerts in the spring in Dresden and Hanover, with one or two others still to be arranged. There was a tentative arrangement with London in the pipeline. Above all he had a new work in his head, relating the arrival of the Holy Family in Egypt. He liked to compose in trains, so perhaps he made an immediate start. At the back of his mind was the plan of an immense opera based on the *Aeneid*, which he had been suppressing as if it were some kind of evil presence.

Over his two visits to Leipzig in ten days Liszt had been impressed by Brahms's civil and respectful behaviour and, not least, after looking again at the C major sonata, by his promise as a composer. He left one day later than Berlioz and returned to his Weimar duties, which included an impending performance of *Tannhäuser* to conduct. Later in the month he returned to Leipzig with Cornelius to hear a dress rehearsal of *Lohengrin*, but three of the singers were ill, and the first performance was delayed once again until 7 January.

Brahms stayed on another week, waiting for some copies of his first publications to be delivered. There is no mention of him hearing any of the *Lohengrin* rehearsals during the week nor of attending the next Gewandhaus concert. We do know that he became fast friends with Julius Grimm, a friendship that outlived any other of his Leipzig acquaintances. On Saturday 17 December he made his first public appearance in a chamber music concert given in the smaller Gewandhaus hall by David and his quartet. Framed by Mendelssohn's D major Quartet, op. 44 no. 1, and Mozart's String Quintet in G minor he played the C major Sonata, op. 1, and the Scherzo, op. 4, the two pieces that he had played most often in the preceding months and which in his view represented the best of his work so far. Pohl reported that his playing dispelled any doubts that Schumann's article had provoked and that all were happy to recognise that he was an unusually gifted musician who would one day prove to be an epoch-making figure in the history of music. The *Signale* said he was a better composer than performer, but he would not have been too unhappy with that.

On the day of Brahms's concert, the 17th, von Bülow, the one member of Liszt's entourage whom Brahms had not yet met, passed through the city *en route* from Dresden to concerts in Bremen but stopped only long enough for a morning meeting with Pohl in Brendel's office. Little did he know that he would one day become one of Brahms's foremost champions in Germany. They soon made good on this missing encounter when Brahms joined Joachim and von Bülow in Hanover on 3 January.

Brahms left Leipzig on Tuesday 20 December with Grimm, who had to see an official in Hanover in pursuit of a position in Göttingen. (He became Wehner's assistant early in 1855.) In his luggage Brahms had the published copies of his op. 1 sonata and the op. 3 songs, also the second set of songs published by Senff. He presented Grimm with the manuscript of the op. 6 songs now that he no longer had need of it, and sent a printed copy of op. 6 to Schumann. The indefatigable Joachim was not in Hanover but in Cologne, giving concerts with Hiller, so Brahms travelled on to Hamburg to rejoin his family in time for Christmas. It is not hard to picture the joy on his mother's face when he arrived back in Lilienstrasse. In the eight and a half months that he had been gone he had perhaps not aged much; he still looked young and slight and boyish. But he had made the transition from unknown to famous; he had met most of the leading musicians in Germany; he had published his first works; he had money in his pocket; and he had launched a career that was to lead to a steady production of some of the finest music of the century, indeed of any century.

CHAPTER 14

The Schumanns in Holland and Hanover

NOVEMBER – FEBRUARY

T HE year 1853 came to an end. In his apartment at 13 Zeltweg, Zurich, Wagner was approaching the end of the first draft of *Das Rheingold* after two months' intensive work. Berlioz was back in the Rue de Boursault, Paris, already composing *L'Arrivée à Saïs* (as it was eventually called), the sequel to *La Fuite en Égypte*. Brahms was at home in Hamburg with his family, all of them full of pride at his extraordinary leap to fame but at the same time knowing he would soon need to seek to consolidate his fortune elsewhere. In Hanover Joachim was starting work on a new overture *Demetrius*, based on a five-act play by Herman Grimm, as a response to the success of his *Hamlet* in Düsseldorf. In the Altenburg in Weimar Reményi was practising Paganini Caprices, while Liszt was as usual engaged on a thousand different tasks: conducting opera, following the court's social round, teaching his students, corresponding with musicians all over Europe, arguing remote theological issues with the Princess, revising old compositions, seeing them through the press, and working on new ones, including the great *Faust Symphony* which came into being in 1854, perhaps occasionally playing the piano.

We will leave our network of musicians there, all of them in the full vigour of life, with many busy and productive years ahead of them. They all turned the calendar page to 1854. It remains to pursue Schumann's story just beyond the end of a year that was decisive for him too, although in his case the future took a very different turn. He did not know it, but the five *Romanzen* for cello and piano (now lost) that he composed in November after a remarkably fruitful few months were his last compositions. At year's end he was actually in a good frame of mind. When the bitter quarrel with the Düsseldorf Musikverein ended in a complete breach in November, he and Clara made up their minds to leave. Where to go, without any prospect of employment? Their preference was Vienna, which was the scene of Clara's most triumphant appearance in her early career. She was there as the eighteen-year-old Clara Wieck in the winter of 1837–8 and had enjoyed extraordinary success. She was even appointed Chamber Virtuoso to the Imperial court. With Robert she had returned there in the winter of 1846–7, but their four concerts had a definitely mixed reception. The last concert was given a boost by the participation of Jenny Lind, the 'Swedish nightingale'. Recent indications were that Vienna would offer the best prospects in 1853, perhaps because they had seen too much of Leipzig and Dresden in the past and because Vienna was after all a city with the resources of the imperial court and a strong tradition of music at many levels.

Before any firmer plans took shape, they seized the opportunity of making

Map 4 The Schumanns' tour of Holland

a concert tour of Holland, made possible by Schumann's abandonment of the Düsseldorf Musikverein. The tour turned out to be a grand success. In the previous summer 1852 they visited Scheveningen in Holland (the nearest coastal point to Düsseldorf) since the doctor suggested sea bathing as good treatment for Robert's complicated ailments. For Clara the month at the seaside was complicated by a miscarriage, but Robert appeared to get a lot better. In Scheveningen they had the company, by chance, of Jenny Lind and, not by chance, of the energetic Dutch musician Johannes Verhulst whom they had known in Leipzig many years before when at the age of twenty-two he was conductor of the Euterpe orchestra there. As a composer he was much indebted to Mendelssohn and Schumann, and he was already one of the foremost Dutch musicians of his time, based now in Rotterdam.

It was with Verhulst's help that they now arranged to give concerts in Holland for the first time. Composers who who were not star pianists could choose to promote their works from the podium. Wagner and Berlioz were in this category, but since Schumann was no longer a pianist and seriously discredited as a conductor, he was often a spectator while others played his music. This would have been a difficulty were it not for Clara's celebrity as a pianist which permitted them to design the tour around her appearances, playing her husband's music much of the time in concerts which also featured his orchestral works. It was essentially her tour, with an immensely demanding programme of solo pieces and concertos. He conducted his own pieces a few times, happily without apparent mishap.

After 1847 Schumann no longer kept such a full diary of his daily doings. His 'Haushaltbücher' continued to record daily events at home in brief with financial bookkeeping, while on his travels he recorded much more. Clara kept a diary too. We thus have a detailed record of the Dutch tour which allows us to see the Schumann ménage at close quarters at a critical time in their lives. Robert was subject as ever to dizzy spells and hearing disorders, while Clara, three months pregnant, was not feeling well, occasionally suffering 'attacks' of different kinds. The weather was very cold. They were accompanied by their maid Bertha and the soprano Mathilde Hartmann, and they were carrying the usual musician's baggage: a trunkful of orchestral parts and concert material.

They left Düsseldorf on Thursday 24 November at around noon, and although Utrecht, the first town to be visited, was only 120 miles away, it took two days to get there. The rail connection with Holland was some years in the future partly because Dutch railways used the broad gauge while German lines were on standard gauge. North from Düsseldorf the line went only as far as Oberhausen; after that a succession of post-chaises took them to Emmerich on the Dutch border where they spent the night. Schumann's painful hearing problem recurred that night but happily went away. A coach ride next morning took them thence across the border to Arnhem where the train connected to Utrecht. They put up at the Kasteel van Antwerpen on the Oudegracht.

In the next twenty-five days they gave thirteen concerts spread between four cities, all quite close together, as Dutch cities are. The concert schedule was:

Saturday	26 November	Utrecht
Wednesday	30 November	The Hague
Thursday	1 December	Rotterdam
Friday	2 December	Amsterdam
Tuesday	6 December	The Hague
Friday	9 December	Rotterdam
Saturday	10 December	Utrecht
Sunday	11 December	Amsterdam
Tuesday	13 December	Amsterdam
Thursday	15 December	The Hague
Friday	16 December	Amsterdam

| Monday | 19 December | Rotterdam |
| Tuesday | 20 December | Amsterdam |

They started in the Gebouw voor Kunsten en Wetenschappen in Utrecht (now housing the Utrecht Conservatoire) where on Saturday 26th the orchestra of the Collegium Musicum Ultrajectinum was conducted by Johann Hermann Kufferath, a German violinist who had studied with Spohr and who had been in charge of Utrecht's music since 1830. There was a single rehearsal at 1 p.m. Clara was feeling so unwell that they thought about cancelling the tour. But she went ahead with the concert and gave the first performance of Robert's *Concert Allegro with Introduction* for piano and orchestra, op. 134, which he had composed in September and which was dedicated to Brahms. She also played some *Lieder ohne Worte* by Mendelssohn and Beethoven's 'Waldstein' Sonata. Mathilde Hartmann sang a group of solos, and the concert opened with Robert's Third Symphony, the 'Rhenish'. The reception was noisily enthusiastic, especially since after Clara had played an encore she realised that they were calling 'Doctor!' Doctor!' in response to which Robert had to come on and take a further bow. Robert was annoyed by people chatting and drinking tea in the gallery, but touched by the applause. Clara concluded that the Dutch were much more musical than the Rhinelanders.

Next day, Sunday 27th, they took a six-hour journey by 'fast coach' through Leiden to the Hague. They didn't get there until 8 p.m., but even so they disliked the receptionist at the Hotel Doelen where Mozart had once stayed, close to the concert hall, so they went to the Hotel Paulez across the road (where the American embassy is now) instead. On the Monday morning Verhulst arrived, to their delight. They revisited Scheveningen, closely adjacent to the Hague, to gaze at the sea and to visit their landlady from 1852 and her daughter Gerritje. Back at the hotel Johann Heinrich Lübeck came to introduce himself. He was another German musician who had been director of the Hague Conservatoire since 1827 and was conductor of the orchestra in the brand new Diligentia Hall (which still stands), where they were to appear.

On the Tuesday they looked at Chinese and Japanese antiquities in what is now the Mauritshuis, whose ground floor then comprised a 'Cabinet of Curiosities'. (The paintings were upstairs.) There was no rehearsal until Wednesday morning, the 30th, the day of the concert. The programme was similar to that heard in Utrecht. The Schumann symphony was the Second, in C major, this time conducted by Robert himself. Overtures by Beethoven and Weber were conducted by Lübeck, and Clara gave the *Concert Allegro* its second hearing. Her main solo piece was Mendelssohn's *Variations sérieuses*. Mathilde Hartmann sang the same solos as before.

Early next morning, Thursday, in glorious winter weather, Verhulst led them to Rotterdam, where they rehearsed at 11.30 a.m. for the evening concert. The music society there, Eruditio Musica, was founded in 1826 and still run by the very capable Wouter Hutschenruyter, with Verhulst acting as his assistant. Their hall (no longer standing) had better acoustics than the Diligentia in the Hague. This time Robert conducted his Third Symphony and Clara played Robert's A minor Piano Concerto. Mathilde Hartmann's place was taken by a Dutch singer Sophie Offermans–van Hove who included an aria by Verhulst in her selection. Robert was greatly impressed by the orchestra, especially their playing of Beethoven's overture *The Consecration of the House*, and the audience's enthusiasm was noiser than in both Utrecht and the Hague.

The concert did not end until eleven o'clock, yet when they returned to their hotel, the Bath, they were greeted by a special welcome. A hundred singers and a group of wind players assembled in front of the hotel and performed, according to Clara, for nearly an hour in icy cold. They sang by torchlight some extracts from Schumann's cantata *Der Rose Pilgerfahrt*, which dated from 1851, and a wind arrangement of Schumann's *Birthday March*, originally a piano duet for children. Did they know they were honouring the Schumanns' youngest child Eugenie tucked up in bed in Düsseldorf, whose second birthday it was? Robert made a speech of thanks, to which the president of the Rotterdam Musical Society welcomed them formally to the Netherlands. Verhulst and Hutschenruyter were obviously the instigators of this touching little entertainment in their honour. Clara again found herself reflecting how undeserving and disrespectful the citizens of Düsseldorf were in comparison with the Dutch.

They did not get to bed until after midnight but had to be up at six next morning to leave for Amsterdam (the short night did not preclude the bedtime intimacy

49 The Bazaar, The Hague

which Robert's coded diary always records). The weather was still bright. With the train the fifty-mile journey took only three hours. They just had time to check in at the Hôtel des Pays Bas on Doelenstraat and then get to the Felix Meritis Society's hall on the Keizersgracht (which still stands) for a noon rehearsal. They were greeted by a collection of Amsterdam's leading musicians, including Johannes Bernardus van Bree, the orchestra's conductor and an able composer. Clara played the Beethoven 'Emperor' Concerto and van Bree conducted Robert's Second Symphony, with the usual supporting items. Mathilde Hartmann was back as their vocal soloist, sounding nervous, as Robert thought. Gales of applause greeted Clara even after the first movement of the concerto.

Those three consecutive concerts in three cities called for a rest of three days, two of which were spent in Amsterdam, visiting the zoo and walking about the city. Mathilde Hartmann left the party to visit friends. Social calls from Amsterdam's musicians filled the rest of their time, making plans for concerts later in the tour. On Monday morning (5th) they left the Hôtel des Pays Bas, feeling cheated by the enormous bill, and headed for the Hague again. Lübeck and his colleagues were there to greet them, although Clara was not feeling at all well. In the evening they explored a very crowded Christmas bazaar, amazed at the expensive gifts, and then went to a rehearsal of Robert's Piano Quintet which started at 10.30 at night.

This second concert in the Hague (on Tuesday 6th) included a full performance, with Clara as piano accompanist, of *Der Rose Pilgerfahrt*. Perhaps the chorus had been part of the demonstration in Rotterdam a few evenings earlier. Lübeck conducted. Clara and some string players prefaced it with Robert's Piano Quintet while the composer sat discreetly in the audience. Sophie Offermans, whom Robert described as an 'interesting' woman, sang songs by Robert and Verhulst, who had rejoined the Schumanns that morning. At the end, when Robert was finally winkled out of his seat in the audience and made to take a bow, one of the singers put a laurel wreath on his head, and he never noticed. 'But we did,' said Clara, 'and that's how it should be.'

Once again Verhulst led them back to Rotterdam on the Wednesday morning through the mist that had settled in, back to the Bath Hotel. Thursday included a lunch at the Verhulsts' house and a dinner given by Schutze van Houten, president of the Rotterdam Musical Society, at which a local violinist played Mendelssohn's concerto with Clara at the piano. Friday (9th), with the sun breaking through the mist, was another concert day for Clara. In the afternoon there was an organ recital in the Zuiderkerk by Jan van Eijken which included two of Robert's fugues on the name BACH as well as music by Bach, Mendelssohn and Gade. It was extremely cold, and no doubt Clara gave it a miss since she had a strikingly heavy part in the chamber concert that evening in the smaller concert hall on Bierstraat. She played the Beethoven 'Appassionata' Sonata, her own *Variations on a Theme by Schumann*, and some smaller solos. She accompanied Sophie Offermans in two Verhulst songs and with a string quartet played Robert's Piano Quintet. Her only break was when the quartet played Robert's A minor quartet, op. 41 no. 1.

Next morning, Saturday 10th, was another early start, this time for Utrecht. On the train they were accosted by a young cellist named Bernhard Hildebrand-Romberg, who was booked to play in the same concert in Utrecht. He was a grandson of the cellist-composer Bernhard Heinrich Romberg, who died in 1841 and whose *Concerto Suisse* he was due to play. Once again they had to go straight into a rehearsal with the concert that same evening. The only Schumann work was the overture to *Genoveva*, which Robert conducted. Clara played Mendelssohn's G minor Piano Concerto and the usual group of smaller pieces. Yet another attraction on the programme was the Italian clarinettist Cavallini, the same virtuoso who had appeared in Berlioz's festival concert in Baden-Baden in August. Schumann called it a 'curious' programme because it contained no vocal items, which concerts normally did in those days. The days of all-orchestral concerts were some way in the future.

Sunday morning breakfast was with Kufferath, the local conductor, before they took the train for Amsterdam, in which, Robert observed, hardy Dutchmen were sitting next to an open window in the freezing weather. The room in the Hotel Rondeel being too gloomy, they went back to their old room down the street at the Hôtel des Pays Bas, having first expostulated with the landlord about the charge for their previous visit. One of the Amsterdam musicians, Wittering, held a reception for them with a soirée to follow in which Clara played Robert's *Études symphoniques*. A quartet played three movements of Robert's quartet op. 41 no. 2 and young Romberg, who had travelled with them from Utrecht, played a piece by his grandfather.

The next soirée was on Tuesday 13th at the Odeon, a small hall with good acoustics (which still stands). Clara was once again playing Robert's Piano Quintet, once again with a different string quartet, led by the conductor van Bree, who was also an excellent violinist. She again performed the 'Appassionata' and accompanied Mathilde Hartmann, back from wherever it was she had gone, in a group of songs. After the concert they feasted on oysters, with a relatively quiet day to follow. Robert was beginning to long for home.

On Thursday 15th they were back in the Hague for the third time for a private soirée as guests of the royal family in the Hague. Lübeck's position as court conductor enabled him to arrange a performance at court hosted by Princess Luise, sister of the King of Prussia and wife of Prince Frederick of the Netherlands, the king's uncle, and a military man who had fought at both Leipzig in 1813 and Waterloo in 1815. Perhaps, like his niece Sophia, Grand Duchess of Sachsen-Weimar and a pupil of Liszt, he was musical as well as military, yet the assembled notabilities, his guests, paid no attention whatever when Clara played, chatting noisily throughout. She played a colossal programme, including the 'Waldstein', Mendelssohn's *Variations sérieuses,* and other pieces by Mendelssohn, Chopin and Heller, but nothing by her husband. Enraged, she stormed out, diva-like, stepping out into the snow in her satin concert shoes. Robert had to endure the question 'And are *you* musical too?'

50 Clara Schumann, by Carl Sohn

This was the only shadow across the Dutch tour, since audiences were everywhere else spontaneously cheering his music and her playing. She had felt unwell early on, but they were both overwhelmed by the response of Dutch audiences; they could not help comparing them to the incivility, as they saw it, of Düsseldorfers. The vitality of music in Holland at this time was one of Europe's best-kept secrets, perhaps hidden because none of their musicians rank among the composers we still honour today. Berlioz's overture *Les Francs-juges* was performed in Holland thirty-eight times between 1844 and 1866, a far higher figure than in England or France, yet he never went there. Although many Dutch musicians were trained in Germany and spoke good German, Holland was often left out of German and French musical enterprises, which makes the Schumanns' tour somewhat incidental to our story, however heart-warming it was at a time when they both needed some blandishment.

And so it went on. Next day, Friday 16th, there was an orchestral concert in Amsterdam with Clara accompanied by the Felix Meritis orchestra; then they went back to Rotterdam the day after. On Monday 19th Clara played a concert there, and then back to Amsterdam for her final appearance in the French Theatre on the

20th. The other participants on this occasion were so bad that Robert went home early. In each city they were besieged by well-wishing musicians inviting them to receptions and smaller gatherings. Clara felt gradually better throughout the tour, especially since she was well received everywhere she played (except at court).

But the demands of such a tour were exorbitant. Few musicians today, even in perfect health, would put up with such a strenuous schedule. There was little respite. It was bitterly cold and they still had a laborious journey ahead of them. Leaving Amsterdam on Wednesday 21st they took the train to Arnhem, but the diligence from there to Emmerich, where they again stopped for the night, was miserably uncomfortable. The rest of the journey was slow and cold. 'Tired horses', commented Schumann, when he might equally have been referring to themselves. They got home to Bilkerstrasse late on the 22nd for a joyous reunion with their children.

They returned just in time to see Joachim, who was passing through town after his concerts in Cologne. Much music was played, and Robert gave him the manuscript of his Fourth Symphony, which he kept for the rest of his life. Clara's Christmas present to Robert was her portrait, very beautifully painted by a local artist, Carl Sohn. Schumann's chief preoccupations were now the compilation of a book of his collected writings and an anthology of poetry called *Dichtergarten*. For a spell the literary Schumann replaced the musical Schumann.

Any opportunity to make music away from Düsseldorf was welcome to them, especially when it took the form of a visit to Hanover at the invitation of Joachim. When Schumann wrote to Joachim on 8 January 1854 he was in an especially good mood. On 19 January they took the train to Hanover where they were met at the station by Joachim and Brahms and were put up at the Hotel Royal nearby. As they dined out together that evening they were joined by Brahms's new friend Julius Grimm. Joachim, the tireless traveller, had just been to Weimar to visit Liszt and to Leipzig, where he played his own violin concerto and gave the second performance of the *Phantasie* Schumann had recently written for him. His plans for the Schumanns' visit originally included an orchestral concert on the 21st, followed a week later by a performance of *Das Paradies und die Peri*, a full-scale choral work on Thomas Moore's *Lalla Rookh* first heard in Leipzig in 1843, to be conducted by Schumann himself. This was to be prepared by Eduard Hille, the local chorus master (sometimes confused with Ferdinand Hiller). But in Joachim's absence the plan had been sabotaged, perhaps by Fischer, the city's second conductor, and the piece was abandoned. In the orchestral concert Clara played the 'Emperor' Concerto, Joachim played the new *Phantasie* and then, after some smaller items, conducted Robert's Fourth Symphony. The orchestra played superbly, as they had for Berlioz two months before. King Georg was of course there to hear it.

The next day they went to Meyerbeer's *Les Huguenots* at the opera, although Clara and Brahms left early. Schumann's intense dislike of the work was public and well-known, so it is odd that he went to hear it at all. Wilhelmine Clauss, the nineteen-year-old pianist who lived in Paris and was one of the star visitors in London during Berlioz's visit there, arrived in Hanover that day and was rapidly the cause of such tension that Clara decided to go home. Bitter words were exchanged over we know not what, but things were soon smoothed over and Clara stayed on. The two women and Joachim made music together, which Schumann observed as a 'rare collaboration'.

Clara played twice at court, to the delight of King Georg, who threw out generous compliments at both of them. The second performance included much of Robert's music, which affected the King deeply, especially *Der Dichter spricht* at the end of *Kinderszenen*.

Above all they relished the congenial company of the young trio, Joachim, Brahms and Grimm. There was much music-making, with Joachim on the violin and Clara or Brahms at the piano. Besides Beethoven and Mendelssohn they played music by Joachim, by Clara, by Robert, and occasionally something by Brahms, who remained largely silent. Clara was in fact especially touched by Brahms's taciturnity. 'He hardly speaks at all,' she wrote, 'and if he does it's so soft I can't understand him.' Joachim seemed more serious than before, although some merry hours passed. One evening as things reached a particular peak of jollity, Joachim went out saying he had to go and see his landlord about a key. While the others were remarking on his thoughtfulness he reappeared with some bottles of champagne which he had just gone out to buy. From that point on champagne was always referred to by all of them as 'house-key'.

Schumann too was notoriously taciturn. But on another occasion the men were at a restaurant (Clara being now in her fifth month of pregnancy was no doubt glad to be left in the hotel) when he was drawn into telling stories about his past, including the well-known incident of which he might in other company have felt embarrassed: his failure to write correctly for trumpets and horns at the opening of the First Symphony, the 'Spring' in B flat. To the astonishment of the other diners he stood up and imitated the tortured noise horns make on the two 'stopped' notes, the effect his piece would have had if he had not been advised to correct it:

Ex. 5 Schumann, Symphony no. 1, first movement, bars 1–2

On their last evening in Hanover, the 29th, Clara and Joachim played Robert's *Romanzen* for cello (in a violin version), then Clara played three movements of one of Brahms's sonatas, followed by Robert's D minor Violin Sonata, op. 121. Next day Joachim, Brahms, Grimm and Hille saw them off at the station, Robert clutching a box of cigars which Joachim had pressed upon him.

Back home in Düsseldorf Robert resumed work on his anthology, sorting through some Greek and Roman poetry, and he corrected proofs of his collected writings for the Leipzig publisher Wigand. It might seem curiously valedictory to publish one's literary œuvre at the age of forty-three, but he had given up contributing criticism to the musical press some years before. The 'Neue Bahnen' article in October was the meteoric appearance of a writer who was known to have laid down his pen. With his career as a conductor in shreds, he believed all the more in an abundant future as a composer soon to be resumed, especially since recent months had been so productive. For the anthology he made several visits to the city library, although Clara thought it was bad for him to be reading Latin and Greek again after such a long interval.

On Friday 10 February the long-feared disaster struck, like the last act of a five-act tragedy. He suffered some excruciating pain in his ears, hearing persistent notes and chords. For several days he was plagued by headaches and by hearing music which, ironically, sounded exquisite but caused him great pain. In lucid intervals he went to the library with Dietrich to work, but the music gave him no rest and he could not sleep. He noted 'wonderful pain' and 'wonderful music' in his notebook, but the symptoms were bad.

After a week of this he got up in the night and wrote down a theme which he said an angel had sung to him. His vision of angels soon turned into something much more alarming, alternating back and forth in his deranged mind between good and bad spirits. Things came to a head on Sunday 26 February when he worked himself into a high state of tension playing the sonata of a young friend. He ate a large supper, then suddenly stood up and said he must go into an asylum since he could no longer control his mind. The doctor was sent for while Robert laid out the things he was going to need.

'Robert, are you leaving your wife and children?' Clara asked.

'It won't be long,' he replied. 'I'll soon be back, cured.'

The doctor persuaded him to go to bed and forbade Clara to stay with him. A male nurse was called while she slept in the next room. Next morning he worked a little at his desk. After lunch Clara went out of the room for a while leaving their daughter Marie with him. When he walked out of the room Marie thought he would be back in a minute, but suddenly the maid Bertha rushed in to say he had gone. Dietrich and their friend Dr Hasenklever ran out to look for him but could not find him. Not long afterwards he was brought back in such a pitiable state that Clara was told to go to her blind friend Rosalie Leser for the day so as not to be upset.

In broad daylight Schumann had turned left out of their house on Bilkerstrasse, left into the narrow street that leads down to the river and on to the long bridge that crossed the Rhine. It was raining and cold. He was wearing felt slippers and had taken only a coat over his house clothes. The bridge was not, as one might imagine, a mighty span rising high above the water, but a 'Schiffsbrücke' constructed from boats lashed together allowing openings for river traffic to pass through, so the walkway was only a foot or two above the surface. It was a toll bridge, but having

51 The Schiffsbrücke, Düsseldorf

no money he offered the tollkeeper his handkerchief as a pledge. Two fishermen saw this strange behaviour, watched him head out to the middle of the bridge and jump in. If he meant to drown himself he had little chance of doing so with so many people around. The fishermen fished him out. He tried to jump in again from their boat, but they stopped him. Eight men were needed to carry him, shivering and dripping wet, back to Bilkerstrasse.

The doctors advised Clara to stay at Rosalie Leser's and not to see him in this state. Next day he sent her a message to say he was getting on well but at the same time insisted to the doctors that he be sent to an asylum. They agreed that was the best course and arranged for him to be taken to an asylum at Endenich, just outside Bonn. On the Friday Brahms's arrival from Hanover was a great comfort for Clara, and on the Saturday Schumann was taken away by the doctor, never to return. Clara then went back to her home. Brahms and Dietrich stayed with her that evening; next day Joachim joined them. A chapter in their lives was closed.

Epilogue

THE remaining years of the 1850s saw a widening of the schism in German music whose early shoots we have seen beginning to push through the surface in 1853. As usual there were both aesthetic and personal perspectives. In the previous generation it had been possible, in fact normal, to combine a fresh Romantic sensibility with a respect for classical traditions, as in Mendelssohn, with his fragrant evocations of Scotland and Italy alongside his devotion to Bach, or in Schumann, whose earnest study of fugue went hand in hand with a poetic love of butterflies and moonlight. Berlioz displayed scant interest in the classical heritage, being impatient with Bach and Haydn and admiring Mozart and Gluck exclusively for the solemnity and passion of their operas. For him music had above all to be expressive. The issue that confronted a young musician in 1853 was whether to follow Wagner's siren call to an all-embracing music drama, uncompromising in its message of modernity and infused with humanity of every kind, or whether to seek beauty and profundity in the language of music itself, unsupported by philosophy or emotional dynamics. The second of these options was both old and new, since its roots lay in eighteenth-century practice but its principles had never been articulated, at least not in modern terms. It is hardly a coincidence that in 1853 the gospel of that faith was being written in Vienna by the critic Eduard Hanslick, whose epoch-making book *Vom Musikalisch-Schönen* was published in Leipzig the following year. Its prophetic message was that music need not look outside itself for its subject-matter, indeed it does not even need subject-matter; the emotion that music generates in us is different from and independent of emotions arising from other human experience. Hanslick's arguments struck at the core of Romantic assumptions about expression and meaning, and they brought him inevitably into conflict with Wagner and Liszt. In contrast, after Brahms's move to Vienna in 1862 he and Brahms became friends, with Hanslick consistently and forcefully supporting Brahms in the press.

As is usually the case in such debates, the fork in the road that faced musicians of the 1850s was defined as much by critics, particularly Brendel in the *Neue Zeitschrift für Musik*, as by the musicians themselves. This journal saw the future in the Wagnerian music-drama and the Lisztian symphonic poem rather than in symphonies and sonatas, even though it was generous to Brahms whenever his new works appeared. Bischoff's *Niederrheinische Musikzeitung* meanwhile did all it could to belittle what soon came to be called, with inflammatory effect, the 'New German School'. By 1855 Joachim was more or less openly criticising the musicianship of his former mentor Liszt, a defection made inevitable by his close friendship with Brahms. Wagner confessed he was later surprised by the vehemence of Joachim's hostility to Liszt and himself, but he had already caught a scent of it in

Basel and Strasbourg. For Joachim and Brahms a loyal attachment to Schumann's music and to his widow was to be interpreted as a statement of their position. Behind Brahms's extraordinary path to fame in 1853 lies a conviction more solidly implanted in him than in Joachim or anyone else that he had no intention of ever following the Lisztian or the Wagnerian path. Joachim in company with Schumann and Brahms came to focus on the development of instrumental music as growing out of Beethoven's quartets and sonatas, not focussed narrowly on the enormous Ninth Symphony.

In 1860 Brahms proposed to Joachim that they should issue a public statement of their protest against the view that the New German School represented the leadership of German music. Many were asked to sign, but only four did: Brahms, Joachim, their friend Grimm, and Bernhard Scholz, at that time Hanover's kapellmeister. It appeared in the Berlin *Echo* and took the form of a direct challenge to the *Neue Zeitschrift für Musik*. In the long run it probably did more harm than good, since Brahms often in later years preferred to stand aloof from partisanship of that sort.

The other musical issue that divided opinion was what we would now call performance practice. Brahms and Joachim became proponents of the view that respect for the classics requires us to play their music as they wrote it, as nearly as possible. In this they were of like mind with Berlioz, who protested strongly against the disfigurement of music of the past by ornamentation and improvisation not sanctioned by the composer. Liszt meanwhile considered the art of interpretation to be essentially creative: the performer's duty was to recreate the music of the past in the spirit of the present. Adaptations of Bach's organ music in his hands, for example, became contemporary piano music of high virtuosity. The fact that modern thinking has almost entirely annihilated Liszt's approach from our consciousness should not disguise the immediacy of the issue in the 1850s, when it was by no means obvious that old music should be dressed in its original garments and not brought up to date.

At the personal level, a split may be traced back to Clara Wieck (as she then was) reporting to her fiancé Robert her disgust with Berlioz when he failed to review her Paris recital in 1839 with the enthusiasm she felt to be her due. Berlioz and Schumann had established a fair level of mutual admiration which was sustained through Berlioz's visit to Leipzig in 1843. But Schumann's shyness, Clara's hostility and the lack of a shared language made closer intimacy almost impossible. Schumann's early enthusiasm for the *Symphonie fantastique* left no mark on his own music; Düsseldorf never featured on Berlioz's German itineraries in the 1850s, and their correspondence dried up.

The Schumanns' relationship with Liszt was more complex, for although the two men held each other in high regard and dedicated important works to each other, Clara never liked Liszt's piano playing and regarded him as a demonic and destructive influence. Liszt felt increasingly uncomfortable during his visits to Düsseldorf both before and after Schumann's final crisis. Having little capacity for personal enmity, Liszt kept up his friendship with Joachim and Brahms as long as they were willing to respond, although they inevitably all went their separate ways in later years.

The polarity and the genius of Wagner and Brahms gave them virtually complete dominance over German music in the last decades of the century to the point where secondary composers were shamefully overshadowed. Verdi achieved the same supremacy in Italy. In France the opposite happened, since Berlioz had never commanded a strong enough following to dominate the next generation. A large number of composers emerged instead, responding to the richness of *belle époque* culture and standing unmistakably aloof from German models, even when they yearned to borrow Bayreuth's colours.

After 1860 the musical map of Europe changed profoundly, even before the revolutionary works that Wagner had been composing since 1853 were performed and known. Musical activity in Russia grew rapidly into a flourishing harvest, with conservatoires in St Petersburg and Moscow and a crop of composers soon to be heard and taken seriously in the west. In Bohemia, too, national colour gave local musicians an identity they had never enjoyed before: Smetana's first operas appeared in 1866. The picturesque, naïve phase of Romanticism gave way to something more searching, self-conscious and dangerous. Dilettantes and amateurs faded into the background, and many of the institutions still in place today, such as conservatoires and orchestras, took on a new solidity and seriousness. Music of the present had to compete more and more with music of the past, although it would be a long time before contemporary music was treated as an eccentric curiosity for devotees only. In the 1850s contemporary music was the first concern of all composers, obviously, but also of all performers, all critics and all audiences. New works were news, as well they might be, since an extraordinary number of enduring masterpieces were taking shape at that time on paper and in the brains of a group of composers each one of whom

> did bestride the narrow world like a Colossus.

I T may be helpful, finally, to outline the later adventures of the main characters in our story:

Schumann was confined to the Endenich asylum until his death over two years later, on 29 July 1856. Clara was instructed not to visit him, and it was not until a few days before his death that she finally insisted on being allowed to see him. During his confinement he was visited by a small group of devoted friends: Brahms, Joachim, Dietrich, Wasielewski and occasionally Bettina von Arnim. His fundamental illness was almost certainly syphilis contracted as early as 1831, with persistent neurological problems in a personality with depressive inclinations. Part of this no doubt supplies the secret of certain aspects of his music, but his genius remains otherwise a miracle of nature.

Clara Schumann bore her last child, Felix, on 11 June 1854. She never remarried but fiercely guarded her husband's name and reputation. She lived until 1896, widely respected as a leading pianist and teacher of her time and in modern times as a composer also. She lived in Berlin, Baden-Baden and Frankfurt, and remained on the closest terms with Brahms, fourteen years her junior, throughout her life.

Brahms outlived Clara Schumann by one year. After early hints of something more passionate, they remained loyal and devoted friends until her death. He never married. His friendship with Joachim cooled somewhat when they were living far apart, but the Violin Concerto of 1877 was a sincere tribute to his friend. Their intimacy was seriously impaired in 1881 when Brahms took Joachim's wife's side in a marital dispute, but they patched it up in 1887 when Brahms composed the Double Concerto. He met Wagner just once, in Vienna on 6 February 1864. The meeting was cordial and Brahms played his *Variations on a Theme of Handel*. Of Berlioz's music *La Fuite en Égypte* remained the one piece he liked, although he once conducted *Harold en Italie* in Vienna on 8 November 1874.

Joachim lived until 1907, universally recognised as one of the great violinists of his time, especially as an exponent of chamber music and the concertos of Beethoven and Brahms. In 1863 he married the mezzo-soprano Amalie Weiss but separated from her in 1881. He remained very attached to Gisela von Arnim, who married the playwright Herman Grimm in 1860. He named his two sons Hermann and Giseler. In 1868 he moved from Hanover to Berlin as the first director of the Musikhochschule. He never abandoned composition, but the intensity with which it engaged him in 1853 was not sustained, and his works are rarely played today.

Berlioz completed *L'Arrivée à Saïs* in April 1854 followed by *Le Songe d'Hérode*, thus making the full trilogy *L'Enfance du Christ*. Its success in Paris in December 1854 encouraged him to plan the opera *Les Troyens*. On visits to Weimar in 1855 and 1856 Princess Carolyne urged him to compose the music, whatever its fate might be. The opera was completed in 1858 but only a part of it was performed in his lifetime, in Paris in 1863. After *Les Troyens* he composed the comic opera *Béatrice et Bénédict* for Bénazet's theatre in Baden-Baden, where it was performed in 1862. His wife Harriet died in March 1854 and he married Marie Recio in October of that year. She died in 1862, and he lived on until 1869.

Liszt completed at least five symphonic poems as well as the *Faust Symphony* in 1854. In 1858 the hostile reaction to Cornelius's *Der Barbier von Bagdad* in Weimar caused him to resign his post. His son Daniel died in 1859 and his daughter Blandine in 1862. His mother died in 1866. In the last twenty years of his life he divided his time between Rome, Weimar and Budapest with a large output of choral music and piano music. He and the Princess were never married. He took minor orders in the Catholic Church in 1865 and died in Bayreuth in 1886.

Wagner completed the first draft of *Das Rheingold* on 14 January 1854 and the full score in May. *Die Walküre* was finished in 1856, *Siegfried* in 1871, and the complete *Ring des Nibelungen* in 1874. It was first performed as a cycle at the opening of the first Bayreuth Festival in 1876. In 1857 he became closely involved with Mathilde Wesendonck and broke off work on the *Ring* to compose *Tristan und Isolde* and then *Die Meistersinger von Nürnberg*. He was permitted to enter most German territories after 1861. He finally separated from Minna in 1862 and she died in 1866. In 1870 he married Liszt's daughter Cosima, previously married to von Bülow. He died in Venice in 1883 and Cosima lived on until 1930.

Von Bülow married Liszt's daughter Cosima in 1857, who left him for Wagner in 1869. He conducted the first performances of Wagner's *Tristan und Isolde* in 1865 and *Die Meistersinger* in 1868. He maintained careers as solo pianist and conductor throughout his life and became a champion of Brahms's music, conducting the first performance of the Fourth Symphony in 1885. He died in 1894.

Cornelius composed the comic opera *Der Barbier von Bagdad* which, when played in Weimar in 1858, aroused the controversy that led to Liszt's resignation. He became a fervent Wagnerian and wrote two more operas. His choral music and songs are particularly estimable, and his output of poetry was impressive. He died in 1874.

Reményi was allowed back to Hungary in 1860. He worked intermittently there and in Rome with Liszt. He continued to tour worldwide and was one of the first European musicians to tour Australia, south-east Asia and South Africa. He died in 1898 in San Francisco while playing a concert.

Bibliography

T HE bibliography is divided into three categories: general reference works, bibliographies for the six principal composers (with Clara Schumann included with her husband) divided into letters, biography, and the catalogue of works, and additional bibliographies for individual chapters. The general reference works and composers' bibliographies have been drawn upon throughout the book.

GENERAL REFERENCE WORKS

Hugo Riemann, *Dictionnaire de Musique*, ed. Georges Humbert (Paris, 1899).
Die Musik in Geschichte und Gegenwart, ed. Ludwig Finscher, 2nd ed. (Kassel, 1994–).
Grosses Sängerlexikon, ed. K. J. Kutsch and Leo Riemens, 3rd ed. (Bern, 1997–).
The New Grove Dictionary of Music and Musicians, ed. Stanley Sadie, 2nd ed. (New York, 2001).
Hans Kobschätsky, *Streckenatlas der deutschen Eisenbahnen 1835–1892* (Düsseldorf, 1971).

COMPOSERS

BRAHMS

Letters

Briefwechsel, 15 vols. (Berlin, 1908–22). [Relevant volumes are nos. 4 (to Julius Grimm), 5–6 (to Joachim), 14 (to Breitkopf & Härtel and Senff), and 15 (to Franz Wüllner).]
Clara Schumann, Johannes Brahms: *Briefe aus den Jahren 1853–1896*, ed. Berthold Litzmann (Hildesheim, 1970).
Kurt Stephenson, *Johannes Brahms in seiner Familie: der Briefwechsel* (Hamburg, 1973).
Die Briefe an Johannes Brahms / Hans von Bülow, ed. Hans-Joachim Hinrichsen (Tutzing, 1994).

Catalogue

Margit L. McCorkle, *Johannes Brahms: Thematisch-Bibliographisches Werkverzeichnis* (Munich, 1984).

Biography

Florence May, *The Life of Johannes Brahms*, vol. I (London, 1905).
Max Kalbeck, *Johannes Brahms*, I, Erster Halbband: *1833–1856* (Berlin, 1912).
Karl Geiringer, *Brahms: His Life and Work* (Boston, 1936).
Renate and Kurt Hofmann, *Johannes Brahms Zeittafel zu Leben und Werk* (Tutzing, 1983).
Styra Avins, *Johannes Brahms: Life and Letters* (Oxford, 1997).

JOACHIM

Letters

Briefe von und an Joseph Joachim, ed. Johannes Joachim and Andreas Moser (Berlin, 1911–13).
Johannes Brahms, *Briefwechsel*, vols. 5–6 (Berlin, 1908–22).

Biography

Andreas Moser, *Joseph Joachim: ein Lebensbild*, 3rd ed. (Berlin, 1904).

SCHUMANN

Diaries

Robert Schumann, *Tagebücher*, Bd. III, ed. Gerd Nauhaus (Leipzig, 1982).
Robert et Clara Schumann: Journal intime, ed. Yves Hucher (Paris, 1967).

Letters

Robert Schumanns Briefe: Neue Folge, ed. Gustav Jansen (Leipzig, 1904).
Schumann Briefedition (Cologne, 2008–) [in progress].

Biography

Georg Eismann, *Robert Schumann* (Leipzig, 1956).
Schumanns rheinische Jahre, ed. Paul Kast (Düsseldorf, 1981).
John Daverio, *Robert Schumann: Herald of a 'New Poetic Age'* (Oxford, 1997).
Ernst Burger, *Robert Schumann: eine Lebenschronik in Bildern und Dokumenten* (Mainz, 1999).
Berthold Litzmann, *Clara Schumann: ein Künstlerleben nach Tagebüchern und Briefen* (Leipzig, 1907).

Catalogue

Margit L. McCorkle, *Robert Schumann: Thematic-Bibliographic Catalogue of the Works* (Mainz, 2003).

LISZT

Letters

Franz Liszt's Briefe, ed. La Mara, vol. I (Leipzig, 1893).

Briefe hervorragender Zeitgenossen an Franz Liszt, ed. La Mara, Bd. I: *1824–1854* (Leipzig, 1895).

Briefwechsel zwischen Franz Liszt und Hans von Bülow, ed. La Mara (Leipzig, 1898).

Franz Liszt's Briefe an die Fürstin Carolyne Sayn-Wittgenstein, ed. La Mara (Leipzig, 1899).

Briefwechsel zwischen Franz Liszt und Carl Alexander, ed. La Mara (Leipzig, 1902).

Helene Raff-München, 'Franz Liszt und Joachim Raff im Spiegel ihrer Briefe', *Die Musik* I/III (1903), pp. 1272–86.

Franz Liszt's Briefe an Baron Anton Augusz 1846–1878, ed. Wilhelm von Csapó (Budapest, 1911).

Friedrich Schnapp, 'Unbekannte Briefe Franz Liszts', *Die Musik* 18 (10 July 1926).

The Letters of Franz Liszt to Marie zu Sayn-Wittgenstein, ed. Howard Hugo (Cambridge, MA, 1953).

Correspondance, ed. Pierre-Antoine Huré and Claude Knepper (Paris, 1987).

Charles Suttoni, 'Franz Liszt's Published Correspondence: an annotated bibliography', *Fontes artis musicae* 26/3 (1979), pp. 191–234.

Charles Suttoni, 'Liszt Correspondence in Print: an Expanded Annotated Bibliography', *Journal of the American Liszt Society* 25 (January–June 1989).

Charles Suttoni, 'Liszt Correspondence in Print: a supplementary bibliography', *Journal of the American Liszt Society* 46 (Fall 1999).

Letter of 12 July 1853 to Bénazet. Schneider Catalogue no. 456 (2011).

Biography

Lina Ramann, *Franz Liszt als Künstler und Mensch*, 3 vols. (Leipzig, 1880).

Alan Walker, *Franz Liszt*, Vol. II: *The Weimar Years* (New York, 1989).

Adrian Williams, *Portrait of Liszt* (Oxford, 1990).

Ernst Burger, *Franz Liszt: A Chronicle of His Life in Pictures and Documents* (Princeton, 1989).

BERLIOZ

Letters

Hector Berlioz, *Correspondance générale*, vol. IV: *1851–1855*, ed. Yves Gérard and Hugh Macdonald (Paris, 1983).

Biography

The Memoirs of Hector Berlioz, tr. and ed. David Cairns (London, 1969).
David Cairns, *Berlioz: Servitude and Greatness* (London, 1999).
Michael Rose, *Berlioz Remembered* (London, 2001).

Catalogue

D. Kern Holoman, *Catalogue of the Works of Hector Berlioz* (Kassel, 1987).

WAGNER

Letters

Richard Wagner, *Sämtliche Briefe*, vol. V (Leipzig, 1993).

Biography

Richard Wagner, *My Life*, tr. Andrew Gray (Cambridge, 1983).
Woldemar Lippert, *Wagner in Exile*, tr. Paul England (London, 1930).
Ernest Newman, *The Life of Richard Wagner*, vol. II: *1848–1860* (London, 1933).
Max Fehr, *Richard Wagners Schweizer Zeit*, 1. Bd. *(1849–55)* (Aarau and Leipzig, 1934).
Martin Gregor-Dellin, *Wagner-Chronik: Daten zu Leben und Werk* (Munich, 1972).
Martin Gregor-Dellin, *Richard Wagner: His Life, His Work, His Century*, tr. J. Maxwell Brownjohn (New York, 1983).
Stewart Spencer, *Wagner Remembered* (London, 2000).

Catalogue

John Deathridge, Martin Geck, Egon Voss, *Verzeichnis der musikalischen Werke Richard Wagners und ihrer Quellen* (Mainz, 1986).

ADDITIONAL BIBLIOGRAPHY

Chapter 1

Hannoversche Zeitung, 1853.

Hannoverscher Anzeiger, 1853.

Heinrich Ehrlich, *Aus allen Tonarten. Studien über Musik* (Berlin, 1888).

Georg Fischer, *Musik in Hannover*, 2nd ed. (Hanover, 1903).

Erich Rosendahl, *Geschichte der Hoftheater in Hannover und Braunschweig* (Hanover, 1927).

Gwendolyn Dunlevy Kelley and George P. Upton, *Edouard Remenyi: Musician, Litterateur, and Man* (Chicago, 1906).

Kurt Stephenson, 'Der junge Brahms und Reményis "Ungarische Lieder"', *Studien zur Musikwissenschaft*, Bd. 25: *Festschrift für Erich Schenk* (Graz, 1962).

Heinrich Sievers, *Hannoversche Musikgeschichte*, 2 vols. (Tutzing, 1984).

Hans Küntzel, *»Aber Fesseln tragen kann ich nicht«: Johannes Brahms und Agathe von Siebold* (Göttingen, 2003).

Aus Ferdinand Hillers Briefwechsel, ed. Reinhold Sietz, *Beiträge zur rheinischen Musikgeschichte*, vol. 28 (Cologne, 1958).

Katharina Loose, 'Kompositorisches Erinnern im Horntrio op. 40 von Johannes Brahms', Brahms Symposium, Kiel 2011 (forthcoming).

Chapter 2

Illustrated London News, 1853.

The Times [London], 1853.

The Musical World [London], 1853.

John Ella's diaries, courtesy of Christina Bashford.

Louis Spohr's Selbstbiographie, 2 vols. (Cassel and Göttingen, 1861).

Francis Hueffer, *Half a Century of Music in England, 1837–1887* (London, 1889).

Adolph Schloesser, 'Personal Recollections', *The R.A.M. Club Magazine* no. 32 (February 1911), pp. 5–6.

Robert Elkin, *Royal Philharmonic: the Annals of the Royal Philharmonic Society* (London, 1946).

A. W. Ganz, *Berlioz in London* (London, 1950).

Charles Stuart, '*Benvenuto Cellini* in London', *The Musical Times* 94 (1953), pp. 399–401.

Harold Rosenthal, *Two Centuries of Opera at Covent Garden* (London, 1958).

George Rowell, *Queen Victoria Goes to the Theatre* (London, 1978).

Clive Brown, *Louis Spohr: a Critical Biography* (Cambridge, 1984).

Peter Bloom, 'Episodes in the Livelihood of an Artist: Berlioz's Contacts and Contracts with Publishers', *Journal of Musicological Research* 15 (1995), pp. 219–73.

Sarah Hibberd, 'Benvenuto Cellini in London' (unpublished paper, 2002).

The Musical Voyager: Berlioz in Europe, ed. David Charlton and Katharine Ellis (Frankfurt am Main, 2007).

David Charlton, 'Berlioz's *Benvenuto Cellini*, London 1853: rejection and its complexities', *The Berlioz Society Bulletin* 176 (May 2008), pp. 36–46.

The Met Office National Meteorological Archive.

Chapter 3

Neue Zeitschrift für Musik [Leipzig], 1853.

Weimarische Zeitung, June 1853.

Eduard Genast, *Aus dem Tagebuche eines alten Schauspielers*, 4. Teil (Leipzig, 1866).

William Mason, *Memories of a Musical Life* (New York, 1902).

Helen Raff, *Joachim Raff: ein Lebensbild* (Regensburg, 1925).

O. Goldhammer, 'Liszt, Brahms und Reményi', *Studia Musicologica Academiae Scientiarum Hungaricae* 5 (1963), pp. 89–100.

Jutta Hecker, *Die Altenburg: Geschichte eines Hauses* (Berlin, 1983).

James Deaville, 'A "Daily Diary of the Weimar Dream": Joachim Raff's Unpublished Letters to Doris Genast, 1852–1856', in *Liszt and His World*, ed. Michael Saffle (Stuyvesant, NY, 1998), pp. 181–216.

Joseph Joachim, *Hamlet* [manuscript], Sotheby's, London, 9 June 2010.

Chapter 4

William S. Newman, *The Sonata Since Beethoven* (New York, 1983), pp. 385–8.

Richard Wagner in Zürich, ed. Werner G. Zimmermann (Zurich, 1986).

Ulrich Enzensberger, *Herwegh: ein Heldenleben* (Frankfurt, 1999).

Chris Walton, 'Wagner-Quellen in der Zentralbibliothek Zürich: Verleger, Kopisten, Dirigate', in: *»Schlagen Sie die Kraft der Reflexion nicht zu gering an«*, ed. Klaus Döge, Christa Jost, Peter Jost (Mainz, 2002), pp. 92–111.

Chris Walton, *Richard Wagner's Zurich* (Columbia, SC, 2007).

Chapter 5

Journal des débats [Paris], 23 February 1851.

Journal des débats [Paris], 29 August 1853.

Neue Zeitschrift für Musik [Leipzig], 1853.

Badeblatt [Baden-Baden], August 1853.

Intelligenzblatt [Frankfurt], August 1853.

Hector Berlioz, *Les Grotesques de la musique* (Paris, 1859); in English as *The Musical Madhouse*, tr. Alastair Bruce (Rochester, NY, 2003).

Hector Berlioz, *A Travers Chants* (Paris, 1862).

Heinrich Ehrlich, 'Ein ungedruckter Brief von Hector Berlioz', *Die Gegenwart* XV/11 (15 March 1879).

Joseph Wechsberg, *The Lost World of the Great Spas* (New York, 1979).

Giacomo Meyerbeer, *Briefwechsel und Tagebücher*, Bd. 6, ed. Sabine Henze-Döhring (Berlin, 2002).

Hector Berlioz in Baden-Baden, ed. Rainer Schmusch and Joachim Draheim (Baden-Baden, 2003).

M. W. Rowe, *Heinrich Wilhelm Ernst: Violin Virtuoso* (Aldershot, 2008).

Chapter 6

K. Baedeker, *The Rhine and Northern Germany* (Koblenz, 1870).

Hermann Deiters, *Johannes Brahms: a Biographical Sketch*, tr. Rosa Newmarch (London, 1888).

Hoffmann von Fallersleben, *Mein Leben* (Berlin, 1894).

Wilhelm von Wasielewski, *Aus siebzig Jahren* (Stuttgart, 1897).

Carl Reinecke, *"und manche liebe Schatten steigen auf": Gedenkblätter an berühmte Musiker* (Leipzig, 1900).

Eric Sams, *Brahms Songs* (London, 1972).

Siegfried Kross, 'Brahms und das Rheinland', in *Musikalische Rheinromantik*, ed. S. Kross, *Beiträge zur Rheinischen Musikgeschichte*, Heft 140 (Berlin, 1989), pp. 93–105.

Hans Küntzel, *»Aber Fesseln tragen kann ich nicht«: Johannes Brahms und Agathe von Siebold* (Göttingen, 2003).

Doyle, New York, auction of 20 April 2011 [Album of Arnold Wehner].

Chapter 7

A. B. Granville, *The Spas of Germany* (London, 1839).

Hans von Bülow, *Briefe*, II. Band (Leipzig, 1899).

Karl Baedeker, *Austria-Hungary* (Leipzig, 1911).

Alexander Buchner, *Franz Liszt in Bohemia* (London, 1962).

Carl Gustav Carus, *Lebenserinnerungen und Denkwürdigkeiten* (Weimar, 1966).

Joseph Wechsberg, *The Lost World of the Great Spas* (New York, 1979).

James Deaville, 'A "Daily Diary of the Weimar Dream": Joachim Raff's Unpublished Letters to Doris Genast, 1852–1856', in *Liszt and His World*, ed. Michael Saffle (Stuyvesant, NY, 1998), pp. 181–216.

Ian Bradley, *Water Music: Music Making in the Spas of Europe and North America* (New York, 2010).

Chapter 8

Robert Bailey, 'Wagner's Musical Sketches for *Siegfrieds Tod*', in *Studies in Music History: Essays for Oliver Strunk*, ed. Harold Powers (Princeton, 1968), pp. 459–94.

Curt von Westernhagen, *The Forging of the 'Ring'*, tr. Arnold and Mary Whittall (Cambridge, 1976).

Robert Bailey, 'The Structure of the *Ring* and its Evolution', *19th Century Music* 1 (July 1977), pp. 48–61.

John Deathridge, 'Wagner's Sketches for the *Ring*', *Musical Times* 118 (May 1977), pp. 383–9.

Richard Wagner in Zürich, ed. Werner G. Zimmermann (Zurich, 1986).

Ute Harbusch, 'Rheingold aus La Spezia – Richard Wagner und Italien', in *Italien in Aneignung und Widerspruch*, ed. Güter Oestetle, Bernd Roeck and Christine Tauber, Reihe der Villa Vigoni 10 (Tübingen, 1996), pp. 116–36.

Ulrich Enzensberger, *Herwegh: ein Heldenleben* (Frankfurt, 1999).

Chris Walton, *Richard Wagner's Zurich* (Columbia, SC, 2007).

Chapter 9

Karlsruher Tagblatt, 1853.

Karlsruher Zeitung, 1853.

Weimarische Zeitung, June 1853.

Neue Zeitschrift für Musik [Leipzig], 1853.

Niederrheinische Musik-Zeitung [Cologne], 1. Jg., 29 October 1853, pp. 140–41.

Richard Pohl, *Hektor Berlioz: Studien und Erinnerungen* (Leipzig, 1884).

Karl Gustav Fecht, *Geschichte der Haupt- und Residenzstadt Karlsruhe* (Karlsruhe, 1887).

Hans von Bülow, *Briefe*, II. Band, ed. M. von Bülow (Leipzig, 1899).

William Mason, *Memories of a Musical Life* (New York, 1902).

Friedrich von Weech, *Karlsruhe: Geschichte der Stadt und ihrer Verwaltung*, III. Band (Karlsruhe, 1904).

Heinrich Ordenstein, 'Die Musik', in *Die Stadt Karlsruhe: ihre Geschichte und ihre Verwaltung*, ed. Goldschmidt (Karlsruhe, 1915).

Karlsruher Theatergeschichte (Karlsruhe, 1982).

Giacomo Meyerbeer, *Briefwechsel und Tagebücher*, Bd. 6, ed. Sabine Henze-Döhring (Berlin, 2002).

Hugh Macdonald, 'Liszt as Conductor', in *Beethoven's Century: Essays on Composers and Themes* (Rochester, NY, 2008), pp. 65–78.

Chapter 10

Neue Zeitschrift für Musik [Leipzig], vol. 39, p. 185 (28 October 1853).

Albert Dietrich and J. V. Widmann, *Recollections of Johannes Brahms* (London, 1899).

Peter Cornelius, *Ausgewählte Briefe*, ed. C. M. Cornelius (Leipzig, 1904).

Wilhelm von Wasielewski, *Robert Schumann: eine Biographie* (Leipzig, 1906).

Albert Dietrich, Robert Schumann and Johannes Brahms, *FAE*, ed. Valentin and Kobin (Magdeburg, 1935).

Arthur Helps and Elizabeth Jane Howard, *Bettina: a Portrait* (London, 1957).

Wolfgang Boetticher, 'Cornelius und Robert Schumann', in *Peter Cornelius als Komponist, Dichter, Kritiker und Essayist*, ed. Hellmut Federhofer and Kurt Oehl (Regensburg, 1977), p. 49.

Chapter 11

Neue Zeitschrift für Musik [Leipzig], 1853.

Weimarische Zeitung, June 1853.

Hans von Bülow, *Briefe*, II. Band, ed. M. von Bülow (Leipzig, 1899).

William Mason, *Memories of a Musical Life* (New York, 1902).

Jacques Hillairet, *La Rue de Richelieu* (Paris, 1966).

Jules Janin, *735 Lettres à sa femme*, tome II (Paris, 1975).

Curt von Westernhagen, *The Forging of the 'Ring'*, tr. Arnold and Mary Whittall (Cambridge, 1976).

Joël-Marie Fauquet, *Les Sociétés de Musique de chambre à Paris de la Restauration à 1870* (Paris, 1986).

Kenneth Hamilton, 'Not with a bang but a whimper: The death of Liszt's *Sardanapale*', *Cambridge Opera Journal* 8/1 (1996), pp. 45–58.

Chapter 12

Neue Zeitschrift für Musik [Leipzig], 1853.

Hannoversche Zeitung, 1853.

Hannoversche Anzeiger, 1853.

Georg Fischer, *Musik in Hannover*, 2nd ed. (Hanover, 1903).

Erich Rosendahl, *Geschichte der Hoftheater in Hannover und Braunschweig* (Hanover, 1927).

Heinrich Sievers, *Hannoversche Musikgeschichte*, 2 vols. (Tutzing, 1984).

Klaus Blum, *Musikfreunde und Musici: Musikleben in Bremen seit der Aufklärung* (Tutzing, 1975).

Chapter 13

Neue Zeitschrift für Musik [Leipzig], 1853.

Signale für die musikalische Welt [Leipzig], 1853.

Recent Music and Musicians As Described in the Diaries and Correspondence of Ignatz Moscheles (New York, 1873).

Peter Cornelius, *Aufsätze über Musik und Kunst*, ed. Edgar Istel (Leipzig, 1904).

Matthias Brzoska, 'Berlioz und Gouvy oder: Vier Symphoniker im Bayrischen Hof', in *Théodore Gouvy (1819–1898): Bericht über den Internationalen Kongreß*, ed. Herbert Schneider (Hildesheim, 2008), pp. 457–76.

Otto Haas Catalogue 43 (2008) [poster for concert of 10 December].

Chapter 14

K. Baedeker, *Belgium and Holland: Handbook for Travellers* (Koblenz, 1869).

Clara Schumann, 1819–1896: Katalog zur Austellung, ed. Ingrid Bodsch and Gerd Nauhaus (Bonn, 1996).

Index